THE GOOD, THE BAD, AND THE UGLY
PHILADELPHIA FLYERS

HEART-POUNDING, JAW-DROPPING, AND GUT-WRENCHING MOMENTS IN PHILADELPHIA FLYERS HISTORY

Adam Kimelman

TRIUMPH
BOOKS

This book has previously been catalogued by the Library of Congress as:

Kimelman, Adam, 1975–
  The good, the bad, and the ugly Philadelphia Flyers: heart-pounding, jaw-dropping, and gut-wrenching moments in Philadelphia Flyers history / Adam Kimelman.
    p. cm.
  ISBN-13: 978-1-60078-021-9
  ISBN-10: 1-60078-021-0
  1. Philadelphia Flyers (Hockey team)—History. I. Title.
  GV848.P48K56 2006
  796.962'640974811—dc22

                          2008029116

This book is available in quantity at special discounts for your group or organization. For further information, contact:
  Triumph Books LLC
  814 North Franklin Street
  Chicago, Illinois 60610
  (312) 337-0747
  www.triumphbooks.com

Printed in U.S.A.

ISBN: 978-1-60078-876-5

Design by Patricia Frey

All photos courtesy Getty Images unless otherwise noted

CONTENTS

FOREWORD

The good, the bad, and the ugly. Why would I be asked to write the foreword for such an important book chronicling the history of one of professional hockey's most storied franchises? I suppose if one were to assimilate my career with the Flyers as an analogy, I have been involved with all three.

By no means is that to suggest my career as a Flyer was of greater importance than anyone else who ever wore the orange and black, but I can attest to the importance and value placed on pulling on that sweater. I always felt, even before I arrived here—and certainly after I arrived—as though the Flyers organization should have been an Original Six franchise because of its rich tradition.

I also know why the Philadelphia Flyers are such a revered franchise, and as a player, why so many athletes want to play in this city, for this organization, and more importantly this ownership. Mr. Snider is the epitome of class, professionalism, philanthropy, and most importantly, leadership. Therein lies the secret to why Philadelphia is such a desired destination for free agents and players in general league-wide. Mr. Snider cares about this city (look at the facilities), the people of this city (just ask the kids involved in the Ed Snider Youth Hockey Foundation), and his players (just ask Joe Watson, Dave Schultz, Bob Kelly, Bernie Parent, Bob Clarke, and anybody else who ever played here). In a business that says owners owe the players nothing but a paycheck, those same people don't know Mr. Snider and his moral convictions.

So what is the good, the bad, and the ugly? Well, I will let the stories you will read here satisfy your fascination for the bad and the ugly; I will touch on only the good.

For me, the good is the people of Philadelphia. Some may believe I overstate my affection for Flyers fans, but I am very sincere when I say the people here salvaged my career. The joy of playing professional hockey climaxed for me in Philadelphia— always there for games and always there when the community asked for generous support of whatever the cause may be. There was and still is no other place I wanted to play than right here in front of the greatest fans in the world.

So please enjoy the following stories, insights, and memories as much as I enjoyed being a part of your history.

—Keith Primeau

ACKNOWLEDGMENTS

The book you hold in your hands today wouldn't exist without the help and support of some very important people.

I came to the Flyers, and hockey in general, fairly late. I was in Hebrew school at M'Kor Shalom synagogue, and one of my classmates, Scott Fleishman, would bring a dozen and a half bagels to class from his father's store, The Bagel Shop, on Chapel Avenue in Cherry Hill. He also would bring in his tiny Sony Watchman, and an entire class, including our teacher, Mr. Pont, would gather around the five-inch screen to watch Flyers playoff games against the Penguins and Canadiens in 1989. I quickly was hooked by the speed and passion of players like Dave Poulin, Ron Sutter, Mark Howe, and Rick Tocchet, plus the seemingly psychotic netminder, Ron Hextall.

From there, I began watching hockey, and playing with friends, and now I've moved on to writing about hockey for a living. And I consider it a life very well lived.

Thanks go to Michael Emmerich and the folks at Triumph Books for believing that I could pull off this project, and to Adam Motin for giving me a second bite at the apple, so to speak, with this Version 2.0 of *The Good, the Bad, and the Ugly: Philadelphia Flyers*. It's interesting in that prior to the first version of this book coming out, the longest story I had ever written was a 35-page honors thesis in my senior year of college. Hopefully this is a little more interesting.

I owe a tremendous debt of gratitude to all the people who gave their time to speak with me for the book. Talking with all of them reinforced something I already knew—hockey people are the best people in sports, and sometimes just in general.

A number of research materials were hugely important to putting this book together, most notably Jay Greenberg's *Full Spectrum, Walking Together Forever* by Jim Jackson and *Orange Black and Blue* by Chuck Gormley.

Credit also goes to the Flyers' senior director of communications Zack Hill, who was indispensable in helping me track down a few Flyers of the past.

Peter Anson's outstanding website, FlyersHistory.net, provided box scores from every game in club history and also made for an invaluable resource.

Most of all, I have to thank my wife, Sheryl, and my kids Breanna and Logan, who continue to allow me to live in my little hockey world.

I also have to thank you, the reader, for taking the time to give this book a read. I hope you're entertained and educated, and if you like it, please encourage as many of your friends and family members to pick up a copy as possible. I have two kids, and they'll need to go to college someday.

To quote the immortal Gene Hart: "Good night, and good hockey."

THE BEGINNING

BLISSFUL IGNORANCE

In the early 1960s Ed Snider wasn't the multimillionaire sports and entertainment mogul he is today.

Snider was living in Washington, D.C., where he co-owned a record company. In New York on business, Snider met up with a friend, Juggy Gayles, presumably to go to dinner. However, Gayles had a different idea.

"He had seats at the old [Madison Square] Garden," Snider said, "and he said, 'Come on, my buddies and I are going to the game and I'll take you.' I said, 'What game?' He said, 'Rangers and Montreal.' I said, 'What are you talking about?' That's how little I knew."

For Ed Snider, hockey was love at first sight. Actually, it was love for Gump Worsley.

Growing up in Washington, Snider followed the Washington Redskins, and as a kid enjoyed the old Washington Senators, but he had never seen anything like pint-sized Gumper the goalie.

"Maybe it was the fact that he didn't look like an athlete or that he wasn't wearing a mask, I'm not sure," Snider said in *Full Spectrum*. "But I know I was fascinated with Worsley. I thought, 'This is the greatest spectator sport I've ever seen.'"

Not long after that, Snider's record company hit a bad patch, and he and his partner sold out.

1

In 1964, Snider, along with a brother-in-law, Earl Foreman, and one of Foreman's law clients, developer Jerry Wolman, purchased the Philadelphia Eagles. Snider, who owned a 7-percent stake in the team, moved to Philadelphia to become the team's treasurer.

That winter Snider was in Boston on business when he went with friends to a Celtics–76ers NBA game. Who won was irrelevant; in the end, it was the city of Philadelphia that came out on top.

As Snider's group was leaving Boston Garden, Snider noticed a line at the ticket window. It was a remarkably long line for a late Sunday afternoon.

"I asked my friend, 'What is that line for?'" Snider said. "And he said, 'It's for the hockey game tomorrow.' I said, 'Are they in the playoffs? Big rivalry?' He said no, they put a thousand seats on sale for every game and people line up the night before to buy them. They're in last place, but it doesn't matter, the fans here just love hockey."

By 1965 Snider's main task was financing Wolman's dream of a multi-purpose stadium that could house his Eagles and the Philadelphia Phillies (Wolman also owned their home, Connie Mack Stadium). The building was going to be erected on the south end of Broad Street, near the Philadelphia Navy Yard.

During a meeting with Bill Putnam, an executive with Morgan Guaranty Trust Company in New York—Putnam had helped set up the loan that allowed Wolman's group to buy the Eagles—Putnam told Snider he was leaving Morgan to move to Los Angeles and run Jack Kent Cooke's sports properties. Cooke was a minority owner of the Redskins and also owned the Los Angeles Lakers. He was planning on building a new home for his basketball team in suburban Inglewood, California. For a second tenant in his Fabulous Forum, Cooke had applied for a National Hockey League expansion franchise.

Snider was shocked. "I said, 'Wait, what did you say? They're expanding in the National Hockey League?' There was nothing in the papers here—the only story had been a six-paragraph blurb buried in the *Philadelphia Daily News*. Nobody knew anything. He

NEAR-SALE

The evolution of the Philadelphia Flyers was proceeding slowly when it nearly stopped cold. A pair of outside investors had approached Jerry Wolman and offered him $1 million for the rights to the franchise, with the money to be split equally among the four prospective owners.

Jerry Schiff, Ed Snider's brother-in-law, agreed with Wolman to sell. But Snider and Bill Putnam said no sale, killing the deal.

"He [Wolman] thought hockey was going to fail and he wanted to sell the franchise before we got started," Snider said. "I said no, so he got angry. He wanted to sell the franchise to people who wanted to move it to somewhere in New York."

Snider believes that decision led to Wolman firing him from the Eagles the night of the Flyers' home opener.

said the National Hockey League is going to double in size, and he named a bunch of cities. I asked about Philadelphia, and he said, 'I'm sure Philadelphia would be one they would consider, but there's no arena, there's no anything.'"

While Putnam was explaining the NHL's grand plan to add six new teams, an earlier meeting with Philadelphia 76ers owner Ike Richman rebounded into Snider's mind. Richman had approached Snider about convincing Wolman to build a new home for his basketball team. The 76ers had been playing at Convention Hall, near the University of Pennsylvania, but he wanted a new, modern building. At the time, Snider had told Richman that the Eagles weren't in the arena-construction business.

Suddenly pieces of a puzzle began coming together in Snider's mind—the NHL's expansion, the growing population of the Philadelphia region thanks to the rapidly developing southern New Jersey suburbs, and an NBA team looking for a new building.

Snider was sure hockey would work in Philadelphia. He knew the passion of Philadelphia sports fans, how they lived and died with the local teams. If Boston fans would stand in the cold to buy tickets for a last-place hockey team, he knew Philadelphia fans would love the NHL just as much if they were exposed to it.

What Snider didn't know was the ignominious history of hockey in Philadelphia. Most fans don't know the Flyers were not Philadelphia's first NHL team.

In the 1920s former light-heavyweight boxing champion Benny Leonard owned the Pittsburgh Pirates, but by the end of that decade, the team needed a new arena. During construction, the team was moved to Philadelphia and renamed the Quakers.

The Philadelphia Quakers' one season of existence, the 1930–31 season, was historical for one reason: sheer ineptitude. In 44 games, the team went 4–36–4. The four wins are the fewest ever posted by an NHL team, and the .136 winning percentage remains the second-lowest in league history. After the season, Leonard folded the franchise. He lost so much money on the team he was forced to return to prizefighting.

There also were a number of failed minor-league hockey experiments in town.

The Philadelphia Arrows of the Canadian-American Hockey League played at the Philadelphia Arena on Market Street from

GIRARD BANK

After raising barely enough money to buy the team, Ed Snider had debts to repay, including a $500,000 loan from ARA's Bill Fishman.

Snider and partner Joe Scott went bank shopping for a loan.

"I went to banks ... and they said, 'What's a hockey puck?'" Snider said. "One guy thought it was soccer. Another banker fell asleep while we were talking to him."

Their seventh stop was Girard Bank, which was placed down the list due to its conservative reputation. Snider didn't know Girard president Steve Gardner had grown up in Boston as a hockey fan, as had vice president Bill Baer, who also was a Philadelphian.

Girard gave the Flyers $1.5 million, and Snider was able to make good on all his debts.

When he founded the Flyers in the 1960s, Ed Snider wasn't the sports powerbroker he is today, but it was his passion for hockey that drove him to bring an NHL team back to Philadelphia.

COLOR SCHEME

Ever wonder why the Flyers look like they skated out of a Halloween catalogue? There are two reasons.

"The hot colors are always more attractive from a marketing standpoint," founding team president Bill Putnam said in *Full Spectrum*. "Since Detroit and Montreal already used red in their color schemes, the closest the Flyers could get was orange."

The other reason?

"The fact that I graduated from the University of Texas, where the colors are orange and white, might have had something to do with the choice," he said.

After black was added to complete the scheme, Putnam was told the NHL logo also was orange and black. Putnam offered to use just orange and white, but league president Clarence Campbell gave his blessing and the black stayed.

1927 to 1935; the team later became a minor-league affiliate of the New York Rangers and was renamed the Ramblers. The Ramblers played until 1941, when they were renamed the Rockets, then folded in 1942.

The Philadelphia Comets of the Tri-State Hockey League blinked in and out of existence in four months, just in time to lose all 16 games they played in the 1932–33 season.

The Philadelphia Falcons played in the Eastern Amateur Hockey League from 1942 to 1946, and then ceased play until the 1951–52 season. The second version of the Falcons, though, didn't make it to the 1952 part of their schedule, as the team was disbanded in December 1951 due to poor attendance.

According to Philadelphia hockey historian Bruce Cooper, hockey's death knell in the city could best be summarized in a quote from Peter A. Tyrell, president and general manager of the Philadelphia Arena, when he announced the Falcons' folding: "The attendance this season to date has proven that there are not enough Philadelphians interested in hockey to warrant its continuance."

The Philadelphia Rockets of the American Hockey League gave the town another shot, playing from 1946 to 1949. They barely lasted the first season, though, as the Rockets went 5–52–7, for a winning percentage of .078, an all-level record of futility that remains today.

The Philadelphia Ramblers of the Eastern Hockey League played decent but undistinguished hockey from 1955 to 1964 before moving to Cherry Hill, New Jersey, and becoming the Jersey Devils.

Snider knew nothing of this inglorious hockey history; for today's Flyers fans, his ignorance is their bliss.

"I was young and full of enthusiasm," Snider said in the Flyers video, *Twenty-Five Years of Pride and Tradition*. "I had seen hockey and loved it. I had seen its success in the six cities that had it. But I didn't realize the history of hockey in Philadelphia or in other places. Maybe if I had, I wouldn't have gone through with it."

Snider suggested to Wolman that they should build an arena—the parking lot of the previously planned stadium was a desired location—and apply for an NHL franchise. Wolman thought it would be a good idea, and they planned to move forward.

First for Snider was a visit to Bill Jennings, president of the New York Rangers and the head of the expansion committee.

A number of cities already had submitted bids, among them Pittsburgh, Buffalo, Los Angeles, Baltimore, and Vancouver, but Snider said Jennings was ecstatic when the idea of a team in Philadelphia was mentioned.

THE BIRTH OF THE LOGO

Mel Richman Inc., a Philadelphia advertising and graphic design company, was hired to create the Flyers' logo and uniforms.

Team president Bill Putnam suggested a winged skate for the logo, but artist Sam Ciccone drew a stylized *P* with four wings to connote speed. An orange dot was placed in the middle of the *P* to symbolize a hockey puck.

Simple and effective, it remains nearly unchanged more than 45 years later.

WHAT'S IN A NAME?

A number of names were suggested for Philadelphia's expansion hockey team, from Lancers and Raiders to Ice-Picks, Acmes and Scars and Stripes.

But it was Phyllis Foreman, Ed Snider's sister, who blurted out "Flyers."

"I was thinking of people skating and sliding around the ice," she said in *Full Spectrum*. "And 'Flyers' just popped into my head. Everybody thought it was great."

There was a name-the-team contest run by Acme supermarkets, but the only vote that counted came from Snider, who favored "Flyers."

Officially, Alec Stockard, a nine-year-old boy from Narberth, Pennsylvania, was named the winner, and took home the grand prize of a 21-inch color television, plus two inaugural season tickets.

Of note is the fact that Stockard spelled it "Fliers." No one is sure how the *i* became a *y*.

"He was just glad I showed up," Snider said. "It's a great metropolitan area, a great rivalry for New York. He was great to me from the day I met him."

Jennings gave Snider the bid parameters. First, there was a $10,000 application fee. Also, there needed to be an arena with a seating capacity of at least 12,500. All applicants would have to make presentations to the NHL Board of Governors, outlining why the NHL would work in their area. And there was a $2 million franchise fee.

Snider was on board, and said his only request was that his bid be kept secret so it would be the only one coming out of Philadelphia. Jennings agreed.

Snider took his arena plan to Philadelphia city councilman Paul D'Ortona and Mayor James Tate. The mayor especially was pleased that a 15,000-seat, privately financed arena could be built in the parking lot of what eventually would become Veterans Stadium, and fast-tracked the project.

Now all Snider had to do was prepare the franchise presentation.

First he enlisted Putnam, who decided working for the demanding Cooke was not the job for him. He joined Snider,

Wolman, and Jerry Schiff, a brother-in-law of Snider, as the nascent club owners. It was agreed Putnam would own 25 percent and hold the title of team president, while Schiff, Wolman and Snider each would own 22 percent. The remaining nine percent was purchased by friends of Wolman and Snider.

A five-page brochure was printed to explain to NHL owners that with a population base of 5.5 million and three established professional sports franchises, the hockey team could join the Phillies, Eagles and 76ers in the pantheon of Philadelphia sports.

On February 8, 1966, at the St. Regis Hotel in New York, Wolman and Putnam met with the NHL Board of Governors and made their pitch.

The next day, the phone rang in Putnam's hotel room. It was Jennings. "You're in," was all he said.

Snider, who had stayed behind in Philadelphia, joined Mayor Tate at City Hall to announce plans for the new arena. Not long after, office space was rented on the ground floor of the Life of Pennsylvania Building, at 15th and Locust Street. Bud Poile, the 42-year-old general manager of the San Francisco Seals of the Western Hockey League, was hired as the club's first general manager. The first coach was 43-year-old Keith Allen, then the coach/GM of the Western League's Seattle Totems.

Team colors of orange, black and white were chosen, and uniforms and a logo—a winged *P* with an orange puck in the center—were unveiled, as was the name—the Philadelphia Flyers, a suggestion first made by Phyllis Foreman, Snider's sister.

The foundation was set, but one item still remained—raising the $2 million franchise fee.

Snider thought he'd get half that amount from Wolman, but when Wolman tried to sell the team out from under him, Snider decided to trade his 40 percent stake in the arena for Wolman's 22 percent share of the franchise. Snider also bought out Schiff, becoming majority owner of the club.

The moves left Snider in a difficult spot. "I had never wanted to own more than 22 percent of the team," he recalled in *Full Spectrum*. "I didn't think I could afford it."

The fledgling Flyers surprised the league when they plucked little-known goalie Bernie Parent from the Boston Bruins in the NHL's 1967 expansion draft.

In fact, he couldn't. Snider remortgaged his home and started borrowing money from banks: $25,000 from one, $50,000 from another.

Despite not being part of the ownership group, Snider still thought Wolman would make good on his promise to foot half the expansion fee. But with the June 5, 1967, deadline approaching and Wolman having financial difficulties, Snider knew something was wrong.

"To my recollections," Snider said in *Full Spectrum*, "It was seven to 10 days before the money was due that Jerry told me he didn't have it."

Snider previously had lined up a $1 million loan from Fidelity Bank. Now he needed to scramble to replace Wolman's money.

The team's television rights for the first three seasons were sold to Kaiser Broadcasting, which owned Channel 48, for $350,000. Snider also took out a $150,000 loan independently.

Still a half-million dollars short, Snider went to Bill Fishman, president and founder of ARA Services (today known as ARAMARK), which already had invested $2 million to provide food services at the planned arena. Snider asked Fishman for a loan, and Fishman was agreeable if a bank would take his personal ARA stock as collateral. Provident Bank said yes, and on deadline day, Fishman wrote a check for $500,000 to the Philadelphia Hockey Club.

Snider took the check, plus the other $1.5 million, to Fidelity Bank to make the wire transfer to Putnam, who had gone to Montreal to deliver the franchise fee to the NHL and for the expansion draft.

And then the lights went out.

"There was a blackout in Philadelphia," Snider said. "Everything went dead. They couldn't wire [the money]. They're waiting in Montreal and nothing's happening. We couldn't communicate by any way, phone or otherwise."

At approximately 10:23 AM, a power failure shut down a 15,000-square mile area, ranging from New Jersey south to Maryland and west to Harrisburg.

The NHL needed confirmation of the Flyers' money by 2:00 PM, or all the hard work put in by Snider, Putnam and others would go for naught.

At noon the power came back on in Center City Philadelphia. Fidelity was able to establish a communication link with a bank in New York, which was able to wire the money to Royal Bank of Canada in Montreal. Putnam ran the $2 million check to the Queen Elizabeth Hotel, saving the day—and the Flyers—for Philadelphia.

"How could something like that happen?" Snider asks now with a laugh that only 45-plus years of success can allow. "It happened. That's how we started."

THE EXPANSION DRAFT

The first step in building the Flyers' inaugural roster was Snider's purchase of the Quebec Aces of the American Hockey League for $350,000.

Then came the NHL's first-ever expansion draft, held June 6, 1967, in Montreal. The six established clubs each were allowed to protect 11 skaters and one goalie. After a team lost a skater or a goalie, it could protect one more of the like. After it lost a second player, it could add one more to its protected list. After that, every remaining player was up for grabs, with the exception of players with fewer than two years of professional experience (NHL or minor leagues).

The Flyers were to pick second among the six new clubs—the California Seals, Los Angeles Kings, Pittsburgh Penguins, St. Louis Blues and Minnesota North Stars were the others—in the two-round goaltender portion of the draft, and fifth in the 18-round skater-selection process.

The Flyers, led by general manager Bud Poile and coach Keith Allen, focused on young players.

"I think we reached a consensus almost from the start that we were going to think young," Poile said in *Full Spectrum*. "We didn't just want to have a team that could be competitive with the new clubs, but one that in a few years could compete with the old ones."

Allen, Poile and top scout Marcel Pelletier had spent the 1966–67 season scouring minor-league outposts throughout North America.

"We'd go on the road, usually alone, for as many as two weeks at a time," Pelletier recalled in *Full Spectrum*. "I'd played in St. Paul [in the Central League], so I had a real good idea of the players in that league. Bud and Keith had been in the Western League, so they knew that, too. We also scouted the American League heavily. The National League we did less. We knew what was there."

One of the players Pelletier, a former minor-league goalie, had seen was a Boston Bruins goaltending prospect toiling for the Oklahoma City Blazers of the Central Hockey League. After Los Angeles took veteran goalie Terry Sawchuk with the first pick, the Flyers shocked the draft room by taking 22-year-old Bernard Parent.

In 39 games as a rookie in the 1965–66 season, Parent had posted a 3.69 goals-against average for a Bruins team that finished fifth in the six-team NHL. He fared slightly better in his second campaign, in Oklahoma City, finishing with a 2.70 GAA and four shutouts in 14 games after winning just four of his 18 games with the Bruins.

"He was supposed to be immature," Pelletier said in *Full Spectrum*. "And he probably was. But when I saw him play at Oklahoma City, I thought he looked like the perfect goalie."

Parent wasn't overjoyed at the thought of heading to an unknown hockey land.

"I was a little disappointed because I was leaving an original team for an expansion team," he said. "Little did I know it would turn out real good."

After the Flyers picked Parent, they hoped to land a veteran with their next choice. The pickings were slim, though, when their next turn came up, so with the 11th selection, the team chose Parent's partner in Oklahoma City, Doug Favell.

With their first pick in the skater selection, they chose 27-year-old Chicago Blackhawks defenseman Ed Van Impe. After five years in the minor leagues, Van Impe had just finished a distant second to Bobby Orr in voting for the Calder Trophy, the NHL's rookie of the year award.

Like Parent, Van Impe wasn't happy to land with an expansion team. He said in Jim Jackson's history of the Flyers' championship teams *Walking Together Forever*: "I had spent five years in the minors trying to work my way up to Chicago and finally accomplished that the season before expansion. We had an outstanding year, finishing in first place during the regular season. When I was picked by the Flyers, it was like starting all over again. The Stanley Cup was something I never even thought could happen in Philly. I can't even say I had mixed feelings. I was very, very disappointed."

Next for the Flyers was defenseman Joe Watson, Orr's 23-year-old road roommate.

"Talk about depression," Watson said in *Walking Together Forever*. "A guy told me I just got drafted by the Philadelphia Flyers, and I said, 'Who? What are you talking about? What the hell is Philadelphia?' I knew nothing about it."

After Watson, the Flyers took 22-year-old center Brit Selby from Toronto. Selby had been the 1966 Calder Trophy winner, but a broken leg the following season limited him to just six games, and the Leafs had given up on him.

Next was 29-year-old center Lou Angotti from Chicago, of whom Pelletier said, "We thought he'd be a character guy and a good two-way player." Angotti became the Flyers' first captain.

After Angotti, they selected 28-year-old right wing Leon Rochefort from Montreal, and then Chicago farmhand defenseman John Miszuk, 26.

They next opted for 30-year-old Boston blueliner Dick Cherry, who was so happy at his selection he promptly retired to become a schoolteacher.

The Flyers then chose Montreal minor-league defenseman Jean Gauthier, left wing Don Blackburn from Toronto, center Garry Peters from Montreal and center Jimmy Johnson from the Rangers.

They then went back to Boston for tall, skinny forward Gary Dornhoefer, 24. Dornhoefer had failed to stick in the NHL in three previous tries with the Bruins, but unlike his draft brethren, he was ecstatic to be going to Philadelphia—or anywhere else, for that matter.

"I didn't know that much about Philadelphia, but it really didn't matter where I played, I just wanted to play in the National Hockey League," he said. "I was thrilled about it."

Rounding out the Flyers' 20 draft picks were veteran forwards Forbes Kennedy (from Boston), Pat Hannigan (Chicago), Dwight Carruthers (Detroit), Bob Courcy (Montreal), and Keith Wright (Boston), and defenseman Terry Ball (New York).

During and immediately after the draft, teams made substantial offers for Parent, Van Impe and Watson, but Poile stood by his word of keeping young players rather than the veterans the established teams were trying to foist onto the new teams.

The new Flyers met for their first training camp in Quebec City on September 10, 1967. But there was discontent in the air, as Watson and Van Impe refused to show up and Parent nearly walked out of camp over a contract issue. Days before the regular season, Parent signed his $20,000-a-year contract; Van Impe inked a two-year, $45,000 deal; and Watson agreed to a two-year, $38,500 deal.

Those were the final additions to the opening-day roster—Parent and Favell in goal; Watson, Van Impe, Gauthier and Miszuk on defense, joined by Jim Morrison and John Hanna off the Quebec roster; centers Angotti, Kennedy and Peters, plus Ed Hoekstra from Quebec; left wings Selby and Blackburn, plus Bill Sutherland from Quebec; and right wings Rochefort, Dornhoefer and Hannigan, plus Quebec's Wayne Hicks.

The group finished the exhibition season in Providence, Rhode Island, then flew to Philadelphia, where the new Flyers got their first look at their new home.

It was far from love at first sight.

Watson's first image of the city came as the team's bus from the airport drove past the massive crushed-car graveyard next to the Penrose Avenue bridge.

"I looked over to the right and saw this big machine crushing cars," he said in *Walking Together Forever*. "I asked the driver about

FLYERS' FIRSTS

On October 11, 1967, at the Oakland Coliseum, the Flyers made their NHL debut.

Coach Keith Allen's starting lineup had Lou Angotti, Brit Selby and Wayne Hicks at forward, Jean Gauthier and John Miszuk on defense and Bernie Parent in goal.

Angotti took the first-ever Flyers penalty—for interference—just 22 seconds into the game.

And at 10:07 of the second period, Bill Sutherland scored the first Flyers goal.

it, and he told me that the mafia ran the machine and that people were still in the cars as they were being crushed. I said to myself, 'What in the world am I doing in a city like this?'"

Van Impe shared Watson's opinion. He went to an Eagles game and saw planes toting banners that read "Joe Must Go," meaning coach Joe Kuharich. When the Eagles players were introduced, they all were booed. "One defensive back got especially bad treatment," Van Impe recalled in *Walking Together Forever*. "I found out he had a tough game the week before. I was wondering what kind of town was I in. What the hell was I doing there? It was an eye-opening experience."

THE FIRST SEASON

The Flyers' inaugural season started October 11, 1967, with a 5–1 loss to the California Seals at the Oakland Coliseum. Bill Sutherland scored the Flyers' lone goal.

Three nights later they played the Los Angeles Kings at the team's temporary home in Long Beach while the Forum was being built in Inglewood. Despite Sutherland's second goal and a strong effort in net from Doug Favell, the Flyers lost 4–2.

With three days off before their next game, the Flyers flew home, where they were to be honored with a parade through Center City. When the team arrived at the airport, a rousing 35 fans greeted them. The next day, the team officially was welcomed to town at City Hall. Mayor James Tate sent his regards, but had other business to attend to. So did most of Philadelphia.

"We come to Philadelphia, they're having a parade down Broad Street to welcome us to the city," Joe Watson recalled, "and there's more people in the parade than watching it."

Bernie Parent had an idea why no one came. "That's because they advertised Joe Watson was going to be in the parade," he said with a laugh.

Watson wasn't laughing when he recalled the day to author Jay Greenberg in *Full Spectrum*: "About halfway down to the Spectrum, I swear to gosh, there was this guy there giving us the finger. He yelled, 'You'll be in Baltimore by December.' I'll bet there were 20 people, tops, all the way down Broad Street, who actually stood there to watch. All the rest were people on lunch hour wondering who the hell we were."

Parent, ever the optimist, wasn't upset by the low turnout.

"It's understandable because nobody knew about the Flyers," he said. "What they wanted to do was introduce the players to the city, but it was the first step toward a long journey. It wasn't an established team. It was something new in the city. I've always been the type of person, take one step at a time. That didn't bother me at all. ... In my mind, I was [more] preoccupied with performing well than with how many people we had at the parade."

Two days after the parade debacle, the Flyers hit the road again, this time in front of a sparse crowd of 5,234 in St. Louis. The Flyers trailed 2–0, but Lou Angotti scored with 35 seconds left in the second period to tie the game, and then Ed Hoekstra scored with 7:40 left in the third to give the Flyers their first-ever lead. Favell made it stand up, and the Flyers had their first victory.

On October 19 the Flyers played their first game at the Spectrum, against the Pittsburgh Penguins, but only 7,812 showed up. The ones who stayed away missed little, as the game's only goal came 2:59 into the third period, when Hoekstra knocked down a Pens clearing attempt, Sutherland shoved a Leon Rochefort rebound into the net, and the Flyers left with a 1–0 win.

With Gordie Howe in town a day early for a promotional press conference, the Flyers scored their first five-figure attendance mark—10,859—for their first game against an established team, a 3–1 loss to the Detroit Red Wings.

Slowly, though, things began to build as the Flyers started to string some wins together. In early November they went to Montreal and returned home with a 4–1 victory. The next day, in front of 9,188 at the Spectrum, the Flyers played the famed Canadiens to a 1–1 tie. A week later they beat the Bruins at Boston Garden and four days after that they beat the New York Rangers 3–2; the 11,276 in attendance that night at the Spectrum gave the team a standing ovation.

The winning continued as the Flyers climbed over their expansion brethren to claim the top spot in the West Division, the exclusive home of the six new clubs.

In early February the Flyers drew their first set of consecutive sellouts, as scalpers were getting $10 for tickets with a face value of $3.25. The Flyers didn't let the fans down, beating Chicago and Toronto.

The sweet breeze of success, though, can change directions awfully fast. In fact, it changed to a gale-force gust that blew the roof off the Spectrum.

It's an exaggeration that the Spectrum became the world's first retractable-roof stadium on February 17, 1968. On a day when winds whipping off the Delaware River reached nearly 50 mph, pieces of tar paper covering the roof were blown away, leaving a 100-foot-long-by-50-foot-wide spot of exposed sheet metal. There was no real hole, but light was visible through perforations in the sheet metal.

Mayor Tate agreed with a *Philadelphia Inquirer* editorial that said the building should be shuttered, but after meeting with Spectrum officials and representatives from McCloskey and Co., the architectural firm that built the Spectrum, the building stayed open but under the city's watchful eye. Days later, though, a city inspection called the damage "freakish," and the building was declared safe.

On March 1, with workers continuing to repair the arena's roof, more wind gusts tore off three layers of roofing paper and decking. This time there were three different holes, with the biggest 20 feet by 40 feet.

"This is a very windy area," Snider said of the South Philadelphia sports complex. "The architects had not done the wind-tunnel studies that they should have done. The roof was made of this material [but] it wasn't a solid roof. You had the structure, but in between you had this material that wasn't solid. So some of it blew off and a little hole was seen up there. There was no structural damage, but it became a political football, and the goddamn mayor closed us down."

The team split its last seven "home" games between Madison Square Garden in New York, Maple Leaf Gardens in Toronto, and Le Colisee in Quebec City.

The Flyers may have been headed to the playoffs in their first season, but Snider had little opportunity to enjoy it. He was more concerned about trying to keep the team in business for a second season.

"We're closed down for the last seven home games of the season," he said. "We had to refund the money, and I didn't have

ED SNIDER, YOU'RE FIRED

The Flyers' home opener, October 19, 1967, should have been the crowning moment of Ed Snider's life.

Instead, he lost a job and was forced to change careers.

While building the Flyers and the Spectrum, Snider maintained his job as treasurer of the Philadelphia Eagles. But his relationship with Eagles owner Jerry Wolman, who had helped Snider build the team and the arena, had fallen into disrepair. And after the Flyers' home opener, Wolman fired Snider from the Eagles.

While no real reason ever was given, today Snider says, "It was a blessing in disguise."

HAROLD BALLARD

Harold Ballard's offer of Maple Leaf Gardens for the Flyers to use for a "home" game against the Boston Bruins while the Spectrum was out of commission in 1968 might sound like a magnanimous gesture, but it came with a price.

According to team president Bill Putnam, the Leafs kept 50 percent of the gate revenue for what was a "home" Flyers game.

"Then he kept our program money and sent us a bill for the ambulance service," he said in *Full Spectrum*.

---

any money. We were mortgaged. We were getting the season-ticket money to pay the players. Everything was ahead of time. We had almost sold out all those games because we were headed to the playoffs, people were getting excited. I didn't know where the money was going to come from."

Girard Bank once again came to Snider's rescue. The bank previously had loaned the owner $1.5 million to pay off debts incurred in creating the team. Bill Baer, who was the bank's vice president, asked Snider what he needed. The owner said $1 million.

The money was in the team's account the next day.

"They saw our situation had been getting healthier and they wanted to protect their investment," Snider said in *Full Spectrum*. "I'm forever grateful. Without people like that, I never would have made it."

Despite their odd travel schedule, the team persevered and clinched the West Division title March 30, 1968, despite a 2–0 loss to the Pittsburgh Penguins. They received help from the re-named Oakland Seals, who got a late goal to tie the Los Angeles Kings and allow the Flyers to take the top spot by one point, despite finishing with a 31–32–11 record.

In goal, Parent and Favell each posted sub–2.50 goals-against averages, and each had four shutouts. Rochefort and Sutherland each scored 20-plus goals, and Angotti had team highs of 37 assists and 49 points.

Off the ice, the Flyers averaged 9,625 fans per game for their 30 home contests, including three sellouts.

The first round of the playoffs saw the Flyers face the St. Louis Blues, a team the Flyers had lost to just once in 10 regular-season meetings. GM Bud Poile predicted a four-game sweep but the Blues won Game 1 at the reopened Spectrum 1–0 on a third-period goal by Jimmy Roberts.

Rochefort broke a 3–3 tie early in the third period of Game 2 as the Flyers earned a 4–3 series-tying win.

Game 3 in St. Louis was postponed for two days following the assassination of Rev. Dr. Martin Luther King Jr. When play resumed, the Flyers lost Gary Dornhoefer to a broken leg but were able to rally from a pair of one-goal deficits. They tied the game 2–2 when Joe Watson's shot bounced off the Blues' Gary Sabourin and into the net with 6:06 left in regulation.

Early in the second overtime, a Flyers defensive-zone breakdown left Larry Keenan unguarded on the post, and he scored past a helpless Parent at 4:10 of the second extra session to put the Blues ahead two games to one.

Coach Keith Allen, switching goalies each game, went back to Favell for Game 4, but the Blues scored twice shorthanded to take a 5–2 victory and a commanding 3–1 series lead.

Parent made 30 saves in Game 5 at the Spectrum, and Rosaire Paiement, just called up from Quebec City, had a hat trick as the Flyers routed the Blues 6–1.

Allen stuck with Parent for the crucial Game 6, and the netminder made his coach look good, stopping 38 of 39 shots in regulation. But the Blues' Glenn Hall was just a little better, and as the final moments of the game approached, the Flyers trailed 1–0.

As the clock closed in on all zeroes, Allen pulled Parent for an extra attacker. The Flyers held the puck in the Blues' end, and when Hall slid out of position on Ed Van Impe's pass to Andre Lacroix, the diminutive French-Canadian scored into a gaping net to force overtime. Parent stopped Red Berenson on a two-on-one break in extra time, and once again the teams went to a second overtime. At 11:18 of the second extra session, Don Blackburn's backhand lob from the blue line went off a Blues player and past Hall for a 2–1 Flyers victory.

For Game 7 back at the Spectrum, Blues coach Scotty Bowman dug into his bag of tricks and pulled out 43-year-old defenseman Doug Harvey, who had been a player/coach for the Blues' AHL team in Kansas City.

With the future Hall of Famer controlling the action in the St. Louis end, the Flyers were limited to 27 shots. The Blues scored first, but Sutherland tied the game when he tipped a Forbes Kennedy shot past Hall for a second-period power-play goal. The game turned, though, when defenseman Larry Zeidel accidentally tipped a puck into the Flyers' net to put St. Louis ahead 2–1, and Berenson scored into an empty net late for a 3–1 Blues victory.

The Flyers' first season might not have ended in Stanley Cup success, but not too many expansion teams can claim to have won a division title in their first season. And it more than set the stage for the next 45-plus years, which featured many more highs than lows.

THE GOOD

BUILDING THE BULLIES

The Flyers' first season ended in a seven-game first-round playoff loss to the St. Louis Blues. Their second season ended the same way, only it took the Blues just four games to dispatch the Flyers.

Snider still considered himself a newcomer to the game of hockey, but he was no dummy. He noticed what was happening on the ice and wasn't the least bit happy.

His Flyers were getting their asses kicked—literally and figuratively.

"We played St. Louis, and they had the Plager brothers [Barclay and Bob] and [Noel] Picard, and these guys were tough fighters," Snider said. "We had all these little French guys."

Those little French guys—Jean-Guy Gendron, Andre Lacroix, and Simon Nolet—had helped the Flyers win the West Division their first season and finish third the next.

"Teams had in those days what they called a policeman," Snider said. "When [Toronto's] John Ferguson takes on Simon Nolet, Simon Nolet didn't do bad in that fight, but he should have gotten the hell beat out of him. He was so scared. But when I see those kinds of things, I think, who said there can only be one policeman? We're not going to be intimidated."

Snider was determined to make his team bigger and tougher. He relayed that message to general manager Bud Poile and assistant GM Keith Allen.

Bobby Clarke quickly became one of the Flyers' best players and leaders when they picked him in the second round of the 1969 draft.

"We might not be able to skate with these guys, we may not have the talent the Original 6 [teams] have, but we'll build our team with one thing: We can be as tough as anybody else," Snider said. "Let's just go out and get tough guys, and nobody is going to intimidate or beat up our players ever again."

That declaration by Snider started the ball rolling on the franchise's greatest success.

The transformation from victim to Bully began at the 1969 NHL Draft. The Flyers had the sixth overall pick, which Poile used on a center from the Cornwell Royals of the Quebec Major Junior Hockey League named Bob Currier, much to the displeasure of some at the Flyers' draft table.

The team's scouts, especially Jerry Melnyk, wanted a smallish kid from Flin Flon, Manitoba, who had some skill, but was a diabetic. After hearing Poile tab Currier, Melnyk left the draft table. Snider had a great deal of respect for Melnyk, who had played on the Flyers' inaugural team but had to retire after suffering a heart attack. Melnyk wanted to move home to Edmonton, so Snider hired him as a Western Canadian scout.

Snider sent Allen to follow Melnyk.

"Keith comes back and says Melnyk said he was shocked because there's this kid, Bob Clarke, plays for Flin Flon, that Jerry says could step on the ice and be our best player right now," Snider said.

Clarke had posted back-to-back seasons of 50 goals, 150 points and 120 penalty minutes. He had the mix of skill, toughness and physicality Snider was looking for.

"I said to Bud Poile, what about this kid Clarke?" Snider said. "He said, 'I took Currier. A guy I know tells me he's great, a can't-miss guy.' I said our scouts, particularly Jerry Melnyk, think Bob Clarke is the kid. What if he's there in the second round? He said we already have a center, I don't need another center."

Snider was incensed. He told Allen that if Clarke was available in the second round, that he demand Poile select him. Clarke's diabetes had scared off the rest of the league, but in the second round, with the 17th overall choice, the Flyers picked Bobby Clarke.

Later in that 1969 draft, the team used its fifth-round pick (No. 52) on a winger from Waldheim, Saskatchewan, named Dave Schultz. One round later, the team picked 6'2" defenseman Don Saleski, a native of Moose Jaw, Saskatchewan.

The following year, the club drafted Bill Clement in the second round and "the Hound," Bob Kelly, in the third.

Allen, who had replaced Poile as general manager following the 1970 season, knew of a defenseman playing for Hershey, the Boston Bruins' American Hockey League affiliate, that the Boston front office didn't think too much of. The Bruins saw Barry Ashbee as nothing more than a career minor-leaguer, slow to recover from back surgery that had forced him to miss the entire 1966–67 season. Allen saw a player who could provide toughness and veteran leadership, so on May 22, 1970, in his second trade as GM, Allen sent Darryl Edestrand and Larry McKillop to Boston for Ashbee.

Another Allen deal, a three-way trade involving the Bruins and Maple Leafs, allowed the Flyers to get forward Rick MacLeish. The cost, though, was high, as goalie Bernie Parent was sent to Toronto.

The Flyers, especially Snider, knew what they had in Parent, but it was a move that had to be made for the good of the organization.

"I cried when he left," Snider said of the January 31, 1971, deal. "I put my arms around him because the guy did everything right. He was a great guy, great player, but we didn't have any assets to build with. ... We would never win the Cup in Parent's lifetime if we didn't make some moves."

Snider wasn't the only one crying.

"It was a bad time," Parent said of the trade.

In January 1972 "Cowboy" Bill Flett and Ross Lonsberry came aboard in a seven-player deal with the Los Angeles Kings. That summer, the seventh overall pick in the draft was used on a high-scoring winger from Callander, Ontario, named Bill Barber. Defensemen Tom Bladon and Jimmy Watson were picked in the second and third rounds, respectively. In December 1972 Andre "Moose" Dupont was acquired in a trade with the St. Louis Blues.

Allen had hired Fred Shero in 1971 to lead the team. Shero had been coaching the New York Rangers' Central Hockey League affiliate in Omaha.

"I didn't know Freddie well, but I had followed his career, and he had won everywhere," Allen said in *Full Spectrum*. "The only thing that made me wonder was why [Rangers GM] Emile Francis had given other guys a chance [to coach the Rangers] and never given one to Freddie. But his record was so good, and I'd never heard anyone say a bad word about him."

Shero had schooled himself in the emerging Russian style of play, where teams attacked in five-man groups. But his Flyers took it to another level. They didn't just attack the other team's net—they attacked the other team.

"It was an eye for an eye, a tooth for a tooth," Joe Watson said on the *History of the Philadelphia Flyers* 40th anniversary DVD.

With Schultz, Kelly, Dupont and Saleski, the Flyers didn't just beat teams—they beat them up.

They left a trail of bloody, broken players and teams in their wake, none more impressive than what Schultz did to Chicago's Keith Magnuson, who was among the elite tough guys in the early 1970s.

BULLIES NICKNAME

The Flyers marauded through the NHL in the early 1970s, and there to chronicle it was *Philadelphia Bulletin* writer Jack Chevalier.

After watching the Flyers ransack Atlanta like General Sherman on January 3, 1973, he filed: "The image of the fightin' Flyers is spreading gradually around the NHL and people are dreaming up wild nicknames. They're the Mean Machine, the Blue Line Banditos, and Freddy's Philistines."

On the flight home, Chevalier called the newsroom and asked "Blue Line Banditos" be changed to "Bullies of Broad Street." Pete Cafone wrote the headline that accompanied the story that ran in the paper on January 4, 1973: Broad Street Bullies Muscle Atlanta.

"Chicago came into the Spectrum, and Schultz kicked the shit out of Magnuson," Snider said, still smiling 40 years later at the image of Schultz's best punch bloodying the mouth of the Blackhawks' defenseman.

It was the beginning of things to come.

The Flyers marauded through the NHL, earning the scorn of many but pride and reverence from their growing legion of fans. The media added to the Flyers' growing mystique. Writers from other towns called the Flyers animals and barbarians. The Philadelphia press had another name for it, coined by *Philadelphia Bulletin* writer Jack Chevalier and editor Pete Cafone, who together created the name Broad Street Bullies in the paper on January 3, 1973. The players didn't really care about the nickname, but they relished the reputation.

"Intimidation was not my goal," Snider said. "We became intimidators because we were so strong and tough. My goal was ... to [not] be intimidated. It was never to be the intimidator."

Teams grew fearful of the Flyers, afraid of their growing legion of loud, bloodthirsty fans, and afraid of coming into the lions' den known as the Spectrum.

Larry Hillman, a defenseman on that team, told writers, "You can see teams coming in here a little worried. They're hearing that we're a bunch of animals. Some guys don't want any part of that."

"Number one, you had the noise factor," remembered Gary Dornhoefer. "You couldn't even hear yourself talk on the ice, that's how loud it was. And because we played a very physical game, the combination of both made it a very intimidating place to play."

The Philly Flu became a common ailment among visiting hockey players.

"In that era, you come into the Spectrum, we think nothing about winning and we think nothing about taking advantage of you," Kelly said. "No one was going to come into our house and intimidate us or beat us."

"Everybody loved to hate us," Orest Kindrachuk said on the *History of the Philadelphia Flyers* DVD. "We loved to be hated. It

Rick MacLeish was acquired in a trade to help beef up the Flyers' lines in January 1971.

inspired us even more. Going into someone else's building and taking two points from them was all we cared about. We didn't care how. We didn't care where. We just wanted to win the games."

With all the pounding the Flyers' bullies were doing, it was opening space for the team's highly skilled forwards.

In the 1972–73 season Clarke had 37 goals, 67 assists and a team-best 104 points, and after the season won the Hart Trophy as league MVP and the Lester B. Pearson Trophy as the league's best player as voted by the players.

Flett scored 43 goals, and Dornhoefer and Barber netted 30 each.

MacLeish, who regained a full-time roster spot after moving to center with Richmond in the AHL, became the eighth player in league history to that point to score 50 goals. He had been considered a bust as a left wing, but said the move to center changed his career.

"When I first came up with Philadelphia I was a left wing," MacLeish said. "I couldn't use my skating and stickhandling ability on the wing. ... Keith Allen made me a centerman and it clicked. Next year I came up from Richmond, I was a centerman and I made the team."

The Flyers finished with 85 points, good for second place in the West Division, earning them a first-round playoff meeting with the Minnesota North Stars. Despite this being the franchise's fourth playoff appearance in six seasons, the Flyers had yet to win a series.

That was about to change.

The best-of-seven series was tied 2–2, with Game 5 at the Spectrum on April 10, 1973. MacLeish netted his second power-play goal of the game early in the second period, giving the Flyers a 2–1 advantage.

The lead held until Bill Goldsworthy beat Doug Favell at the 13-minute mark of the third period, forcing overtime.

And that's when Dornhoefer scored one of the most memorable goals in team history.

He rushed down the left slot, eluded Barry Gibbs' poke-check attempt, pulled the puck from his forehand to his backhand as he cut in front of the net, and deposited a shot behind North Stars goalie Cesare Maniago, just before Tom Reid upended him. The goal gave the Flyers the win and the series lead, and two days later they closed out the North Stars for the first playoff series win in team history.

Dornhoefer's goal is immortalized in a large bronze statue— Dornhoefer parallel to the ground, arms and stick extended, as the puck sits in the back of the net—that for years sat outside the Spectrum and now is part of the Xfinity Live! complex. "I don't even know how I scored," Dornhoefer told reporters that night. "I just remember getting the puck at center ice, and fortunately it stayed right with me. You could try that play again a hundred times and it wouldn't work."

The momentum from the Minnesota series lasted just one game and two days as the Flyers drew the powerful Montreal Canadiens in the conference finals. They won Game 1 on a MacLeish overtime goal, but the Flyers dropped the next four games.

Despite the heartbreaking loss, there was a breakthrough.

"We went over the hump with Minnesota," Barber said. "We flew out of Minnesota and went right to Montreal. We beat them the first game, in their own building in overtime, then they beat us four straight. But there were games that we knew then that, with maturity, there was something there. We woke them up. We woke the league up."

The next year would see them wake up even more people.

Favell had been the starting goaltender in what had been the Flyers' most successful season to that point in the club's history, but team management thought that to reach the next level, an upgrade was needed in goal. "It wasn't any particular goal or goals in the Montreal series," Keith Allen said in *Full Spectrum*. "It was just the realization that Dougie was the kind of goalie who could win you a series in four straight or lose you one in four straight."

While Favell was winning games in Philadelphia, Parent was remaking his game. What began as an unwanted move from Philadelphia became cushioned by a season and a half sojourn into the reservoir of hockey knowledge known as Jacques Plante, Parent's idol growing up and his teammate with the Leafs.

"I'm always one of those guys that looks at the glass as half-full rather than half-empty," Parent said. "My approach there was, it was sad when I first heard [of the trade], but after a while, I concentrated on the team that made the trade for me rather than the team that traded me. Because you get traded, then you have sad feelings. But if you look at the other side of the coin, you're going to a team that made the move for you.

"At the same time, little did I know I was going to spend two years in Toronto with Jacques Plante. Spending two years with him took me from a raw goalie talent and he helped me become a better goalie."

In 1972 Parent returned to Philadelphia—as a member of the Philadelphia Blazers of the World Hockey Association. That stint lasted just one season, as once paychecks stopped coming, Parent stopped playing. He watched as his old teammates made their first significant playoff run.

"It's always difficult to be a spectator," Parent said. "All your life when you're playing, you're a performer. Just being a spectator was difficult. Little did I know that the universe was guiding me with the right people, the right places, at the right time. Everything had to happen to put me in the right place at the right time with the Flyers."

The following season, Parent needed a job. And the Flyers needed an upgrade in net.

Since the Maple Leafs still owned Parent's NHL rights, Allen and Leafs GM Jim Gregory worked out a deal—Favell and a 1973 first-round draft pick to the Leafs for Parent and a 1973 second-round pick.

On May 15, 1973, the final piece of the puzzle was put in place as Parent returned to the Flyers.

"It was a great feeling," Parent said. "I knew the team, the team had gotten a lot better, and I knew the team had a chance to do something. I was going back to a team that was ready to explode."

"That was the great move," Snider said of bringing back Parent. "That was the greatest moment. To get him back was such a coup."

The Bullies were built. With the 1973–74 season dawning, it was time to turn them loose.

CUP I

The Flyers reported to training camp in 1973 refreshed and feeling positive after the previous spring's playoff experience, plus the return of goaltender Bernie Parent amounted to an upgrade in net.

"I went to Canada that summer and told everybody that I thought we were going win the Stanley Cup the next year," Don Saleski said in *Full Spectrum.* "Our whole club thought we had a chance."

"We had a good mixture, that was the key," Bill Barber, who was starting his first full NHL season, said. "We had [veterans] Barry Ashbee, we had Eddie Van Impe and Joey Watson and Ross Lonsberry. Then we had the in-between group with Clarkie and Schultzy, guys a little older. Then there were guys like Tommy Bladon and myself, we were a younger group there. We had a mix of three different age groups. All of them complemented each other."

The 1973–74 Flyers started with a bang as Kate Smith appeared live to sing "God Bless America." Opening night was Smith's first live performance for Flyers fans, but her rendition of the patriotic song already had become a regular event at the Spectrum. On December 11, 1969, Flyers vice president Lou Scheinfeld shocked the 10,059 in attendance by opting for Smith's version of "God Bless America" rather than the traditional "Star-Spangled Banner."

"I thought I'd do something to shake things up," Scheinfeld said in *Full Spectrum.* "I listened to tapes and records of various patriotic songs, tested them over the PA system in an empty Spectrum, and decided on Kate."

Ed Snider was furious, but the Flyers won that night. Scheinfeld returned to the "Star-Spangled Banner" two nights later, but the Flyers lost. When he played "God Bless America" before the next home game, the Flyers beat Pittsburgh 4–0, and newspapers noted the Flyers were 2–0 when Smith sang. Snider's anger quickly abated.

Over the following years, Snider and others within the organization had tried to get Smith to sing live, but to no avail.

Unbeknownst to the club was the fact that Smith's uncle, Fred Ditmars, lived in West Philadelphia and had been sending the singer newspaper clippings chronicling the "God Bless America" phenomenon. It was enough for Smith to tell her agent to make a deal with the Flyers.

When the Flyers realized they usually won the games in which Kate Smith opened by singing "God Bless America," a Philadelphia tradition was born.
Photo courtesy AP Images.

"The cheers went right through me," Smith said after her opening-night performance. "I've played before larger crowds, but I've never had a bigger ovation. It was fantastic, and I'm sorry that is such a mediocre word."

The Flyers beat the Leafs that night 2–0, running Smith's record, live or on tape, to 29–3–1.

The 1973–74 Flyers cruised to their first 50-win season and won the West Division with 112 points.

Bobby Clarke led the team with 35 goals, 52 assists and 87 points, the fifth-highest total in the league. Barber added 34 goals, and Rick MacLeish and Ross Lonsberry scored 32 apiece. Dave Schultz added 20 goals and a league-high 348 penalty minutes.

In net, Parent had arguably the finest season ever for a player at his position. He played a remarkable 73 of 78 games, setting a league record that stood for 17 seasons. He set another NHL standard with 47 wins in a day when there was no overtime or shootouts (the mark stood until the 2006–07 season, when the rules had been changed so ties were eliminated). He also posted a league-low 1.89 goals-against average and an NHL-leading 12 shutouts.

Parent became the first Flyer to win the Vezina Trophy, sharing the award with Chicago's Tony Esposito, and he finished second to Phil Esposito in balloting for the Hart Trophy, awarded to the league MVP.

And for leading the Flyers to their best season ever, coach Fred Shero won the initial Jack Adams Award as league coach of the year.

The Flyers swept Atlanta in the first round of the playoffs, then took a 2–0 series lead against the Rangers in the conference finals, but dropped the next two games. They also lost Bob Kelly to a season-ending knee injury in Game 3 and Barry Ashbee in overtime of Game 4 with what became a career-ending eye injury.

The Flyers, also now missing an injured Bill Clement, won Game 5 at the Spectrum 4–1 , but lost Game 6 at Madison Square Garden by an identical score.

That set up Game 7 at the Spectrum. The Flyers drew first blood—literally—when Schultz pounded Dale Rolfe in the first period.

"That took something out of New York," Shero told reporters. "They didn't do as much hitting after that."

The extra space allowed Orest Kindrachuk and Gary Dornhoefer to drive to the net for rebound goals to give the Flyers a 3–1 lead. But at 8:49 of the third, Dornhoefer allowed Steve Vickers to get away from him and score to make it 3–2. Rather than berate Dornhoefer for his gaffe, Shero went a different way.

"Shero left our line [Dornhoefer, Lonsberry and MacLeish] on the ice, and 30 seconds later I was able to get that goal back with a goal," Dornhoefer said. "He had confidence in the line by letting us stay out there after the goal was scored."

It actually took just 12 seconds, as Dornhoefer got in front of Rangers goalie Ed Giacomin and scored to restore a two-goal lead.

Pete Stemkowski scored for the Rangers to make it 4–3 with 5:26 left, but the Flyers kept the Rangers to the outside and milked time off the clock. When it was over, the Flyers had become the first expansion team to beat an Original 6 club in a playoff series.

To win the ultimate prize, they'd have to do it again.

The Boston Bruins entered the Stanley Cup Final a heavy favorite. They were well-rested, having a week to sit and watch the Flyers battle the Rangers after they had dispatched the Chicago Blackhawks in six games.

The Bruins' Phil Esposito was coming off a league-record 68-goal season, and his 145 points earned him the Art Ross Trophy as the league's leading scorer, as well as the Hart Trophy as NHL MVP. Bruins players took the top four spots in the league scoring race, as defenseman Bobby Orr had finished second with 122 points, followed by Esposito's linemates—Ken Hodge with 105 points and Wayne Cashman with 89.

Orr, though, was the key to the Bruins' success. Considered the best player in the game at the time, he was in the midst of a stretch of six straight seasons finishing in the top three in league scoring, including winning a pair of Art Ross trophies, and he had won the seventh of his eight straight Norris trophies as the league's best defenseman.

But rather than fear Orr, Shero devised a different plan: Dump the puck in Orr's corner at all times. Shero wanted Orr to carry

Dave Schultz cross-checks Wayne Cashman in the 1974 Stanley Cup Finals.

the puck, which would allow the physical Flyers forwards to use him for target practice on the forecheck. Over a long series, the hope was Orr would wear down.

Game 1 started with Boston taking a 2–0 lead, but goals by Kindrachuk and Clarke tied the game 5:32 into the third period.

Cowboy Bill Flett had a chance to put the Flyers ahead on a three-on-two break, but his shot hit the post. At the other end, Orr put the Bruins on top when his blast through traffic went between Parent's pads with 22 seconds left.

POST-GAME ENTERTAINMENT

A city watched, listened and cheered on May 19, 1974, when the Flyers won the Stanley Cup.

But no one beside the players, their families, and members of the organization know how beautiful the post-game celebration was. Rather than go inside the victorious locker room for interviews, NBC, which was televising the game, immediately cut to the movie *The Raiders*.

Despite the 3–2 loss, the Flyers were confident.

"We'd outplayed them, and they knew it," Clarke said in *Full Spectrum*. "We were in better shape than the Bruins."

Game 2 saw the Bruins again take a 2–0 lead, but again the Flyers battled back. Clarke redirected a Flett shot past Bruins goalie Gilles Gilbert, and then an unlikely Moose Dupont score evened the game with just 52 seconds left to force overtime.

Midway through the extra session, the surprising trio of Clarke, Flett and Schultz got the puck in front of the Boston net, with Clarke lifting the winner over a sprawling Gilbert at 12:01. It was the Flyers' first win at Boston Garden since their first trip there in their inaugural season.

Despite losing Dornhoefer to a separated shoulder, the Flyers outworked the Bruins at the Spectrum, taking Game 3 4–1.

MacLeish and Schultz gave the Flyers a 2–0 lead early in Game 4, but the Bruins tied the game before the first period was over on scores by Esposito and Andre Savard.

The game remained tied into the latter stages of the third period. Barber, a left wing playing on the right side for Dornhoefer, dumped the puck into the Bruins' end. Lonsberry held Orr up enough so the defenseman couldn't clear the puck, and Barber grabbed it off the boards and fired a shot over Gilbert's glove with six minutes left, snapping a nine-game goal drought and giving the Flyers a 3–2 lead.

Clarke then fed Dupont, who walked past Esposito and scored with 3:20 left, icing the 4–2 win and giving the Flyers a three-games-to-one stranglehold on the series.

Back in Boston for Game 5, Orr scored twice in the second period to snap a 1–1 tie and propel the Bruins to a 5–1 win.

Game 6 of the series was Sunday, May 19, 1974. The Flyers had a second chance to close the best-of-seven series, and no one in black and orange wanted to see Boston Garden until next fall.

"I don't think anybody would have been very comfortable going back," Clarke said.

When the players arrived in the locker room Sunday morning, there was a nine-word message scrawled on the blackboard: "Win together today, and we will walk together forever."

The Flyers were ready to throw everything they had at the Bruins in Game 6. They even brought in their secret weapon: Kate Smith, booked for an appearance on *The Mike Douglas Show* in Philadelphia the next day, was a no-brainer choice to sing "God Bless America."

"What could be better than being linked with something so wholesome as good, clean sport?" Smith rhetorically asked *Philadelphia Bulletin* writer Joe Adcock.

The Flyers gave the Bruins the game's first two power plays, but got a four-on-three advantage when Terry O'Reilly was sent off for tripping Barber at 13:58, followed by Orr and Clarke getting whistled for matching roughing minors at 14:22 after a goalmouth scrum.

Midway through the advantage, MacLeish beat Gregg Sheppard on a faceoff in the right circle, then got in front of the net and tipped a Dupont point shot past Gilbert at 14:48 of the first.

MacLeish, traded by the Bruins to the Flyers in 1971, described that night as "the best feeling I've had in my life."

"Only Rick could have done what he did," Snider said. "He had such great hand-eye coordination."

"It was simple," MacLeish said. "I won the draw, and just skating toward the net the puck came there and I tipped it. It's something you practice in practice [but] you don't think you'll ever get the opportunity. But I did."

Parent made the lead stand up. In one of the greatest big-game performances of all time, he stopped all 30 Bruins shots. His biggest save came with just under three minutes left, when

Hodge ripped a low slap shot from the just above the left faceoff circle that looked destined for the inside of the far post, but Parent kicked out his right pad to knock the shot aside.

"It was the best game he's ever played in his life," MacLeish said. "To shut them out like that, 1–0, it was unbelievable."

"We threw everything we had at them in the sixth game and still needed a special effort from Bernie," Clarke said. "Parent in that particular game played the best game any player's ever played for the franchise."

As time ticked down, orange streamers started raining down from the Spectrum roof. Snider may have disagreed with the city's exaggerated ruling of the roof blowing off in 1968, but he was ecstatic on this night six years later that it might happen again.

Gloves, sticks and players all flew into the air in celebration, and Gene Hart jubilantly screamed for all to hear: "The Flyers win the Stanley Cup! The Flyers win the Stanley Cup! The Flyers have won the Stanley Cup!"

Fans leapt the boards, some already with bottles of champagne, while the players engaged in the traditional post-series handshake. Many of the 17,000-plus were crowding onto the ice as Clarke and Parent, trailed by teammates, attempted a victory lap with the Cup.

They didn't get far, but that didn't mean they partied any less.

"I thought it was a wonderful thing when people stepped on the ice," Parent said. "I always said 75 percent of our success was our family at the Spectrum. I always felt it was 18,000 people and us playing against you. I was very happy when they jumped on the ice. It was as much their Stanley Cup as it was ours."

For his remarkable play, Parent was awarded the Conn Smythe Trophy as most valuable player for the playoffs. In 17 games, he went 12–5 with a pair of shutouts and a 2.02 goals-against average.

Parent also became the first goalie to win the Vezina and Conn Smythe trophies in the same season, and he's one of just two players in NHL history to win the Vezina, Conn Smythe and Stanley Cup in the same season.

It was just the fourth time since 1925 the greatest title in sports had been won by the slimmest of margins, and it's happened just one time since.

The next day was the victory parade, with players, coaches and other team officials piling into convertibles in the Spectrum parking lot for a ride up Broad Street and along Chestnut Street that ended at Independence Hall.

Police expected a crowd of a few hundred thousand for the first championship celebration in town since the 1967 Philadelphia 76ers won the NBA title. Instead, a throng estimated at 2 million people overwhelmed the officers—and nearly overturned the cars carrying the players.

The car carrying Clarke and Ed Van Impe never made it to Independence Hall. Parent's car had to be stopped for fear of celebrating fans flipping it. Tom Bladon abandoned his car and walked, while MacLeish ended up with a bruised arm and Don Saleski had the sleeve of his jacket torn off by fans crazed at being so close to these champions.

Al Piazza was one of those 2 million. "I have a picture of Bernie Parent. It was something," the lifelong South Philadelphia resident and 45-year Flyers fan said. "I can remember that day, walking to Broad Street, it was bedlam. It was like that on the streets to Broad. It was just crazy. The day they won, South Philly was crazy, people hanging out of cars on Oregon Avenue.

"It was like the astronauts [returning from space]. In Center City, the tickertape was unbelievable. And it was played over and over on the news."

The parade was a special day for everyone associated with the Flyers, but it meant a little bit more to one three-year-old boy.

"My dad told me the first parade was for my birthday," Brian Hart, Gene Hart's son, said.

Lauren Hart, Gene's daughter and the Flyers' anthem singer, was only five years old at that first parade, but the memory of the event remains as clear today as it was on that day more than 35 years ago.

"When we got there, my father and Don Earl [Gene's broadcast partner] were supposed to ride in an open convertible right behind the Cup [and] the wives and children were all going to go on a bus behind. I remember my father grabbing us all and pulling all three kids and Don Earl's wife and my mom, and we all got into that two-seat convertible," she said. "Had he not done that, we would not have had that experience. And I remember people hanging from lampposts and street signs, and people wanted to shake my dad's hand."

When the parade—or at least most of it—reached Independence Hall, each player was introduced. Snider told the crowd, "They deserved the title. They've worked hard. We've got the number-one team in the world in the number-one city in the world."

Then it was Shero's turn, and the coach set the stage for the next season. "This is the greatest team in the league," he told the crowd, "and we're going to win it again next year."

CUP II

Coach Fred Shero made the declaration that the Flyers would win the Stanley Cup again in the 1974–75 season. It was up to GM Keith Allen to put the players in place to make it happen.

Allen wasn't interested in changing too much of a good thing. He did, though, believe the team needed more scoring, so five days after winning the Cup, he got a player he had been lusting after for a number of years: Reggie Leach.

Leach had been a teammate of Bobby Clarke's for three seasons in junior hockey with the Flin Flon Bombers, including one remarkable campaign when Leach had 87 goals and 131 points in just 59 games.

With Cowboy Bill Flett's scoring going down and his alcohol consumption going up, Allen—living up to his nickname of Keith the Thief—sent Al MacAdam, Larry Wright, and a 1974 first-round pick to the California Golden Seals for Leach, and three days later shipped Flett to the Toronto Maple Leafs.

Leach immediately was installed on Clarke's line, with Bill Barber completing the trio.

It was a gutsy move, as Leach had unmistakable talent—the Boston Bruins thought so when they made him the third overall

---

BILL CLEMENT TRADE

When Bill Clement scored the insurance goal in the Cup-clinching win against the Buffalo Sabres in 1975, technically speaking, Clement wasn't even a Flyer.

Earlier in the game, Flyers general manager Keith Allen had agreed on a deal that would send the young center to the Capitals, along with defenseman Don MacLean and a first-round draft pick, for the Caps' number-one overall selection in the 1975 draft.

---

selection in the 1970 draft—but in five NHL seasons Leach's best output was 23 goals.

"[Leach] has never played with a good team or a good center-man as a pro," Allen said in making the deal. "He has a chance to be a star." By Christmas the Flyers had reeled off 10- and 12-game unbeaten streaks. Backstopping their effort seemingly on an every-night basis was Bernie Parent. As great as the goalie had been the season before, he was even better in 1974–75. In his first 37 starts, Parent had 26 wins and seven shutouts.

And not only was he making an impact on the ice, he was bringing newfound attention to the sport. On February 24, 1975, a masked Parent became the face of hockey when he appeared on the cover of *Time* magazine.

When the magazine hit newsstands, Parent had played in 53 of the Flyers' first 60 games, posting a 33–12–8 record with nine shutouts and a 2.13 goals-against average, while the Flyers were 35–16–9 overall. Bumper stickers that read "Only the Lord Saves More Than Bernie Parent" began popping up on cars at all points of the Delaware Valley.

Clarke wasn't joking when he said in the *Time* story, "Bernie makes you feel like you can walk on water."

The Flyers ran roughshod over the league, with a 16–1–2 finishing kick, propelling them to league-highs of 51 wins and 113 points, one more in each category than the season before.

"We just played along," Rick MacLeish said. "We never lost two games in a row. We only lost one game, never two games in a row. That was our mindset—never lose two games in a row. It worked out for us."

Parent, playing 68 of the 80 games, totaled league-best totals of 44 wins, a 2.03 goals-against average, and 12 shutouts.

Offensively, the Leach-Clarke-Barber triumvirate dominated the league. Leach, nicknamed the Rifle, finished with 45 goals. Clarke had 89 assists and 116 points, and won his second Hart Trophy as league MVP. Barber finished with 34 goals, 37 assists and 71 points.

Together, the LCB Line totaled 106 goals and 265 points, and had a plus/minus rating of plus-178. Leach, who had been a minus-61 in 1973–74 with California, finished plus-53. Clarke led all NHL forwards with a plus-79, while Barber was a plus-46.

"I think it was three different kinds of players," Barber said as to why the line worked so well. "Reggie had the cannon of a shot. I complemented in the sense of playing more detailed in all three zones and making sure I was accountable defensively. Clarkie was tenacious in his forecheck and anticipation of the puck. We all complemented one another. We knew where each other was, we always backed one another. We always took the sure route on things. We were three different players, but we could all score a little bit. We were tough to contain. Reggie could really gun the puck, so [defenses] tried to focus in on him. I was open a little bit. Reggie and I fed off ourselves quite a bit for rebound goals. It was one of those unique things."

The first-place Flyers opened the playoffs against the Toronto Maple Leafs. Parent was outstanding, keeping the Leafs off the scoreboard for a total of 143:16, covering the final 29 seconds of the second period of a 6–3 win in Game 1 and lasting through the first 2:47 of Game 4.

The Leafs made one last stand at home in Game 4. Barber scored in the second period to put the Flyers up 3–2, but Ron Ellis scored with 6:37 left in the third to force overtime.

Early in extra time, it was an unlikely pair combining to eliminate the Maple Leafs. Dave Schultz and Moose Dupont had combined for just 20 goals during the regular season, but it was Schultz who intercepted a Toronto pass and dropped the puck for Dupont, whose wrister from about 20 feet out beat goalie Gord McRae and closed the series.

On the flight home, the players grooved to a new song that was set to debut on Philadelphia Top 40 AM radio—Schultz's single, "Penalty Box." Some of the lyrics: "Love is like an ice hockey game, sometimes it can be rough/You got me checking and holding and hooking and then you blow the whistle on me." Despite the lyrics and overall lack of singing ability, the fact that

Bernie Parent (left) and Bill Clement (right) clasp hands as NHL President Clarence Campbell (second from left) presents them with the Stanley Cup after their victory over the Buffalo Sabres on May 27, 1975. Bobby Clarke (second from right) gives a big, gap-toothed grin.

Schultz's name was attached sent the song soaring up the charts, and records flew off the shelves.

The Toronto challenge answered, it was on to the conference finals against the New York Islanders, who in the previous round had become just the second team in league history to overcome a 3–0 deficit in a best-of-seven series when they got past the Pittsburgh Penguins in the quarterfinals.

The Flyers felt confident—until a Gary Dornhoefer shot hit Parent on an unprotected part of the netminder's knee. Parent couldn't get back on his feet, and backup Wayne Stephenson, who had played just 12 games all season—and not at all in the previous six weeks—was pressed into action.

Stephenson was up to the challenge, however, shutting out a young Islanders squad—which featured much of the core of the dynastic team that would win four straight Cups in the early 1980s—and Clarke scored the overtime winner in Game 2.

With Parent back for Game 3, the only goal came from Leach, who looped a backhander over Chico Resch's glove 30 seconds into the third period.

Once again, the Isles were down 3–0 in a series. Once again, they mounted a comeback.

The Islanders won 4–3 in Game 4 on an overtime goal by Jude Drouin, and they won Game 5 in a 5–1 rout, handing the Flyers their first home playoff loss in two years.

At Nassau Coliseum for Game 6, the teams were tied 1–1 early in the third when Flyers rookie defenseman Larry Goodenough gave the puck away to the Islanders' Gerry Hart, who rifled a shot over Parent's glove to give the Isles a series-tying 2–1 win.

Their season on the line, the Flyers brought a little extra ammunition for Game 7. Kate Smith was secreted into Philadelphia, and once again her rendition of "God Bless America" drove the 17,077 Spectrum denizens into bedlam.

The Flyers' performance on the ice kept the good feelings rolling. Jimmy Watson forced Eddie Westfall to turn the puck over, and Dornhoefer fired a shot from 40 feet out that beat Resch to the short side, giving the Flyers a 1–0 lead just 19 seconds into the game. MacLeish added a pair of goals, redirecting a Barber shot for a power-play goal at 2:27 to make it 2–0, and then scoring on a wrister to make it 3–1 7:11 into the game. MacLeish capped his night with an empty-net goal for the hat trick, finishing the Islanders and sending the Flyers back to the Stanley Cup Final.

The Flyers' foe in the Final was the Buffalo Sabres. The Sabres had eliminated the powerful Montreal Canadiens in their conference final, led by their French Connection Line of Gilbert Perreault, Rick Martin and Rene Robert. As good as the LCB Line was, the Connection was better, combining for 131 goals and 291 points.

"We were underdogs in the Boston series [in the 1974 Cup Final] and we were underdogs in the Buffalo series," MacLeish said. "They thought they'd walk all over us."

In Game 1 Barber snapped a scoreless tie in the third period and added an empty-net goal late, and Clarke had a goal and two assists in a 4–1 win.

In Game 2 Clarke set up Leach for the game's first goal midway through the second period. After Jerry Korab tied the game early in the third, Clarke took a pass from Barber and scored from the left side of the net at 6:43 of the third. Parent slammed the door the rest of the way, and the Flyers shuffled to Buffalo with a 2–0 series lead.

The fog got the better of the Fog and the Flyers in Game 3.

May 20, 1975, was an unusually warm spring day in Buffalo, and temperatures reached 90 degrees. As the temperature inside Memorial Auditorium—which did not have air-conditioning—matched the outside air, a mist began to rise as the ice started melting under the players' skates. The game was stopped 12 different times so players and arena workers, some holding bed sheets, could skate around the ice to try to dissipate the mist.

"It was weird," Clarke said. "It was 90 degrees outside and no air conditioning in the building. It was tough, not only because of the fog, but you'd get dehydrated. Those were the days where you weren't told to drink to water—you were told not to drink water. They always thought you'd get bloated from drinking water. Wash your mouth out but don't swallow it. You had dehydration problems."

Fred Shero coached the Flyers to two Stanley Cups and a memorable win over the Russians in 1976, but felt his ability to motivate the Flyers was waning by the late 1970s.

Adding to the surreal feeling was a bat that began buzzing the ice. Prior to a faceoff, Sabres forward Jim Lorentz slashed the bat with his stick. It dropped dead onto the ice as players and officials stared at it. Finally, MacLeish scooped up the carcass and dropped it in the penalty box.

"They said it had rabies. I said nah, it's not rabies," MacLeish said. "It was just laying there—dead."

Whatever the bizarre night held, the Flyers looked unstoppable early. Dornhoefer scored off a Barber takeaway just 39 seconds into the game, and then Don Saleski gave the Flyers a 2–0 lead at the 3:09 mark. Danny Gare and Martin scored 17 seconds apart to tie the game, but MacLeish put the Flyers ahead when he scored with 5:47 left in the first. Don Luce tied the game 29 seconds into the second, but Leach again put the Flyers on top until Bill Hajt scored off a Martin rebound midway through the third, which forced overtime.

The longer play went, the thicker the fog got, making the puck harder to see. Play was stopped seven times just in the 18 minutes of overtime. Finally, Robert played a Perreault dump-in along the goal line in the Flyers' end, and from the sharpest of angles, he slid a shot past Parent's skates and into the net.

"I didn't see Perreault's pass," Parent told reporters after the game. "I saw Robert's shot too late for me to come out and stop it."

The Flyers remained confident heading into Game 4, and held a 1–0 lead after 20 minutes on a Dupont goal. That would be as good as the night got for the Flyers, though, as Buffalo scored three times in the second period en route to a 4–2 series-tying victory.

In Philadelphia for Game 5, the Flyers bombarded Buffalo goalie Gerry Desjardins with shots, rather than look for nice set-ups to lead to goals. Schultz started and finished what would become a 5–1 rout, first surprising Desjardins from a sharp angle 3:12 into the game, and scoring on a breakaway to close the scoring. With the win, the Flyers were one game away from their second straight Stanley Cup.

Game 6, on May 27, 1975, was scoreless through the first two periods thanks to Parent, who held off five Buffalo power plays.

Shero, worried that some of his players might be tiring from penalty-killing duties—he used his best players in all situations, including Barber and Clarke as his top short-handed forwards—took the advice of assistant coach Mike Nykoluk and subbed Kelly for Barber on the top line to open the third period.

Clarke won a faceoff back to his defense, and the puck was worked around to Leach along the right wall. He dumped the puck behind the Buffalo net, where Kelly beat Korab to the puck, but Korab momentarily pinned Kelly to the glass. Clarke joined the party behind the goal and bumped Korab hard enough to let Kelly spin away with the puck. Kelly bolted in front to the right of goalie Roger Crozier and slid a backhand to the far side of the net 11 seconds into the frame, and the Flyers held a 1–0 lead.

Kelly celebrated with teammates, but when he returned to the bench, he had a few words for Shero.

"I told Freddy he owed me five dollars," Kelly said.

The reference was to a drill frequently used by Shero in which players had to bull their way from behind the net and score a goal, and anytime they did, Shero would give them a $5 bill. They ran the drill during the final 15 minutes of every practice during the 1974–75 season. And when the moment struck, all the practice time paid off.

The Flyers doggedly protected their goal, and Parent, as usual, was outstanding. His best save came late, when Barber failed to clear the puck and Craig Ramsay blindly whacked it with his backhand to an open Luce, who tipped it on net, but Parent made a juggling chest save with less than five minutes left.

The Flyers got an insurance goal when Orest Kindrachuk blocked a Brian Spencer shot and raced the length of the ice to corral the loose puck. Spencer and Korab chased Kindrachuk, and as Spencer caught him, he drilled the winger with a forearm to the head. But Kindrachuk was able to backhand the puck to a trailing Bill Clement, whose shot went between Crozier's pads with 2:47 left to play.

The Flyers' bench emptied onto the ice to celebrate Clement's first—and only—playoff goal as a Flyer. When the final horn sounded, the Flyers again leapt off their bench, this time mobbing Parent. For the second straight season, he had backstopped a Cup-clinching effort with a shutout, the only netminder in NHL history to accomplish the feat.

Parent finished the playoffs 10–5 with four shutouts and a 1.89 goals-against average in 15 games, numbers even better than the previous year. He again won the Conn Smythe Trophy as playoff MVP, and he's the only goalie in league history to win it in consecutive years.

When Clarence Campbell handed the silver chalice to Clarke for a second consecutive season, the captain and the goalie got to skate their celebratory lap around the ice unimpeded—something they didn't get to do the previous year at the Spectrum due to the overzealousness of the fans.

"It was really congested [the previous year]," Barber said. "There were so many people on the ice you never really had the true opportunity. The second time we did it, it was in Buffalo ... it was pretty awesome. It's a memory that sticks with you. There's moments and memories. Memories are special things. Moments are every-day stuff you deal with. They're great memories that are with you the rest of your life."

They say you never forget your first time, but some players considered the second Cup just a bit sweeter.

"I can honestly say it's a better feeling to win two years in a row," Parent told reporters after the game. "When we won last year we were in the clouds. This year it was different because we knew what we were doing and where we were going. We proved to everyone that last year was no fluke."

More than 35 years later, Parent still feels the same way.

"The second one was better," he said. "We could appreciate more what happened. We had the Stanley Cup, and we flew back from Buffalo and had an hour and 15 minutes by ourselves to just reflect on this thing. It was beautiful."

For Kelly, he was just happy to be on the ice when the Cup was won. A knee injury had shelved him for the 1974 title series against the Bruins, and he didn't know until game time that he would be playing in Game 6 against the Sabres, as Shero had considered kenneling the Hound.

"You have to be there in the end to feel like you made a contribution," Kelly told reporters that night.

Kelly then turned and told a man in a suit seated in his dressing stall to get the heck out of there. The man, Pennsylvania Governor Milton Shapp, apologized and walked away.

After the near-riots of the previous year, Philadelphia police had the players ride on flatbed trucks for the parade down Broad Street to a rally at JFK Stadium.

There were 100,000 people packed into the stadium, plus an estimated 2.2 million lining Broad Street for the parade, meaning about 2.3 million—or 300,000 more than the year before—saw the second parade.

There was none of the same pandemonium of the previous year, except for when Parent jumped off a truck and knocked on a door along South Broad Street and asked the homeowner if he could use the bathroom.

There also were none of the same pronouncements from Shero or anyone else. None were needed. Philadelphia was the center of the hockey universe. Anyone who didn't recognize it the previous year certainly knew it now.

DEFEATING THE RED MENACE

The Broad Street Bullies were the ultimate bad guys, a hoard of rampaging monsters, beating teams and beating up people.

They didn't play classy, dignified hockey, but two straight Stanley Cups meant nobody in the City of Brotherly Love really gave a damn.

Ed Snider—credited or blamed, depending on your point of view—thinks the violence has overshadowed the legacy of the championship teams.

"The sad part is," Snider said, "that phase of it has detracted from our Stanley Cup championships. The truth of it is we had phenomenal talent on those teams, great coaching."

But the Flyers were the Broad Street Bullies, and no one likes a bully. But there was this one time …

In 1976 the Soviet government sent a pair of all-star hockey teams to tour North America in their quest to show Communist supremacy over all things in the Western world. The final stop on the Central Red Army team's barnstorming tour was a visit to the Spectrum to play the two-time defending Stanley Cup champions, on January 11, 1976.

The Red Army team had beaten the New York Rangers and Boston Bruins, and even the mighty Montreal Canadiens only could manage a tie.

"It was their all-star team against our regular franchises, and they were winning," Snider said. "They came in here, and we were the defending Stanley Cup champions. We were the team that everybody was hoping would finally beat these sons of bitches. The game had everything; it was mind-boggling."

Philadelphia, the cradle of liberty, the birthplace of the nation, put orange and black right next to the red, white, and blue.

Even other NHL teams were pulling for the Flyers.

"We were hated," Snider recalled, "and suddenly all of Canada wanted us to win."

"In those days it was defeating the Communist lifestyle," Bob Clarke said. "The Cold War was on. It was more than just a hockey game."

Clarke had initiated his own cold war with the Soviets. During the famed 1972 Summit Series, he had slashed Soviet star Valeri Kharlamov hard enough to break the legendary player's ankle.

"It wasn't premeditated," Clarke told reporters in the build-up to the 1976 game. "He had speared me, and it wasn't a clean series from the start."

When the Soviets arrived in Philadelphia, the NHL hosted both teams and the press at a luncheon at the Blue Line Club at the Spectrum.

"The Russian players were on one side, and our players were on the other," Snider said. "Because of the Cold War, the Russians were like slaves—they weren't allowed to do anything, very gruff, angry."

Gene Hart, who spoke some Russian, had taught Snider a few phrases to use to welcome the visitors to town.

"Gene taught me how to say in Russian, 'We welcome you to our fair city and we hope you're enjoying yourselves,' something like that. So I practiced and practiced, got up and I said [in English], 'We're looking forward to the game tonight, may the best team win,' and I sat down. Gene said, 'Did you forget?' I said I looked at those sons of bitches and I couldn't welcome them."

Fred Shero had been a disciple of the Soviet hockey style. Days after the Flyers' first Cup victory, Shero flew to Moscow to attend a coaching clinic led by Anatoly Tarasov, the father of Russian hockey. Shero spoke no Russian and Tarasov spoke no English, but the pair somehow found a way to communicate.

Shero believed the style of play used by the Flyers, where the third forward would stay high in the offensive zone, would cut off the Soviets' favored long passes through the middle of the ice.

That, and the Flyers could bludgeon the Russians senseless.

"I'm not sure the Soviets wanted it with that type of attitude, but that was our type of attitude," Clarke said. "It was going to be ugly. We were going to beat you, and if you were going to beat us, you were going to pay a big price. And they weren't willing to pay the price."

There was more to it than just a hockey game. Clarke remembers people in Philadelphia imploring him and his teammates to do awful things to the Soviets, including winning the game.

"We heard that all the time," he said.

While fans took it personally, so did forward Orest Kindrachuk. Kindrachuk's grandparents were of Ukrainian descent, and had told him about how the Soviets had mistreated their people.

"They told us stories about how tough it was for them over there," he told reporters. "I was so happy to beat them. When I was out there, I didn't want to look at them, hear them."

Snider also had more than just the interest of an owner or a fan. Snider, a Jewish man, hated the Soviets for their treatment of Russian Jews, and long swore that he never would have a Soviet player on his team.

Jewish activist groups marched outside the Spectrum on the day of the game, protesting the harassment and imprisonment of Jews in the Soviet Union. Banners were hung inside the Spectrum, in Russian and English, demanding freedom for Soviet Jews. But all the banners were taken down before the game, as the Soviets said they wouldn't play if the signs were allowed to stay.

Off the opening faceoff, the Red Army team dropped back into its zone and made eight passes before coming forward. Meanwhile the Flyers waited, like hungry lions watching gazelles at a watering hole.

"Shero had been over there and had a little understanding of them," Clarke said. "We had seen them play since 1972, and that's the style they played. Once you had the patience and discipline to just wait, they had to bring the puck to you eventually. They could keep going backward all they wanted, but they have to come forward at some point if they want to score. And once they started coming forward, we took them physically, and then they weren't so eager to come forward."

The Flyers started on the attack early, outshooting the Soviets 10–2, but world-renowned goalie Vladislav Tretiak was up to the challenge. The Flyers even got the game's first power play, when Boris Aleksandrov was sent off for elbowing Gary Dornhoefer in the head 2:24 into the game.

But with Ed Van Impe off for tripping Vladimir Lutchenko at 9:10 of the first, the serious hitting began. Moose Dupont threw a shoulder into Red Army captain Boris Mikhailov at the Flyers' blue line. Then Bill Barber, on the forecheck, rammed Valeri Vasilyev hard into the boards in the Soviet end and then cross-checked Kharlamov in the face.

As Van Impe jumped out of the box, he ran directly at Kharlamov, elbowing him in the head and leaving him face-down on the ice in the Flyers' end.

"He basically ran into my elbow with his head," Van Impe joked in *Walking Together Forever*. "I've always said I just couldn't understand how a world-class player would have wanted to do such a thing."

Snider described the incident a little differently: "Ed Van Impe put one of his famous checks on one of the Russians." He added with a chuckle, "Ed Van Impe wasn't one of the cleanest hockey players."

The Soviet players and their coach, Konstantin Loktev, screamed for a penalty, but the only one coming was a two-minute bench minor to the Soviets for delay of game. Loktev then waved his team off the ice and into the locker room. There was 8:39 left to play in the first period.

"They pulled all the players over in front of the bench and they didn't want to come off for the faceoff," Lou Nolan, the long-time Flyers public address announcer who was stationed next to the Soviet bench, said. "I remember talking to Lloyd Gilmour, he was the referee. We said it [the delay] is an intimidation factor, and he said yeah, I know—give them two minutes for delay of the game. When I announced that two minutes for delay of the game, they went berserk and that's when they left."

Snider immediately ran down to the Soviet locker room, where he met with NHL president Clarence Campbell and NHLPA president Alan Eagleson, who was coordinating the tour.

"We went down, and they said we're not playing," Snider said. "They won't play, they're going to leave. I said, 'What's the status of the payment for this tournament?' They said we haven't given them anything yet. They get the check tonight for all the games. I said to tell them you're not going to pay them. I think we were the eighth game, and it was only, like, $25,000 a game in those days. They were supposed to get a couple hundred grand, but they hadn't been paid anything yet. It was supposed to be settled that night, so I said just tell them they're not going to get paid for the tournament. They told them, they started huddling, then they came back and said, 'We play.'"

After a 17-minute delay, the Russians returned.

"They cried it was too physical, but it wasn't any more physical than what we played against NHL teams," Clarke said. "It was just another form of quitting when they walked off. I don't think the players would have done that. It was their coaches and the people in charge who did that to the players. But the game was over ... I think 10, 12 minutes into the game we knew."

The game resumed with the Flyers on the power play, and 17 seconds later Reggie Leach tipped a Barber shot past Tretiak for the game's first goal.

The Flyers got another when Rick MacLeish's wrister went over Tretiak's glove with 2:23 left in the first.

Even when the Russians had a power play, they seemed to shy away from anything resembling physical play, allowing the Flyers to continue to dominate.

Early in the second, with Dupont in the penalty box for tripping Kharlamov on a breakaway, Don Saleski took a pass from Kindrachuk and cut wide on the Soviet defense. He fired a shot from the right side that handcuffed Tretiak and dropped to the ice. Joe Watson knocked it in, giving the Flyers a 3–0 lead.

Watson, who was far from a prolific goal-scorer—NHL career totals: 835 games, 38 goals—recalled Shero coming into the locker room and saying, "That set the Russian hockey program back 20 years by scoring that goal."

The Red Army got its only goal at 10:48 of the second, when Viktor Kutyorgin scored on the team's sixth shot of the game. That was all the Soviets could manage, as the Flyers' forechecking and tight defense continued to stifle them.

The Flyers made it 4–1 after Clarke drew a hooking penalty on Alexei Volchenkov, and on the ensuing power play fed a cutting Larry Goodenough, who sneaked in from the point and beat Tretiak with a wrist shot at 4:01 of the third.

Shero told reporters after the game that he felt as good after beating the Soviets as he did after beating the Bruins in 1974 to win the Stanley Cup.

The final shot tally was 49–13 for the Flyers, and despite the claims of the Red Army coach, who said the Flyers played "like animals," the animals had just two more penalty minutes than the Soviets, 14–12.

"We made every place they went on the ice miserable for them, and they quit," Clarke said. "They didn't compete."

In the days following the game, something strange happened. The phone calls and letters that used to decry the players and the organization as thugs and bullies had a different tenor. The players were heroes, avenging the honor of their league brethren.

"Probably the only time the league was cheering for us," Clarke said with a smile. "To this day."

FLYERS CARNIVAL

When hockey fans think of the Philadelphia Flyers, there are certain images that jump to mind, mostly big, brawling teams led by Bobby Clarke and Bernie Parent and Dave Schultz.

Another image, though, is just as big, longer-lasting, and certainly more important.

Every year the club hosts the Flyers' Wives Fight For Lives Carnival. The event, which raises money for more than 100 charities in the Delaware Valley, is the biggest one-day charity event organized by a major North American professional sports team.

"There are people that have come for 15, 20 years," said Heather Hatcher, wife of former defenseman Derian Hatcher. "There are people who have been coming since they were little kids and they look forward to it, and it keeps getting better and better every year."

In 36 years, the event has raised more than $25 million.

Most of the money is earmarked for cancer-related charities, with the main recipient the cancer research laboratories at Hahnemann Hospital in Philadelphia.

"It's been a huge success," Doreen Holmgren, wife of former player and current general manager Paul Holmgren, said. "Over the years it just grew and grew to the point where we have our own offices now."

That success wasn't assured in 1977.

Then, Dr. Isadore Brodsky was running the fledgling cancer institute at Hahnemann and was looking to create a board of directors that could help raise funds. One of his targets was his brother-in-law, Sylvan Tobin, who was a minority investor in the Flyers. Tobin arranged a meeting for Brodsky with Ed Snider, who was receptive to the idea of helping Brodsky in some way.

"We had enough dinners," Snider recalled in *Full Spectrum*. "I told them I'd go back to my [hockey] people and try to come up with some fundraising ideas where we could use the Spectrum."

One of those people was Ed Golden, the team's public relations director, and he devised the idea of a carnival. Fran Tobin, Sylvan's wife, and Estelle Brodsky, Isadore's wife and Fran's sister, got ideas from local carnival people for games and supplies, and they gave their ideas and input to the players' wives, who were charged with planning the event.

The idea of giving the wives the job of planning the carnival was an easy one. Most of the women were Canadian citizens and banned by immigration laws from holding full-time jobs.

The first Carnival was held February 1, 1977, at the Spectrum. About 6,500 tickets were printed, and sold for $6 apiece. Between advance sales and walk-ups the day of the event, about 8,000 fans attended the first carnival.

"The carnival games came, and we had no idea what would happen that first year," Brodsky, who died in October 2007, said. "It was snowing and we had horrible weather, but the people kept pouring in."

More than $95,000 was raised at that first event. Some of it came from the winning auction price of $1,055 for Bobby Clarke's 1972 Canada Cup sweater. Fans lined up to pay $1 each to shoot—and mostly score—on goalies Bernie Parent, Gary Inness and Wayne Stephenson. Reggie Leach and Gary Dornhoefer volunteered to sit in the dunk tank. Barry Ashbee and his wife, Donna, spent most of the day retrieving coins tossed at saucers.

The money allowed Brodsky to purchase an electron microscope, which was critical in researching blood disease-causing retroviruses.

"This is a good cause," Parent told the *Philadelphia Daily News* then. "We're all made of flesh. This damn disease can happen to any one of us."

Sadly, he didn't know just how right he was—months later, Ashbee was diagnosed with acute leukemia.

Ashbee was placed in Brodsky's care. Chemotherapy would help, but the disease was ruthless. Within weeks, Ashbee's kidneys shut down, and he died a month after being diagnosed.

The Carnival was made into a yearly event and rededicated to Ashbee's memory. The biggest recipient of money raised by the carnival remains the Hahnemann cancer center, now known as the Barry Ashbee Research Laboratory at the Isadore Brodsky Institute for Cancer and Blood Diseases at Hahnemann.

"It's so big and so important to the organization and cancer research," Clarke said of the Carnival.

Over the last 35-plus years, the event has become so successful other teams have attempted to copy what the Flyers started.

"Even our other local Philadelphia teams have come and mimicked what we do," Holmgren said. "The Eagles and Phillies and Sixers try to do something similar because it's been so successful."

The Carnival has grown to include current players, coaches, and broadcasters from the Flyers and Phantoms plus well-known alums like Parent, Dornhoefer and Bob Kelly.

Former Flyers captain Keith Primeau said he first heard of the Carnival when he was playing for the Carolina Hurricanes.

"It has received a lot of recognition and notoriety, and it's recognized around the league by the fans, by other organizations, by other players, as a tremendous event," he said.

Vincent Lecavalier, who signed with the Flyers in July 2013 after 14 seasons with the Tampa Bay Lightning, said the Carnival was something he also knew about.

"You hear that all around the league, how great that [the Carnival] is," he said. "This is a first-class organization."

The Carnival is one part of Comcast-Spectacor Charities, and wives and girlfriends of players and management members take part in numerous other charitable activities year-round. The signature event, though, remains the Carnival.

"The Carnival is not only our signature fundraising event of the year, but also a wonderful opportunity for the Philadelphia Flyers and their families to give back to the community," said Mary Ann Saleski, senior vice president of Flyers Charities. "With the help of our loyal fans and local corporate community, we are able to donate funds benefiting many worthy non-profit organizations."

Saleski has seen both sides of the Carnival—her husband is former Flyer Don Saleski, and she took part in the planning of a number of Carnivals.

And more than three decades after the idea was hatched, the fans still turn out in droves to not only take part in games, but meet, get autographs from and take pictures with current and former Flyers players and coaches.

"We sell out every year," Holmgren said. "It's always been very successful, come rain, snow, whatever. We have the loyal people coming out. And the players give up their day."

The players' wives also give up a lot. But for them, it's a labor of love.

"We're fortunate enough that we have our names and our husband's names to get out the awareness of cancer and, for me, I have a lot of good friends who are survivors," Hatcher said.

And once one Carnival ends, planning for the next one starts.

"It takes a whole year for us to plan this," Holmgren said. "The minute it's over, we start putting our heads together to start planning how we can make it bigger and better."

THE KIDS AND THE CUP I

The first seeds for the Flyers team that grew to make the 1984–85 Stanley Cup Final were planted in the summer of 1979.

With their first pick, at No. 14 overall, the Flyers chose high-scoring left wing Brian Propp. In the third round, they made what some considered a reach and others viewed as shocking, selecting a relatively unknown Swedish goalie named Pelle Lindbergh.

Jerry Melnyk, the scout who in 1969 fought so hard to convince the Flyers to take a diabetic center from Flin Flon, Manitoba, named Bobby Clarke, raved about Lindbergh. The Flyers knew they wouldn't be getting Lindbergh for at least a year so he could play in the 1980 Olympics, but that was fine by Melnyk. That turned into a bit of foreshadowing of Lindbergh's future success, as overshadowed by the U.S. team's Lake Placid miracle was the fact that Lindbergh was the only goalie to face the Americans and not lose—Sweden and the U.S. played to a 2–2 tie in the opening game for both teams.

Lindbergh played eight games for the Flyers in 1981–82 and 40 relatively unimpressive games the following season. Then a rocky start in 1983–84 saw him serve a four-game sentence with the AHL's Springfield Indians. But with the dawning of the 1984–85 season, rookie coach Mike Keenan declared the 25-year-old Lindbergh his No. 1 goalie.

When Keenan convened his first training camp in 1984, he was looking at the youngest team in the league. The oldest player on the roster was 33-year-old defenseman Miroslav Dvorak, but it was only his third NHL season.

Mark Howe was a veritable graybeard at 29. Ilkka Sinisalo and Brad Marsh were 26; Propp, team captain Dave Poulin and Brad McCrimmon were 25; Tim Kerr was 24; Ron Sutter and Rick Tocchet were 20; and Peter Zezel was only 19.

And not only were the players young, it was Bob Clarke's first season as general manager, and for Keenan, just 34, the 1984–85 Flyers were his first NHL team.

Keenan already had a reputation for having a tongue as sharp as a skate blade. But he had taken Peterborough to the Memorial Cup championship, had won an AHL title with Rochester, Buffalo's minor-league affiliate—beating Maine, the Flyers' minor-league club, in the finals—and led the University of Toronto to the Canadian university title.

"Everybody I talked to said that his style would cause some problems with players, but that he had always won," Clarke said in *Full Spectrum.*

With a first-time NHL coach, a first-time general manager, a roster full of kids and a burden of having gone three years without winning a playoff series, expectations were pretty low— but not for Keenan.

"Some form of excellence," was Keenan's answer to reporters who asked what his goal was for the 1984–85 season. Meeting that level of excellence would not be an easy task.

"He was willing to do whatever it took to get the best out of someone," Poulin said of Keenan. "It's a difficult proposition because there are times you don't want to do what's necessary as a coach. I think the best coaches in many respects have to be unreasonable about what a player goes through. The demands on a player have to be so extreme, and it's very hard to get to that point. That's not a reasonable demand, and Mike was able to make unreasonable demands."

The players gave Keenan what he wanted early, roaring out of the box with a 6–2–2 start through the season's first month.

"Everybody is so enthusiastic," Kerr told reporters. "The expectations, at least from the outside, aren't as great they've been the last few years, and so far we're having fun."

THE GUFFAW

Brian Propp was known as much for scoring goals as he was for his celebration, the Guffaw.

Propp got the idea while attending a Howie Mandel show in Atlantic City during the summer of 1986. Mandel suggested the Guffaw—a short left-to-right wave followed by extending the arm straight up to the ceiling—instead of laughing to confuse the next comic on stage. Propp had other ideas.

"I was thinking about the Guffaw and finally scored my first of the year," Propp writes on his website. "I had the usual crowd of players congratulating me after the goal; then, as I broke away from the pack and headed to center ice, I put my right glove under my left arm and did the 'Guffaw' as I skated toward center ice."

Propp continued the Guffaw for the rest of his career, and still does it for fans at golf outings.

Kerr was having more fun than most. He posted the club's first four-goal game in four seasons October 25 against St. Louis, and a pair November 15—Bob Clarke Appreciation Night—gave him 17 in 15 games.

By December 8, the young Flyers had blazed to a 17–4–5 mark, but over the next two months, they sputtered along at 14–12–2. They recovered to enter early March second to Washington in the Patrick Division, but faced a daunting three-game-in-four-days set that featured a trip to Long Island to face the Islanders and a home-and-home series with the Caps.

The Flyers topped the Isles in overtime when Propp intercepted a pass and fed Poulin for the game-winner. Two nights later at the Spectrum, the Flyers fell behind the Capitals 4–2 midway through the second, but hat tricks by Poulin and Kerr—the latter notching goals 49, 50, and 51 on the season—keyed a 9–6 win.

The next night in Washington, Sinisalo and Derrick Smith scored early, Murray Craven added a goal in the second, and Howe notched an empty-net goal with five seconds left as the Flyers finished with a 4–2 win.

The Flyers shotgunned their way through the rest of the schedule, blowing away 13 of their final 14 foes. Trailing Washington by 11 points on February 9, they won the Patrick Division by 12. They finished with a team-record 53 wins, and their 113 points were four better than Edmonton for tops in the league.

Despite missing four games down the stretch with a knee injury, Kerr led the team with 54 goals, matching his total from the previous season, and 98 points. Propp added 43 goals and 97 points. Sinisalo had 36 goals, and Poulin had 30 to go along with 44 assists.

Howe finished a plus-51 and added 39 assists and 57 points. His defense partner, McCrimmon, posted a plus-52.

In goal, Lindbergh was nothing short of sensational. Playing 65 games, he went 40–17–7 with a 3.02 goals-against average, .899 save percentage and two shutouts. He was rewarded with the first-ever Bobby Clarke Trophy as Flyers team MVP, and later added the Vezina Trophy as top goalie in the league.

The Flyers opened the playoffs against the New York Rangers. They had swept the seven-game season series, averaging more than four goals per game, while the Rangers had sneaked into the playoffs with a 26–44–10 record, the second-worst record ever for a playoff team. The Rangers had amassed just 62 points—51 fewer than the Flyers.

Despite their dominance over their neighbors to the north, Keenan said he sensed fear in his young team.

Some of that could have been the fact that only three players—Kerr, Propp and defenseman Thomas Eriksson—had won a playoff series as a Flyer, and only four others—blueliners Doug Crossman, Brad Marsh, Ed Hospodor and McCrimmon—had won a playoff series at all.

"I could feel the nervousness," Keenan recalled in *Full Spectrum*. "After all we had accomplished, as strongly as we had finished, they weren't sure they could win."

It didn't take them long to learn they could.

Ron Sutter scored on an odd-man rush just 4:04 into Game 1, and then Todd Bergen's long shot deflected off Rangers defenseman Grant Ledyard and past goalie Glen Hanlon. McCrimmon finished a three-on-two break to give the Flyers a 3–0 lead after 20 minutes of hockey.

The Rangers rallied, and when Don Maloney deked Lindbergh and scored 1:17 into the third period, the game was tied 3–3.

Kerr put the Flyers ahead when he scored off a Hanlon giveaway, but Anders Hedberg's goal with 26 seconds left forced overtime.

Any apprehension from regulation was washed away during the intermission, as the Flyers came out flying, outshooting the Rangers 8–1 to start overtime. As the midpoint of the extra session neared, Sutter beat Reijo Ruotsalainen to a McCrimmon dump-in and passed from behind the net to Howe, who had crept to the top of the right faceoff circle. With Lindsey Carson providing a screen, Howe fired a shot that went between Hanlon's pads, giving the Flyers a 5–4 win.

The Rangers scored first in Game 2 when George McPhee tipped a Ron Greschner shot past Lindbergh 61 seconds into the second period. Bergen redirected a point shot by Crossman past Hanlon to tie the game, and then knocked in Marsh's rebound 5:23 into the third. Sinisalo converted a Sutter pass with 2:20 left to ice the 3–1 victory.

At Madison Square Garden for Game 3, the Rangers took a 2–0 lead on goals by Ruotsalainen and Maloney. Zezel got a goal back late after Hedberg was sent off for tripping, and then Crossman scored on a delayed penalty early in the second to tie it. With Kerr off for tripping, Willie Huber scored off a rebound to put the Rangers up 3–2.

But Kerr would make up for his gaffe in an historic way.

Over the next 8 minutes, 16 seconds, Kerr put four pucks into the Rangers' net, three on the power play, and a one-goal deficit became a 6–3 advantage. The offensive explosion set an NHL playoff record for the fastest four goals in a playoff game.

Maloney and Hedberg scored in the first four minutes of the third period, but the Flyers played flawless defense for the final

16, and skated into the second round of the playoffs for the first time since 1981.

The Flyers' foe in the Patrick Division Finals was the Islanders.

Poulin, who sustained partially torn knee ligaments in Game 2 against the Rangers, was out, so into the scoring breach stepped Propp. He had just three goals and eight points in the three previous spring flameouts, but he set up second-period goals by Tocchet and Kerr, and Lindbergh stopped all 22 shots he faced as the Flyers won Game 1 3–0.

The Islanders opened Game 2 hot, throwing 14 shots on Lindbergh and earning three power plays in the first 20 minutes. The Flyers hung tough, however, as Propp had a hat trick, Kerr had a goal and three assists and the Flyers took a 5–2 win and a 2–0 series lead.

The Isles took a 1–0 lead in Game 3 when Lindbergh accidentally knocked Anders Kallur's pass into his goal. But with Paul Boutilier and Ken Morrow in the penalty box Crossman scored on a five-on-three power play to tie the game and then Tocchet scored with 1:12 left to give the Flyers a 2–1 lead after one period.

Sutter and Propp scored to make it 4–1 eight minutes into the second, but Brent Sutter and John Tonelli answered with two of the Islanders' 27 second-period shots, making it a one-goal game with 20 minutes of hockey left.

Rather than wilt, the Flyers strengthened, limiting the Islanders to just four shots in the third, and Sinisalo iced it with an empty-net goal. The 5–3 win put the Flyers one game away from the Wales Conference Finals.

These Islanders had rallied from 3–0 deficits before, and they made a nice first step in that direction in Game 4. Tonelli set up first-period goals by Pat LaFontaine and Bryan Trottier, and when Mike Bossy scored at 8:53 of the second to make it 4–0, Keenan pulled Lindbergh for Bob Froese in what became a 6–2 loss.

After a scoreless first period in Game 5, the Flyers turned on the jets in the second and outshot the Isles 17–8. Less than seven minutes into the period, Zezel entered the zone, dropped a pass for Crossman and drove to the net, where he got tangled with goalie Kelly Hrudey. Hrudey stopped Crossman's shot, but Sinisalo dumped the rebound into an open net.

From there it was all Lindbergh, as he closed the series the same way he opened it, stopping 25 shots to earn his second shutout of the series.

The Quebec Nordiques stood between the Flyers and a berth in the Stanley Cup Final. In an odd quirk of the schedule, the series started in Quebec due to Adams Division teams winning more regular-season games in head-to-head battles with Patrick Division clubs.

Poulin returned for Game 1, but it didn't help as Peter Stastny snapped a 1–1 deadlock at 6:20 of overtime when he rang a long shot past Lindbergh and under the crossbar.

Not only did the Flyers trail in a series for the first time, they also lost Kerr to a sprained right knee ligament in the first period.

While Game 1 had little anger to it, the teams wasted little time finding their hate in Game 2. Tocchet and Pat Price dropped the gloves 30 seconds in, there were three fights alone in the first period and four in the game.

Between all the fisticuffs, Poulin suffered cracked ribs when Mario Marois sticked him, but the grinding captain took a feed from Craven and scored shorthanded at 11:16 of the first.

Craven and Sinisalo notched goals in the second, and after J.F. Sauve scored for the Nords, Joe Paterson, playing in place of the injured Kerr, added an insurance goal and the Flyers evened the series with a 4–2 victory.

Paterson's solid play continued when the series shifted to the Spectrum. He set up Craven for a first-period goal, and after Quebec took a 2–1 lead after one period, he scored 1:41 into the second to tie it, and then drew the second assist on Sinisalo's game-winner. Propp notched an insurance marker, and the Flyers, despite playing without Kerr, Poulin, and McCrimmon, who was lost after a first-period blast into the boards by Wilf Paiement left him with a grotesquely separated shoulder [Dr. John Gregg said the defenseman's shoulder blade was next to his ear], took home a 4–2 victory and a 2–1 series lead.

The Flyers' good fortune ran out three nights later as Quebec jumped to a 2–0 first-period lead. Howe's goal early in the third tied it at 3–3, but the Nordiques scored twice more to take a 5–3 win back to Quebec City.

"You can't be great every night," Lindbergh told reporters.

But he was just that in Game 5. The Flyers had just 12 shots over the first 40 minutes, but only trailed 1–0 thanks to stellar play by Lindbergh, who allowed only Sauve's goal at 7:02 of the second.

Keenan ranted and raved between periods, imploring his young team to push further than they thought they could—another of what Poulin called Keenan's "unreasonable demands."

Whatever he said worked, as Paterson knocked in a Howe pass 60 seconds into the period to tie the game. With five minutes left, Propp sent Craven in alone on goalie Mario Gosselin, and the winger shot high off Gosselin's shoulder for the deciding goal and a 3–2 series lead.

The Flyers returned home with a chance to clinch the series but knew they had to play better.

They did just that, limiting the Nords to five shots in the first period and taking the lead when Tocchet tipped a Howe drive into the net. After penalties 37 seconds apart to Paterson and Propp put the Flyers two men down early in the second, Poulin, wearing a flak jacket to protect his cracked ribs, intercepted a lazy pass by Marois, raced the length of the ice, and buried one of the biggest goals in club history behind Gosselin.

Crossman added a goal as the Flyers and Lindbergh, facing just 15 shots, needed little effort in closing his second straight playoff series with a shutout.

The Flyers, the youngest team in the league, were going to play for the oldest prize in hockey.

With Kerr back in the lineup for Game 1, plus the home-ice advantage, the Flyers appeared to be a team of destiny. But standing in their way were the defending Stanley Cup champion Edmonton Oilers in all their legendary glory—Wayne Gretzky, Mark Messier, Jari Kurri, Esa Tikkanen, Paul Coffey, Kevin Lowe, Grant Fuhr, Glenn Anderson.

"I don't know if there was an awe factor, maybe more of a scared factor," Propp said. "They were all in their prime, and all Hall of Famers. I don't think there was awe, it was, we all have to play our best games if we're going to beat that team."

They didn't look intimidated in Game 1. With a two-man advantage late in the first period, Bergen threw a puck into the crease that Sinisalo knocked in.

In the third, with the score still 1–0, Ron Sutter stole a Coffey pass and scored, and then Poulin stole the puck from Anderson and fed Kerr, who scored to make it 3–0. Poulin added an empty-net goal as the Flyers took the series lead with a 4–1 win. The victory extended the Flyers' win streak against the Oilers to nine straight, a streak that dated back three seasons. But one Flyer knew things going forward wouldn't be easy.

"Historically, in the regular season we beat the Oilers the majority of the time," Howe said. "But the team you saw in the Final was a completely different team. The Oilers were a highly skilled team that played loose and open hockey in the regular season, but in the playoffs, when you talk about all the small details of the game, their attention to detail was as good as any team I've ever seen."

Gretzky found one detail in an Al Morganti story in the Philadelphia Inquirer. Morganti wrote, "Unless they are total frauds, the Oilers should be able to play a lot better." It wasn't meant to be insulting, just Morganti's way of saying the Oilers were the better team and still should win the series.

"That's just how Wayne was, finding motivation from nothing," Morganti said.

The Great One notched the first goal of Game 2, recovering his centering pass from between Howe's skates and scoring.

Kerr, his knee suffering, tied the game after Poulin poked the puck away from Messier, but Willy Lindstrom put the Oilers ahead when he scored from in close, and Dave Hunter added an insurance goal in the Oilers' 3–1 win.

The series moved to Alberta for Game 3, which Gretzky took over in the first period, scoring three times. The Flyers managed a Derrick Smith tally after Gretzky's first two goals, but the Flyers trailed 4–1 entering the third. They limited the Oilers to just two shots in the final 20 minutes, and Howe and Propp each scored to make it a one-goal game, but their last, best chance ended a bounce short. With 15 seconds left, Craven nearly sprung Tocchet on a breakaway, but the pass was just behind the winger, and he stumbled trying to reach back for the puck. The Oilers escaped with a 4–3 win and the series lead.

The Flyers may have trailed just 2–1 in the series, but they were at the end of their collective rope by the start of Game 4. Kerr's knee was bad enough to end his season, and Poulin's ribs had made the captain a shell of himself. Despite that, Craven's shorthanded goal midway through the first gave the Flyers a 3–1 lead.

But their injuries and inexperience, combined with the Oilers' superior skill, allowed the home team to tie the game early in the second, and two goals by Gretzky gave the Oilers a 5–3 win and put the Flyers on the brink of elimination.

Game 5 was an Edmonton whitewash. Lindbergh, who had taken a shot off the back of his knee in the Quebec series, took another when a Mike Krushelnyski drive caught him in the same spot in Game 4. Doctors diagnosed a partially torn quadriceps tendon, meaning Froese, who was less than 100 percent after December knee surgery, had to step into the crease.

The Oilers, smelling blood, poured eight goals past the helpless Froese. Rich Sutter scored twice and Propp added a goal, but it was the Oilers who celebrated their second straight Stanley Cup at home with an 8–3 victory.

"We knew how great they were as individuals, but we were really beat up," Howe said. "McCrimmon was out, Timmy Kerr was out, Dave Poulin was out with broken ribs. I think the only two big scorers we had on our team were Brian Propp and Sinisalo. When you're playing a juggernaut, it's kind of a tough task."

THE KIDS AND THE CUP II

When the Flyers reported for training camp in 1986, it was much the same group that had gone to the Stanley Cup Final two seasons prior.

The kids who had ridden their youthful exuberance to that 1985 Final were two years older in age, but they were a far more mature and hardened group after dealing with the tragic death of teammate Pelle Lindbergh a year earlier.

"The core of the group was the same, but it was two different teams," Dave Poulin said. "That team went through so much with the death of Pelle that it was a more mature team in 1986–87."

Helping the group awake from that nightmare was a rookie goalie who couldn't have been more different from Lindbergh: Ron Hextall. Where Lindbergh was relaxed, Hextall brought a level of intensity that bordered on the fanatical.

"His competitive edge in practice … he wouldn't let you score in practice 10 seconds after the whistle blew and he was skating toward center ice," Poulin said.

"He was such a good competitor," added Howe. "Not only in the games, but every day at practice. The only way you're going to get better as a scorer or a defenseman is to have someone working with you. If I'm trying to keep the puck out of the net, I'm going to want a goalie that's working with me in practice. If I can keep the puck out of my net in practice, I can do it during a game."

"Every time he stepped on the ice, he was full out," recalled Kjell Samuelsson. "Even in practice, if you shot high on him he'd get irritated. He tried to stop every puck coming at him."

Besides Hextall, there were other changes. Rich Sutter, Dave Richter and a draft pick had been traded to the Vancouver Canucks for defenseman J.J. Daigneault. Rambunctious forward Scott Mellanby, a second-round pick in 1984, was signed away from the University of Wisconsin. And undrafted Western Hockey League graduate Craig Berube was signed to a minor-league deal and played seven games with the big club.

GM Bob Clarke raised the bar when he said during camp, "I think it's time for this team to do something."

Hextall gave a glimpse of what was to come opening night against Edmonton at the Spectrum. Jari Kurri gave the Oilers an early lead, but Hextall stoned Wayne Gretzky on a breakaway, and held the fort as Ron Sutter and Peter Zezel gave the Flyers a 2–1 win.

Fiery coach Mike Keenan guided the Flyers to a pair of Stanley Cup Finals.

They won their first six, and were 13–4–2 when Tim Kerr scored four in a row against Chicago on November 20, his fourth hat-trick-plus-one.

Slowly, though, injuries began whittling away at the lineup. Brian Propp had 41 points in 27 games when he fractured his left knee. Ilkka Sinisalo went down with a knee injury, and back issues sidelined Howe and Sutter.

Despite the injuries, the Flyers went 17–10–2 from the beginning of December through the end of January. Propp and Sinisalo returned in mid-February, Howe was back by the end of the month, and the Flyers finished with 100 points and the Patrick Division title.

Kerr totaled 58 goals—his fourth straight 50-goal season—Zezel had a career campaign with 33 goals and 72 points, and Propp had 31 goals in just 53 games.

The revelation, though, was Hextall, who finished with a 37–21–6 record, a 3.00 goals-against average and a .902 save percentage, good enough to earn him the Vezina Trophy [but oddly not the Calder Trophy, which went to Los Angeles' Luc Robitaille].

Hextall also finished with six assists and 104 penalty minutes—the sixth-highest amount on the team—foreshadowing a historical future in both categories.

The Flyers were due to open the playoffs against the New York Rangers, a team they finished 24 points ahead of in the regular season, but there was a bit of trepidation from how the regular season ended—a 9–5 embarrassment against the Islanders. All season there had been tremors of a rebellion against the ultra-intense, volatile Keenan.

"Mike ran such a tight ship," Al Morganti, who covered the team for the *Philadelphia Inquirer*, said. "It was very tense with Mike all the time. There wasn't much fun and games with Mike. It was pretty serious all the time.

"Mike took every loss personally, like, 'They [expletive] me.' I said, 'Mike, sometimes you lose,' but he looked at me like I had three heads. He wouldn't back off."

The Rangers had allowed 323 goals in the regular season, the third-most in the NHL, but the Flyers couldn't get any past goalie John Vanbiesbrouck in a Game 1 loss.

The Flyers got on the scoreboard in the first period of Game 2, went ahead with four seconds left in the second on a Rick Tocchet goal, and dominated in the third en route to an 8–3 series-evening victory.

Hextall was the star in Game 3, holding off a 12-shot Rangers first-period attack. He stopped all 34 shots he faced for the game, and Zezel and Howe scored 13 seconds apart early in the second as the Flyers earned a 3–0 win.

The goalie was his own worst enemy in Game 4, allowing an early Tomas Sandstrom goal, and then getting into a shouting match with Rangers coach Phil Esposito in a series-knotting 6–3 defeat.

Game 5 at the Spectrum could have turned ugly again after Hextall was whistled for clearing the puck over the glass moments after Samuelsson had been sent off for holding, but the netminder kept the game scoreless and it remained that way until Tocchet jammed the rebound of a Derrick Smith shot 2:02 into the second period under Rangers goalie Bob Froese.

Another Hextall gaffe, when he lost a race for the puck into the corner, allowed the Rangers to score into an empty net to tie it. Kerr put the Flyers back in the lead with about six minutes left in the second, and Tocchet scored into an empty net in the third to ice the 3–1 victory.

Game 6 started with the Flyers losing Poulin four minutes in when he needed X-rays on his ribs after being driven into the boards by Ron Duguay. Even without their captain, the Flyers got first-period goals from Smith and Doug Crossman. Brad Marsh and Kerr scored in the second, Lindsay Carson added a goal early in the third, and Hextall stopped all 34 Rangers shots to register the series-clinching 5–0 shutout.

The Islanders arrived at the Spectrum for the Patrick Division Finals an aging, tired club that had survived a four-overtime Game 7 win just two days earlier.

The visitors were missing Mike Bossy and Denis Potvin, but out for the Flyers were Poulin with broken ribs and Murray Craven, who broke his foot during Game 6 against the Rangers.

Kerr was healthy, though, and his hat trick pushed the Flyers to a 4–2 win in Game 1.

Game 2 featured a goaltending duel between Hextall and Kelly Hrudey, which the Isles won when Mikko Makela scored a power-play goal with three seconds left in regulation to hand the Flyers a 2–1 loss.

Al Hill tipped Howe's long shot past Hrudey to open the scoring midway through the first period in Game 3, and then Propp, who had just one goal in his previous 13 playoff games, scored off the rebound of a Tim Tookey shot as the Flyers cruised to a 4–1 victory.

Propp scored again in Game 4 after Alan Kerr had given the Islanders an early lead. Hill scored with 1:25 left in the first to tie the game, but Bryan Trottier beat Hextall 2:50 into the second to put the Isles ahead 3–2.

Kerr tied the game with a power-play goal, and then Tookey, the leading scorer in the American Hockey League making his first foray in the NHL playoffs, scored off a Propp set-up to put the Flyers ahead for good. Kerr and Tocchet added goals as the 6–4 victory gave the Flyers a 3–1 series lead.

The Flyers looked to be on their way to clinching a spot in the next round in Game 5 when Carson blocked a Ken Morrow shot, raced in alone and beat Hrudey 5:56 into the second period for the game's first goal. Instead, the Islanders tied the game late in the second and won it 2–1 on Randy Wood's goal early in the third.

The Flyers lost both Game 6 and Kerr, whose season-long shoulder issues finally forced him out of the lineup.

"It got to a point in that Isles series," he said, "my arm sitting by my side, [my shoulder] would separate. I couldn't even hold a stick."

Without Kerr, Poulin put aside the pain from his broken ribs and set up goals by Dave Brown and Propp, and the Flyers advanced to the Wales Conference Finals with a 5–1 win. Their foes would be the Montreal Canadiens, the defending Stanley Cup champs.

Montreal coach Jean Perron went with goalie Brian Hayward in Game 1, rather than Patrick Roy, giving the Flyers a huge edge in net.

Despite not having Poulin—his Game 7 heroics against the Islanders proved a personal setback—a red-hot Propp one-timed a Crossman pass into the back of the net with 2:09 left in the first. Montreal scored the next two, but Sinisalo answered with a goal to tie the game. After the Canadiens' Bobby Smith and the Flyers' Derrick Smith traded goals in the third, overtime was needed to decide the contest.

WATER BOTTLE

Pelle Lindbergh had suffered from dehydration in the past, so coach Mike Keenan gave him a water bottle to keep on top of the goal during games. No netminder ever had done this before, and the league never objected.

Edmonton coach Glen Sather unleashed one of the more comically famous quotes in NHL history the day before Game 2 of the 1985 Stanley Cup Final.

"Maybe we want a bucket of chicken on our net," he said. "Maybe hamburgers. I mean, if you have a water bottle out there, let's have lunch."

Midway through extra time, Samuelsson sent the puck up the boards to Zezel. As Zezel cut to the net, Guy Carbonneau tackled him and the puck momentarily was lost under the pile of bodies and sticks. It eventually emerged behind Hayward, with Sinisalo getting credit for the game-winning score.

Montreal scored early and often on Hextall in a 5–2 win in Game 2, and they came out fast again in Game 3, firing 21 shots on net and getting rebound goals from Chris Nilan and Chris Chelios in the first period. Pelle Eklund scored twice to spark a three-goal rally that gave the Flyers a 3–2 lead midway through the third, but a Mats Naslund power-play goal at 12:35 of the third tied the game. Tocchet, who committed the penalty that led to Naslund's goal, fed Propp at the hash marks for a score with 3:09 left to give the Flyers a 4–3 win. Perron turned to Roy to start Game 4, but it made little difference as Eklund snapped a 2–2 tie with a goal with 4:11 left in the second, and Mellanby scored 14 seconds into the third. Perron yanked Roy for Hayward, but Eklund scored twice more for his first playoff hat trick as the Flyers won 6–3 and took a 3–1 series lead home to Philadelphia.

Larry Robinson's power-play goal through a Claude Lemieux screen sparked a 5–2 Canadiens win in Game 5, sending the series back to Montreal.

Fireworks started in Game 6 before the puck dropped as a pregame brawl sparked by Shayne Corson and Lemieux scoring into the Flyers' net at the end of warm-ups saw players spill out of both dressing rooms in various states of undress to brawl on the ice. Flyers defenseman Ed Hospodar was ruled the instigator in the attack and was the only player ejected; he subsequently was suspended for the remainder of the playoffs.

Once the game started, it looked like the Canadiens safely could pack for one more trip to Philadelphia. Mike McPhee scored for Montreal less than a minute in, but Poulin, whose broken ribs had forced him out of Game 5, scored shorthanded to tie the game.

The game was tied 3–3 seven minutes into the third period when Tocchet finished a two-on-one with Propp, and the Flyers held on over the final 12-plus minutes to celebrate a 4–3 win and a second chance in the Stanley Cup Final in three seasons.

Just like 1985, their opponent in the Final would be the dynastic Edmonton Oilers.

The Flyers felt many of the lessons learned in losing to Edmonton two seasons prior would be put into practice in the upcoming series.

"We were mentally stronger, mentally tougher, and with the emergence of the Cravens, the emergence of the Tocchets and the other younger players, we were all better as a group," Howe said. "We were tougher mentally as a team, which I think makes you better as a team overall."

All the experience, though, couldn't compensate for the injuries that had decimated their roster. Already without Kerr and with Poulin nursing broken ribs, Howe was hobbled by a charley horse suffered on his first shift of Game 1.

The Oilers' Wayne Gretzky opened the scoring, but Propp answered late in the second when his long shot handcuffed Grant Fuhr and dropped into the net. But the Oilers responded with three goals in an 8:23 span of the third to earn a 4–2 win.

Gretzky scored in the first minute of the second period in Game 2 on a five-on-three advantage, but the Flyers rallied. Ron Sutter dug a puck out of the crease and Derrick Smith pushed it over the goal line to tie the game, and then Propp redirected a Tocchet shot into the back of the net to put the Flyers up 2–1 after two periods. The Oilers came back in the third to tie the game and force overtime when Anderson walked past Crossman to score. In overtime the Oilers swarmed like white-sweatered hornets as a Gretzky drop pass to an open Paul Coffey caught the Flyers with four skaters down low. Coffey got deep and fed a diagonal pass to Kurri, who beat Hextall for a 3–2 win and a sweep of the first two games at Northlands Coliseum.

For Game 3, the Flyers trotted out a video performance of the late Kate Smith singing "God Bless America" to pump up the fans and hopefully court Lady Luck.

It looked like the Lady had run out on the Flyers early when the Oilers took a 3–0 lead. Craven, back in Game 3 from the broken foot that had sidelined him for the previous two series, got the shaft of his stick on a Tocchet shot for the Flyers' first goal, and then a puck bounced off Edmonton's Craig Muni and into the net to make it 3–2.

Mellanby scored through Fuhr's pads 4:37 into the third to tie the game, and 17 seconds later, with the celebration of Mellanby's goal still echoing through the Spectrum, Brad McCrimmon took the puck from Esa Tikkanen, received a return pass from Mellanby, and lifted the puck high above a sprawling Fuhr to give the Flyers a 4–3 lead.

Propp scored into an empty net in the final minute, and just like that, the Flyers had a heartbeat again.

The loss only served to anger the Oilers, who took a 2–0 lead in the first period of Game 4. McCrimmon answered with a long one-timer off an Eklund feed to make it 2–1, but Randy Gregg and Mike Krushelnyski scored to give the Oilers a 4–1 victory.

Hextall, angry at his own play, snapped when Anderson poked him as he was juggling a shot. He took out his frustration on Kent Nilsson with a two-handed stick chop across the back of the winger's legs as he skated near the goal. Hextall was assessed a five-minute major, but stayed in the game.

"That was basically a frustration moment for me," Hextall said. "We were getting beat and I had taken a lot of abuse over the course of the playoffs, and my frustrations came boiling out at that point. Glenn Anderson slashed me right before that, and I said that was enough. [I swung at the] first blue jersey I saw."

Knowing his team was running on fumes—Game 4 had been the Flyers' 23rd playoff game, at the time a league record—Keenan dug deep into his bag of motivational tricks for a special locker room guest for the morning skate prior to Game 5.

The Stanley Cup.

With hockey's Holy Grail sitting in the middle of their locker room, the message was simple: There it is, boys. Go get it if you want it.

Early goals put the Flyers down by two for the third straight game, but Hextall kept things close, and Tocchet scored with 50 seconds left in the first to halve the deficit. Marty McSorley answered with his second of the game to make it 3–1, but a Crossman rocket over Fuhr's glove got the Flyers back within a goal, and Eklund scored on his own rebound to tie it in the second.

Edmonton came out firing in the third, but it was the Flyers who got the go-ahead goal. Propp took the puck from Muni in the Edmonton zone, walked in front and backhanded a pass to Tocchet, who poked the puck past Fuhr to make it 4–3.

There still was 14:34 on the clock and the best team on the planet facing them, but Hextall was up to the challenge, and the Flyers survived for a 4–3 win and a return trip to Philadelphia.

Game 6 at the Spectrum followed the same script as the previous three games. The Oilers took a 2–0 lead, but with Hextall as the last line of defense, the ever-resilient Flyers fired back.

Brown pushed the puck between Kevin Lowe's skates to Carson, who deposited it behind Fuhr at 7:12 of the second, and then Propp tied the game with a power-play goal at 13:04 of the third.

Moments later, on a Flyers rush into the Edmonton end, Kurri picked off a Zezel pass and tried to throw it out of the zone. The puck hit the wall short of the blue line and dribbled toward the edge of the zone.

Daigneault had been trailing the play and was headed for the bench for a line change, but Keenan waved for him to stay on the ice. That allowed him to pounce on the dying quail and one-time a low shot through a Mellanby screen. The Spectrum shook as the Flyers once again had survived to reach a remarkable, previously unthought-of Game 7 back in Edmonton.

"I guess we had a little more to give than everybody thought," Brown said after the game.

There was a two-day break before Game 7 due to scheduling issues at Northlands Coliseum, but the Flyers didn't seem to mind. Back-to-back penalties on Mark Messier and Coffey gave the visitors a two-man advantage, and they capitalized when Craven banked in a shot off Fuhr's skate as the Flyers scored first for the first time in the series.

Messier answered to tie the game, and with 5:01 left in the second, Kurri put a shot between Zezel's skates and inside the right post to put the Flyers into one final hole.

With the lead, the Oilers put the pedal to the floor while the weight of 80 regular-season games and 26 exhausting playoff contests in 54 nights dropped like an anvil on the Flyers' backs. After putting 12 shots on Fuhr in the first period, they managed just 14 the rest of the game.

As Jay Greenberg wrote in *Full Spectrum*, "Hextall and heaven were the only things that could help the Flyers now."

The rookie netminder was brilliant with one exception, when Anderson fired a wicked, sinking slap shot from about 35 feet that went between his pads with 2:24 left to play.

When the final horn sounded, it was the Oilers parading around the rink with their third Stanley Cup in four seasons. Hextall, for all his brilliance, became just the second player from a losing side to take home the Conn Smythe Trophy as playoff MVP.

"That was the best goaltending I've ever seen," Howe said of Hextall. "He was incredible his first year. For the most part, especially in the Final, as good as we played and as close as we came, it wouldn't have been that close without Ron Hextall, there's no doubt about it."

SUPRIMEAU

Coming down the stretch of the 2003–04 season, the list of injured Flyers was growing like a pile of broken sticks.

And when the playoffs started, the Flyers drew about the worst opponent possible for them, from an on-ice standpoint as well as a psychological one—the New Jersey Devils.

An aging, injured team with an inexperienced goalie needed a hero, someone who could throw a team on his back for a two-month death march through the playoff minefield.

Far down the list of hero candidates would have been Keith Primeau. The team captain, he had played just 54 games due to a series of injuries, including a concussion that sidelined him for seven weeks. He had just seven goals during the regular season, and since his epic fifth-overtime goal against Pittsburgh in the 2000 playoffs, Primeau had scored exactly one postseason goal in 31 games.

"It's hard to score in the National Hockey League even in the best of times. It's even harder to score in the playoffs," he said. "A lot of factors go into why numbers are the way they are. I didn't play any different [in 2004]."

But scoring wasn't Primeau's role on that Flyers team. With Ken Hitchcock's arrival as coach in 2002, Primeau was given a new role, that of checking center.

"I think I started to buy into the idea that I was a different player as he was coming in," Primeau said of Hitchcock. "But he gave me the opportunity to really shine in that [defensive] role."

Primeau also had a much larger job, one possibly harder than anything he would encounter on the ice: Providing the buffer between the abrasive Hitchcock and the delicate egos of some of his teammates.

"My message to the guys was, don't listen so much to the delivery as the message," he said. "If you hear the message, 99.9 percent of the time the message is right."

It also helped that he accepted his changing place on the team without complaint. When Primeau came to the Flyers in 2000, he was a top-line center expected to perform offensively. Four seasons later, he was a checker, a mucker and a grinder.

"He became an excellent captain and leader because he first made himself accountable and then made everyone else accountable," Hitchcock said. "He had no problem doing that, and that's why our team played to its potential on a nightly basis, because he made the team play."

"When they see me accept a lesser role, a different role from what I was accustomed to, what was their excuse?" Primeau said. "That's where we transformed." In Primeau's case, that transformation changed him from an ordinary hockey player into a new man for the 2004 playoffs—Suprimeau.

As all journeys do, Primeau's started with a first step—or in his case, a long stride. Many of them, in fact, as midway through the first period of Game 1 against the Devils, he raced into the corner to support Simon Gagne, who had beaten an icing call, and worked the puck back along the wall to Sami Kapanen. Goalie Martin Brodeur stopped Kapanen's shot, but Gagne scored on the rebound, and just like that, the checker had helped set up the game's first score.

Early in the third, he rushed the puck into the offensive zone, barreling down the right side and around Devils defenseman Brian Rafalski. He cut hard on the goal line, and in one deft motion slid the puck under Brodeur, giving the Flyers a 3–0 lead.

The Flyers held on for a 3–2 win, and as would become the norm, Primeau's play was the difference.

Primeau didn't score in Game 2, but he was dominant in the faceoff circle, winning 14 of 22 draws, as the Flyers won again. He was just as good in Game 3, but it took a stellar lunging save by Brodeur to keep Primeau off the score sheet and preserve a 4–2 Devils victory.

In the loss, Primeau's supremacy still could be seen. *Philadelphia Daily News* columnist Rich Hoffman called him a "runaway destroyer," while Devils coach Pat Burns said the best way to stop him was with "a couple of bricks and some cement."

Burns' players tried to take their coach literally in Game 4, showering Primeau with all manners of hacks and whacks, from elbows to gloves to sticks. Primeau took it all with a smile.

"That's good. I like that," he told reporters. "If they're focused on me, it frees up J.R. [Jeremy Roenick], it frees up Rex [Mark Recchi], it frees up Alex [Zhamnov], those guys, to create a little more."

They did just that as Zhamnov scored the second goal of a 3–0 win, a game capped by Primeau tipping a Kapanen pass off Brodeur, then knocking the puck from between the goalie's skates into the net.

But it was more than goals and points for Primeau.

"He has presence, he has accountability," Hitchcock told reporters. "When he sits in the locker room nobody dares not play. He knows that he's carrying a message from the coaching staff through to the players. That's what captains do. ... He has accountability on both sides, in the locker room and in the coaches' office. Players know that."

Primeau looked at it as his duty to not just play well, but to excel, because he owed that much to his teammates.

"They had really pulled up their socks when I was out with my concussion, and I felt they really carried the load that I had left," he said. "I was in an important role, and now I wasn't there. They found a way to persevere. I felt I owed it to them more than anything. That's why I really dug in, because I really felt they carried my weight while I was out."

A 3–1 series lead resurrected talk of the collapse against the Devils in the 2000 conference finals, but Primeau quickly and efficiently chased away the ghosts of failures past, playing physically over 200 feet of ice, dominating in the faceoff circle [winning 16 of 23 draws], and being on the ice in the crucial final minutes of a 3–1 series-clinching victory.

Next was the Toronto Maple Leafs, the team that had extended the Flyers to seven games in the first round the previous year. And with seven overtime periods, it was more like nine games.

"I thought I played better the year before [2003] in the Toronto series," Primeau said of his one-goal, one-assist performance.

He was on the ice for Gagne's late goal in a 3–1 win in Game 1, and again did yeoman's work killing off penalties. In Game 2 he added his fourth playoff point, drawing an assist on Donald Brashear's power-play goal in a 2–1 victory.

The Flyers were pushed around in Games 3 and 4, both losses in Toronto, but when the series returned to Philadelphia for Game 5, Primeau had a little something extra attached to his black sweater.

A cape.

The day before Game 5, Primeau called a team meeting.

"He stepped up in the meeting and laid some things on the line," goalie Sean Burke said. "He told us he would be great today and told us to jump on for the ride."

It turned into the ride of their captain's life.

It started, appropriately, when the Flyers needed him the most: Leading 2–0 but shorthanded in the final two minutes of the first period.

Leafs defenseman Bryan McCabe fumbled the puck at the Philadelphia blue line and Primeau pounced, poking the puck loose and streaking in alone on goalie Ed Belfour. He held off defenseman Brian Leetch, deked Belfour out of the goal and slid a backhander into the gaping net with 1:06 left in the period.

Goal number two came 44 seconds into the second, when he stepped around the Leafs' Aki Berg and re-directed a Gagne pass past Belfour.

He completed his night by shrugging off a Joe Nieuwendyk slam into the boards to finish a give-and-go with Gagne for the hat trick at 3:50 of the third.

Caps rained down on the ice, carried by the throaty, loving screams for their team's newest hero. Besides his three goals were an assist, 10 wins on 15 faceoffs, and a number of bone-rattling body checks.

"He's been our leader on and off the ice," Roenick told the media. "That's what you need from your captain. He had something to prove after Games 3 and 4. He was a real treat to watch."

Primeau didn't score in Game 6, but he didn't need to record a point to earn the second star of the game as the Flyers closed the series with a 3–2 overtime win. He won faceoffs, killed penalties and turned the Leafs' leader, center Mats Sundin, into the

SHUT YER YAP

Ken Hitchcock not only knows how to irritate his players, but opposing coaches, as well.

In the 2004 Eastern Conference Finals against Tampa Bay, Lightning coach John Tortorella took the bait.

The day after Game 2, Tortorella accused Hitchcock of yelling at one of his players, and famously told the coach to, "Shut his yap."

While Tortorella steamed, Hitchcock laughed, replying that the Tampa coach should, "Mind his own business." And when asked if he would take Tortorella's advice and shut his yap, he chuckled and said, "You know me better than that."

Invisible Swede. He refused to budge on puck possession, at one point taking about 20 cross-checks between the numbers from the Leafs' Gary Roberts during a second-period scrum in the corner.

And it was Primeau, more than any netminder, who made the save of the night—and maybe of the season. With their defense corps decimated by injuries, Kapanen, Primeau's closest friend on the team, had been shifted from forward to defense. In overtime, Kapanen stretched to hold the puck in the offensive zone, leaving himself vulnerable, and Toronto's Darcy Tucker arrived with a hit more felt than seen. The force of the blow lifted Kapanen off his feet and turned him parallel to the ice. For a split second he remained airborne, pinned between the Leafs' forward and the wall. When Tucker skated away, Kapanen fell like Wile E. Coyote, landing with an audible splat. Kapanen's body may have landed in Toronto, but his head was in a faraway place. He attempted to skate to the bench, but instead stumbled toward center ice. Primeau opened the bench door, and with one skate barely scraping the rink, used his stick to reel Kapanen in like he was pulling a marlin onto a fishing boat.

"I could see he had no clue as to where he was," Primeau told reporters. "He wasn't sure which way he was facing."

GAGNE'S GAME 6

Five games into the 2004 Eastern Conference Finals, Simon Gagne had one assist. In a newspaper story the day before Game 6, GM Bob Clarke called out his young forward.

"He has to make the decision whether he wants to become a great player in the NHL or whether he will be satisfied being a good player," Clarke said.

Gagne answered with a pair of goals in Game 6, including the overtime winner.

"Usually I don't read the papers, but I got calls from back home and read it," Gagne said. "It was a message he was trying to tell me. I had to find a way to put the puck in."

The save allowed Roenick to jump on the ice and score the series-clinching goal.

Thanks to Primeau, the Flyers were in the Eastern Conference Finals for the first time since 2000, where they faced the Tampa Bay Lightning.

Primeau didn't score in the first two games of the series in Tampa, but his presence on the penalty kill enabled the Flyers to return to Philadelphia with a split. They lost Game 1, but killed four of five Tampa power plays in Game 2 and got a short-handed goal from Kapanen—he used Primeau as a decoy before scoring—in a 6–2 rout.

With the Flyers down 2–0 in Game 3, Primeau knocked a pinballing puck past goalie Nikolai Khabibulin 36 seconds into the third period to halve the lead, but it was as close as the Flyers would get in a 4–1 loss.

In writing about how Primeau had carried the team on his huge shoulders to that point, *Philadelphia Inquirer* columnist Phil Sheridan asked, "How many more of those does Primeau have in him?"

Fans and media alike didn't have to wait long for the answer.

Midway through the first period of Game 4, Primeau helped kill off a double-minor on Simon Gagne followed by a slashing call on goalie Robert Esche, all of which left the Flyers down a man for nearly four straight minutes. Tampa scored just once, and Kapanen, who served the penalty on Esche, jumped out of the box and dragged the puck up the ice. He was stopped near the red line, but Primeau, following the play, jumped on the loose puck. He cut to the middle in the Tampa zone and sent a pass across to John LeClair, who rocketed a shot past Khabibulin to tie the game.

After Recchi's goal late in the first put the Flyers ahead, Suprimeau stepped out of the phone booth one more time.

On a Tampa power play, Lightning captain Dave Andreychuk couldn't control a bouncing puck at the Flyers' blue line. Primeau saw the fumble and jumped toward the play. When Andreychuk batted the puck in the air, the Flyers' Captain Clutch was at full speed as he gloved it down and dropped it on his stick. Gagne broke out with Primeau, who rushed the puck up the right side of the ice and into the Tampa end. He looked to pass across to Gagne, but when Lightning defenseman Dan Boyle slid down to take away the lane, Primeau rocketed a shot high and just inside the right post for a 3–1 Flyers lead.

The goal was Primeau's seventh of the playoffs, matching in 15 games his 54-game regular-season total.

Vincent Lecavalier got a goal back for Tampa Bay with 33 seconds left in regulation, and as the Flyers teetered, Primeau again steadied things. After losing the ensuing faceoff, he charged into the Tampa end, tipped away passes, and pushed the puck into the corner. Taking whacks and hacks, Primeau held possession along the wall, milking the final precious seconds off the clock.

"There are certain stages in your season and certain stages in critical playoff series where captains have to step up, and he stepped up again," Hitchcock told reporters.

"Preems has been that guy we've been looking to and following," LeClair added. "Today he did the same thing. He was the difference out there each time he was on the ice."

And he was out there a lot. He played 31 shifts totaling 22:28 of ice time. It was five shifts and four minutes more than any other Flyers forward.

"Every time I came off the ice, I looked around to Hitch and wanted to go back out again," Primeau said. "I felt I could have played 60 minutes."

In Tampa for Game 5 he only played 20, but it was a night he'd like to forget as he indirectly assisted on a pair of Brad Richards power-play goals—sitting in the penalty box for one, the other bouncing off his shin pad on a faceoff—as the Flyers fell behind 3–0 7:12 into the second period. He set up Patrick Sharp's second-period goal that got the Flyers within 3–2 at 9:34 of the second, but that was as close as they got.

The Flyers flew home to Philadelphia knowing their season was one game from ending.

The day of Game 6, uncertainty filled the Philadelphia air. It wasn't just about one game for the rest of their season; it was so much more than that. The dark cloud of impending labor doom had hung over the entire season as the 2003–04 campaign was the last of the collective bargaining agreement between the players and the clubs. There was more talk of war chests and lockouts and lost seasons than there was of goals, assists and points.

The funeral for the 2004–05 season was being held before it even was born.

And with a veteran group, many of whom were playing in the final years of their contracts—and their careers—some knew this was could be their last, best chance to get their names on the Stanley Cup.

LeClair, Recchi and Vladimir Malakhov already had been part of Cup championship teams, but for many others—Roenick, Burke, Zhamnov, Primeau, Danny Markov, Tony Amonte—they could see more road behind them than ahead. They had no way of knowing it then, but of those nine distinguished veterans, only Primeau still would be wearing a Flyers sweater when the 2005–06 season began.

"We're not sure where this group will be not only a year from now, but three months from now," Primeau said the day before Game 6. "Odds are that there will be changes. And on top of that, there's the collective bargaining agreement. We don't know what to expect. So it's important to take advantage of the opportunity right now."

It wouldn't just take a supreme effort—it would take a Suprimeau one. And the Flyers' Captain Fantastic had one more memorable night left in a two-month run of them.

With his team trailing 1–0, Primeau took a bouncing pass from Roenick into the Tampa end. Unable to control it with his stick, and with a pair of Tampa players hanging on him like a clothesline, he kicked the puck to Gagne, who scored to tie the game. And with 2:59 left in the first, Roenick forced Darryl Sydor to throw a clearing attempt through the slot to Malakhov, who fed Primeau on the doorstep for goal number eight in his remarkable run.

But the Flyers trailed 4–3 when the game's final 20 minutes began.

As the clock ticked down to less than two minutes remaining, the Flyers got the puck deep in the Tampa end, but Martin St. Louis emerged from a scrum and tried to push the puck to Andreychuk. It skittered past him and onto the stick of Flyers defenseman Mattias Timander at the left point. Timander fired a shot that went off Sydor and Khabibulin's blocker, where it dropped to the ice and onto Primeau's right skate. In a play that was one part Pele, one part Gretzky, Primeau kicked the puck across the goal line behind Khabibulin, circled behind the net, and tapped it in for a remarkable game-tying goal with 1:49 left in regulation.

Primeau described his magical goal: "I kind of directed it with my skate and then I thought, 'Oh, don't go in.' I wanted it to go in, but I didn't want it to go in, because I was thinking, 'They are going to review it and it's going to be disallowed.' And all of a sudden it kept coming across the crease and I was coming out the other side, and I got an easy whack at it."

The Wachovia Center shook with the excitement of 19,910 rabid fans proudly clad in their Orange Crush T-shirts.

Those fans didn't know it then, but their heroes on ice would coax one more deafening roar out of them.

With 1:42 left in overtime, Primeau, Roenick and Gagne controlled the puck deep in the Lightning end. Gagne sent a pass behind the net to Primeau, who skated out and slid the puck to Roenick. Roenick threw it across the crease to Gagne, who buried the shot and gave life to Game 7 back in Tampa. Primeau drew an assist, his second of the game. The four-point night was his biggest scoring output of a remarkable postseason. And he saved it for when his team needed him the most.

"You knew if he was on the ice he'd find a way to win that game," Chuck Gormley, who covered the series for the *Courier Post*, said. "And he was on the ice a lot that game. They kept sending him over the boards, and he said let's go. He was obsessed with winning that game, and he did. He did it on his own."

Looking back now, Primeau believes that game not only was his best experience with the Flyers, but possibly in his hockey career.

"I know how many people remember the fifth-overtime game, but for most memorable game, for me, was Game 6 against Tampa Bay. I was so much more involved offensively on the score sheet from start to finish, as opposed to just scoring an overtime goal. That game I remember very vividly, especially being at home. It was such a great atmosphere. That's a point in time I'll never forget."

Neither have the fans. In a 2006 online poll celebrating the 40th anniversary of the franchise, Game 6 of the 2004 Eastern Conference Finals was voted as one of the 10 greatest in team history.

But beyond the fans, Primeau's peers stood in awe of what he accomplished.

"What pleases me about that [Game 6], people tell me what kind of performance it was, how dominant and all those things, but the two greatest compliments I got were from Steve Yzerman and Phil Esposito," Primeau said. "Both those guys have told me face to face that it was the most dominating performance they had ever seen in the playoffs. To receive those kinds of accolades from those people and players is pretty special."

That the dream died in Game 7 with Primeau being held without a point doesn't diminish what he accomplished in the 2004 playoffs.

"Probably the best individual performance that I had seen by a Flyer," Gormley, who covered the team from 1990 until 2011, said. "He literally carried that team on his shoulders. And he was not a Joe Sakic/Wayne Gretzky/Mario Lemieux kind of player. He was a mucker and a grinder and he did things that were uncharacteristic for him."

Added Hitchcock: "Players have a sense that they might not ever get an opportunity to win a championship again. He knew this was the best chance he'd have in his life and he was going to do everything in his power to pull the rest of the players along. All the players in the world, he was a cut above everybody in the whole playoff run."

Primeau finished with nine goals and seven assists for 16 points in 18 games. Of the 234 players who had played at least 100 playoff games to that point, Primeau was the first player in league history to match his career playoff goal total in just one postseason.

He also was a plus-11 while averaging nearly 19 minutes of ice time per game. He killed penalties, played on the power play and skated over 20 minutes in six games, including the final four games of the Tampa series. And he did it all while suffering possibly two concussions during the run.

"It was by far the best period or stretch of my career," he said. "For many reasons: One, it's playoff time; two, the way I was able to produce offensively, especially after the regular season and the role I had taken on under Hitch's system; and because I was getting older and I didn't think I wouldn't ever play again, but I didn't know how many more opportunities I would have. It was an exciting run and a very memorable point in my career."

But when asked to explain how an otherwise ordinary career playoff performer can turn into Superman—or Suprimeau—for two months, he's at a loss.

"Other than coming off a concussion that year, I was healthier than I'd been in a long time because I had just missed six weeks before the playoffs started," he said. "And pucks just started to go in and kept going in. I really don't feel I played any different, but statistically it was a lot different."

LeClair, who had one of the best seats in the house during the historic run, summed it up simply and succinctly: "With the team we had, we needed someone like that. Without someone stepping up like that, we would have been out of the playoffs a lot earlier."

THE COMEBACK

When the Flyers reported for training camp in September 2007, no one knew what to expect as new faces dotted the roster.

There was Danny Briere, the team's new $52 million center, imported to add front-line scoring. And Kimmo Timonen, the All-Star defenseman added to bolster a blue-line corps that had been embarrassed and outskated the previous season.

Other additions included high-scoring forwards Joffrey Lupul and Scott Hartnell, and defenseman Jason Smith was brought in for his toughness and leadership. He was appointed the 16th captain in club history prior to the start of the season.

The chemistry experiment would be how the newcomers would blend with those left over from the previous season's league- and team-worst 22-win, 56-point campaign.

"It's a little bit of the unknown," goaltender Martin Biron told the team's website the first day of training camp. "In the [scrimmages], in the workouts and all of that, you never really know what is going to happen, so you kind of come in pretty much ready for anything."

What coach John Stevens wanted them to be ready to do was work.

"Our motto coming into the season is we have to be willing to earn it," he said. "We have to be willing to earn the respect of the league again."

Their quest for respect got off to a bumpy start. In a preseason game against the Ottawa Senators on September 25, rookie forward Steve Downie, looking to earn himself a spot on the team, instead earned himself a 20-game suspension when he launched himself like a cruise missile at the head of Ottawa's Dean McAmmond.

The Flyers got a little extra bonding time when they traveled to Western Canada prior to starting the season in Calgary.

CHANGING THE ROOM

One of the Flyers' worst losses of the 2007–08 season came March 16 in Pittsburgh, a 7–1 beating reminiscent of the previous season's failures.

Coach John Stevens, looking for some way to shake the team up, called equipment manager Derek Settlemyre and told him to shuffle the dressing stalls in the locker room.

"The next day at practice, we walked in the room and everything was rearranged," Danny Briere said. "We kind of laughed about it. John didn't say anything, [but] it changed the mindset. Instead of thinking about the last game, we were talking about who's my new stall neighbor. I thought that was pretty clever."

The coach looked even smarter when the team went 7–1–1 to finish the regular season.

If anyone was wondering how the new players would jell, that question was answered in the affirmative when Briere scored two goals, including the game-winner with less than two minutes left, in a 3–2 win against the Flames.

"It's a great feeling right now," Briere told reporters after the game. "I can't even explain it. To start like this on a new team is an unbelievable feeling."

The good feelings were tempered six nights later when another belligerent play overshadowed an 8–2 win against the Vancouver Canucks. Mike Richards scored twice and added two assists, but the night was marred when Jesse Boulerice cross-checked the Canucks' Ryan Kesler in the face in the third period, breaking his stick on the center's jaw and earning himself a 25-game suspension.

While the Flyers were pilloried for their overly physical play, they also were winning games. Biron earned back-to-back shut-outs of the Atlanta Thrashers and New Jersey Devils, and when Simon Gagne scored 48 seconds into overtime for a 3–2 win against the Carolina Hurricanes, the Flyers had swept a four-game homestand.

The good feelings wouldn't last long, though. A season-long 16-day road trip started badly and only got worse. During their first stop, Gagne was leveled by a hard hit from Florida Panthers defenseman Jay Bouwmeester that left him with the first of what would begin a season-long fight with concussion problems.

Three nights later in Boston, the Flyers committed their third suspendable offense when Randy Jones drove Bruins forward Patrice Bergeron face-first into the boards behind the Flyers' net. Bergeron suffered a broken nose and what became a season-ending concussion; Jones was given a two-game suspension.

When the teams met in Philadelphia a month later there was another incident. Bruins defenseman Andrew Alberts dropped to his knees to stop a puck from leaving the zone when Hartnell barreled into him. Alberts was knocked out of the game with a concussion and Hartnell earned a two-game suspension.

The suspensions didn't put a damper on the Flyers' physical play, but their winning certainly subsided, as they won consecutive games just once between November 1 and December 22.

They rebounded, though, with an 11–2–1 streak leading into the All-Star break that pushed them to the top of the Atlantic Division and second in the Eastern Conference.

The success wouldn't last, however, as the club flopped out of the break, losing 10 straight games from February 6–23 to plummet from second to 10th in the conference.

Along the way they lost Gagne for the season due to recurring concussion issues. After sitting out most of November and all of December, he wasn't the same player when he returned in early January, playing a perimeter game and scoring just three power-play goals in 15 games; his season ended February 10 against Pittsburgh when Jordan Staal hit him from behind on the first shift of the game.

Gagne's prolonged absences not only took a 40-goal scorer out of the lineup, but sent Briere into a tailspin that nearly ruined his first season in Philadelphia.

Briere had spent his offseason studying Gagne—where the forward wanted the puck, where his scoring zones were. It was beautiful to watch when they were together. In the first eight games of the season, Gagne had four goals and eight points while Briere had four goals and 12 points. Without Gagne, though, Briere struggled to jell with other linemates. Stevens tried Briere with just about every other forward on the roster, and even shifted him to wing for a short time.

"It was frustrating," Briere said, "because for the past four years I had been in Buffalo, I had three different wingers the whole time I was there."

The low point came February 23 at the Wachovia Center as the Flyers lost the game—Bouwmeester's goal tied the game with 3.7 seconds left and Olli Jokinen scored in overtime—and Mike Richards, the team's leading scorer, to a torn hamstring. Meanwhile, Briere's second-period goal was just his third in an 18-game stretch, and he had a minus-23 rating.

"We're just going to have to deal with it right now," Flyers general manager Paul Holmgren told the media. "We're in a tough spot. There's no sense waving the white flag. Everyone else is just going to have to pick it up."

"You're just hoping for a break somewhere," Briere said. "When things start to go wrong or go bad, everything is magnified. All I was hoping for was just a break somewhere, somehow."

That break came in the most unexpected spot.

On February 25 the Flyers toted that 10-game losing streak into Buffalo. It looked like the skid would hit 11 when they fell behind 3–0 14 minutes into the game, but Jeff Carter and Scottie Upshall scored 1:48 apart late in the first, and then R.J. Umberger's power-play goal in the third tied it.

After a scoreless overtime, the game went to a shootout, with the outcome resting on the stick of Briere, the former favorite son in Buffalo who now was booed every time he touched the puck.

"All I was thinking was, this is perfect," Briere said that night. "I can't be in a better position."

Briere skated in on goaltender Ryan Miller, baited him out of position with a forehand deke, and deposited the puck inside the right post.

On one shot, Briere lost about 700 pounds off his narrow shoulders.

"Going in, it was a big game personally," Briere said. "We had been struggling, 10 in a row we lost. ... That game was probably the turnover of the season for us.

"If it wasn't the biggest game of the year, it was close to it. And personally, that was the break I needed to turn things around."

It continued to get better for Briere and the Flyers hours later, when the team dealt promising defense prospect Alexandre Picard and a draft pick to the Tampa Bay Lightning for forward Vinny Prospal. Installed on a line with Briere, magic happened almost instantaneously.

"The way we were doing drills, he was just throwing the puck without looking into areas I like to hang out," Briere said of their first practice. "And for him, he had played with Marty St. Louis and Vinny Lecavalier in Tampa, and that's the way they played. For me, I was just trying to find that chemistry with different guys. I remember that first practice getting really excited. It just felt like we were thinking the same way.

"I think what happened was you start feeling lighter, quicker, more comfortable. That's when things started happening positively for you. Instead of forcing plays and forcing passes, you let things happen. And that helped me play better, play more relaxed and enjoy myself out there."

There was little to enjoy, though, on March 16, when the Flyers were embarrassed 7–1 in Pittsburgh. With their playoff hopes slipping away, Holmgren didn't hide his frustration.

"That was painful to watch," he said. "You've got to question a lot of things. It was a big game. We're in a fight for a playoff spot [and] to have that type of performance is alarming."

What bothered him most?

"Preparation," he said. "We weren't ready to play in a game. The players certainly need to look in the mirror right now, and I'm sure the coaches are looking very closely at their preparation."

Stevens didn't disagree with his boss.

"It starts with me," he said. "I'm the head of this snake, if you want to call it that, and we have a staff here that works diligently to get this team ready to play. At the end of the day I have the responsibility to make sure these guys are ready."

THAT'S THE TICKET

After the worst season in franchise history, the Flyers wanted to do something different for their fans. So they took their tickets and made them something more than a piece of paper with a seat location on it.

"One thing we realized is the fans are what make the organization," Shawn Tilger, the club's senior vice president, business operations, said, "so why not do a tribute to the fans, especially the season-ticket holders?"

Through an e-mail campaign, the club received more than 200 photo submissions from its season-ticket holders, and put the best 44 (preseason and regular season) on the tickets.

They were ready after that game. With a new look to the locker room—Stevens ordered the layout of the room changed—they won four straight and finished the season on a 7–1–1 streak.

They shut out the New Jersey Devils in the second-to-last game of the season to get back into the playoffs, and two days later, after a season-closing 2–0 shutout of the Penguins, the Flyers had the sixth seed in the playoffs and an opening-round date with Southeast Division-champion Washington Capitals.

The Flyers took a two-goal lead into the third period of Game 1 in Washington, but Caps defenseman Mike Green scored twice to tie it. And then forward Alexander Ovechkin, displaying the sublime skills that had earned him the league's scoring title, won it with less than five minutes to play. Ovechkin poked the puck away from Flyers defenseman Jaroslav Modry and then lifted Lasse Kukkonen's stick to steal the puck and score in a disheartening 5–4 loss.

"To start that series, not a lot of people believed we had a chance or that we could win," Briere said. "But that wasn't the mindset in our room. It was totally different in our room. ... Even though we lost and people saw we blew that two-goal lead, for us it was a step in the right direction. We knew if we could play like we did in the first two periods, we could win."

They made the right next step in Game 2. Biron stopped everything thrown his way, and Carter and Umberger scored as the Flyers evened the series with a 2–0 victory.

A raucous Wachovia Center crowd was delighted by a three-point night from Briere and a penalty-shot goal by Richards in a 6–3 win in Game 3. Two nights later Briere tied the game with a power-play goal midway through the third and Mike Knuble scored off his own rebound 6:40 into the second overtime for a 4–3 victory and a 3–1 series lead.

Washington won Game 5, forcing a Game 6 back in Philadelphia. Ovechkin, held mostly in check since Game 1 by outstanding defensive work by Timonen and Braydon Coburn, scored twice, including the winning goal 2:46 into the third period, to force a Game 7 in Washington the next day.

Suddenly Biron became a hot topic. The goalie had gone 0–5 with a 5.95 goals-against average in back-to-back games during the regular season, and his confidence had to be wavering after the team surrendered what had looked to be a commanding series lead, right?

"One of Marty's strengths to me is he's able to brush it off when things go bad," Briere, who played with Biron in Buffalo and has been a close friend for years, said. "It always seems like he's happy. When we lost Game 6 and everyone got on his back and said he can't do this, he can't do that, I knew this is where his personality is going to come into play and help us win this game. He's going to forget about what happened yesterday and he's going to come in and have fun in Game 7."

Biron had more than just fun in Game 7—he had the game of his life.

The Flyers took a 2–1 lead midway through the second period when Patrick Thoreson shoved Shaone Morrison into goalie Cristobal Huet, giving Sami Kapanen an open net to score into. Ovechkin's goal with 4:31 left in the second tied the game, but that was all Biron would allow. He stopped the next 21 shots, including a 16-shot third-period bombardment.

The game went into overtime, and turned when Caps defenseman Tom Poti was sent off for tripping at 4:15. On the ensuing power play, Timonen fired a shot from the left point that Huet stopped, but Lupul, who hadn't scored a goal to that point in the playoffs, poked in the rebound at the 6:06 mark.

Lupul was the hero, but Biron was the real star.

"I guess he answered those questions about back to back," Stevens told reporters. "He was terrific, and he had to be."

Next was the top-seeded Montreal Canadiens, who had beaten the Flyers in all four regular-season meetings. They made it five straight in Game 1, but in irregular fashion.

The Flyers jumped to a 2–0 lead on goals by Umberger and Jim Dowd, but started a series-long trend of handing those leads back by the third period. Andrei Kostitsyn scored midway through the second and Alex Kovalev used a controversially magical piece of eye-hand coordination to tie the game with 3:57 left in the period. Tomas Plekanec fired a shot off a short-handed rush, and the rebound popped in the air. Kovalev appeared to play the puck with a high stick, but replays showed that while the blade of his stick came down on top of the crossbar, the puck hit the middle of the shaft—which was below the crossbar—and the goal was allowed to stand.

Lupul scored 19 seconds into the third to put the Flyers ahead, but Montreal got another break when Richards was whistled for kneeing Kovalev with 1:09 left. Replays, though, showed Richards hit the Canadiens forward with a clean shoulder check when Kovalev tried to jump around him.

Carter lost the ensuing faceoff when his stick broke, allowing Kovalev to score again to tie the game with 28.6 seconds left. The Canadiens' Tom Kostopoulos then won it with a goal 48 seconds into overtime.

Just like he did in Game 2 of the first round, Biron rose to the occasion in Game 2 against Montreal. He stopped 15 of 16 shots in the first period and made 34 saves for the game, while Umberger scored twice as the Flyers took a 4–2 decision and a tied series home to Philadelphia.

Game 3 easily was the wildest of the series. The Flyers took a 3–0 lead in the second period as Upshall capped an end-to-end rush by Lupul, Richards scored on a short-handed two-on-one break and Umberger added a goal off a Carter rebound. But the lead nearly came unraveled 5:17 into the third period as Derian Hatcher was given a five-minute major and a game misconduct for drilling the Canadiens' Francois Bouillon face-first into the boards.

Montreal cashed in twice in a 1:12 span, but that was all they would get. Biron was outstanding as the Flyers were outshot 17–2 in the third period, but skated away with the 3–2 victory and the series lead.

Hatcher breathed a sigh of relief when the final horn sounded.

"It was a horrible feeling," the veteran defenseman said. "Watching those 15 minutes that I wasn't playing, that was a lot more exhausting than playing the game. Mentally it was a lot more stressing."

There was even more stress in Game 4, as the usual script unfolded—the Flyers scored the first two goals, the Canadiens tied the game in a short burst, Biron played like a superhero, and the Flyers eked out a victory.

This time it was Umberger scoring twice more—giving him six in the series—and Briere netting the game-winner in a 4–2 victory.

Biron, though, was the story.

"Marty has set a standard of play for himself that he's able to consistently achieve," Stevens said. "Until you have success this time of year, you really don't know what your standard is. Marty has never been in this situation, he never had a reference point, and now he has a reference point that he can play at a very high level and be the difference in a hockey game, and he was tonight."

The series returned to Montreal for Game 5. Again leading a series 3–1, the Flyers were determined not to make the same mistakes they made against Washington.

"The last Game 5, we played like we were an unsure team," Lupul said. "They [Washington] came out hard and we should have been prepared for that. We'll be prepared for that [against Montreal]."

They didn't look prepared early, as the Canadiens scored the game's first goal for the first time in the series. It actually was the first time they had played with a lead the entire series to

GUTTING IT OUT

Players will do whatever it takes to get their name on the Stanley Cup.

For veteran defenseman and team captain Jason Smith, that meant playing through two separated shoulders while leading the team in the 2008 playoffs with 56 hits and 45 blocked shots, while for fellow blueliner Derian Hatcher, it was blocking out the pain from a broken leg and needing fluid drained from his knee every other day while still playing more than 21 minutes per game.

"I get shivers thinking about it," GM Paul Holmgren said. "It was almost like we'd have to shoot him [Smith] for him not to play. That was his attitude. I've been around hockey a long time and I don't know that I've ever seen anything like that. I don't know how he did it.

"They both are ultimate pros. What they bring to a team, you can't define it."

that point. Umberger scored his seventh of the series to tie it, but midway through the second, the Canadiens led 3–1.

That's when the Flyers turned the offense loose, scoring three times in a 2:58 span to take a 4–3 lead. Umberger continued his dream series, as his wild shot from the point hit Richards' glove and dropped into the goal. Moments later, Umberger took the puck from Montreal defenseman Roman Hamrlik in front of the Montreal net and scored to tie the game. Hartnell completed the comeback when he lasered a shot past Montreal rookie goalie Carey Price to put the Flyers ahead.

Kostitsyn scored early in the third to tie the game, but Upshall tipped a Carter shot behind Price, and then Knuble outraced Chris Higgins to a loose puck for an empty-net goal for a final 6–4 margin.

The Flyers became just the second team in NHL history to win two rounds in the playoffs the season after finishing with the league's worst record.

"For the guys who were doubted last year, it's been a lot of fun and it's a vindication," Knuble said. "We're thrilled where we are and now we can really start thinking, 'Why not us?'"

The Eastern Conference Finals would be dubbed the Keystone Clash, an All-Pennsylvania series between the Flyers and Penguins.

As high as the Flyers were riding, a huge dip came the day before the team was scheduled to leave for Pittsburgh when they learned they would be without Timonen due to a blood clot in his ankle, suffered when he blocked a shot late in Game 5 against the Canadiens.

Facing the Penguins' offensive juggernaut, it was a crushing blow.

"We feel like we've battled through adversity all year long," Briere told reporters before the series started. "Yes, Kimmo is a big part of our team, but at the same time we've been faced with those situations before. We've found ways to pull through, to come together. We believe we can do the same thing."

For a while in Game 1 it looked like they would, thanks to a pair of Richards goals that put them up 2–1 midway through the first period. But the Penguins scored twice before the period ended and added another goal when a cherry-picking Evgeni Malkin scored a short-handed goal for a 4–2 final score.

Less than two minutes into Game 2, Coburn would join Timonen on the sideline after a tipped puck slammed into the left side of his head, leaving him with a face that looked like it came from a Halloween nightmare. A gash in the middle of his head that needed more than 50 stitches to close left him with a scar that resembled a question mark, and his left eye looked like he had gone 12 rounds with Rocky Balboa and Apollo Creed. He also suffered a concussion and didn't play the rest of the series.

Playing almost all of Game 2 with just five defensemen—three of whom were 34 or older—the Flyers held as best they could. The turning point came midway through the third when Downie didn't fight hard enough to clear a puck from the Flyers' end, then compounded the mistake by chasing Gary Roberts behind the net. No one covered Maxime Talbot in front, and he netted the winner off Roberts' pass in what became another 4–2 defeat.

Despite the mistake, Stevens wrote Downie's name into the lineup for Game 3. "There'll be lots more good days for Steve Downie," the coach said.

Game 3 wasn't one of those days.

Pittsburgh started fast, scoring twice in a 2:38 span early in the first, but Umberger scored his 10th of the postseason when he knocked in a Prospal rebound midway through the period.

The game turned in the third when Downie went one-on-four in the Pittsburgh end. Trapped, he threw a lazy pass into the middle of the ice that Malkin intercepted and started back the other way, leading to a Ryan Malone goal that triggered a 4–1 Penguins victory and left the Flyers in a 3–0 series hole.

"You've just got to keep going," Carter said. "We had a 10-game losing streak this year [and] we learned from it. We just have to keep battling. You can't let up—you have to keep going, work harder. We've got one game here to turn things around."

Their season on the line, the Flyers came out angry and effective. Lupul scored when his shot ticked off the stick of Penguins defenseman Hal Gill and got past Pens goalie Marc-Andre Fleury, and Briere made it 2–0 when he found a sliver of space between Gill and Fleury to knock in a rebound. Carter made it 3–0 when he whacked his own rebound out of mid-air.

The Pens got a pair of Jordan Staal goals in the third period to make it a one-goal game, but Biron backstopped a furious final 5:49, and the Flyers remained alive with a 4–2 victory, and even felt a little confident.

"This is the weirdest group I've ever been around," Lupul said. "We seem our most confident when it looks like we're down and out. We're kind of a weird team that way. We play our best when our backs are up against the wall."

Timonen was cleared to play in Game 5, but the Flyers got no extra lift from the return of their best defenseman, as the Penguins' over-abundance of offensive firepower ended the Flyers' fairy-tale season with a 6–0 shellacking.

While there were tears in the aftermath of their season ending, the 2007–08 campaign showed the Flyers' horrendous 2006–07 season was a one-time disaster. "To win the Cup you have to be a good team, but you need some breaks to go your way," Briere said. "I believe at some point things will fall in line with us. That's the way you have to see it. We made some great strides. We gained a lot of experience this year. It's tough to see right away, you're fighting so hard to get to the Stanley Cup Final, it's a tough blow when it happens, when you lose that game that sends you home. But when you sit back and look at all the strides we made this year, the organization is definitely headed in the right direction."

PHILADELPHIA'S CLASSIC MOMENT

The Flyers already had taken part in a Winter Classic, the NHL's outdoor extravaganza, when the game was played at Boston's Fenway Park in 2010, when they were approached again about participating again in the 2012 game.

The difference this time is they would be the host, facing the New York Rangers in a game scheduled for Citizens Bank Park, the home of the Phillies.

"It was a big honor," Flyers president Peter Luukko said. "It puts Philadelphia on the map for a week."

The announcement was greeted with overwhelming approval by hockey fans in the Delaware Valley, with available tickets selling at a lightening pace.

The organization planned a celebration of all things hockey in the region, starting with an alumni game on New Year's Eve that featured players from all generations of the franchise facing Rangers alums. From the Stanley Cup teams there were Joe and Jimmy Watson, Orest Kindrachuk, Bob Kelly, Larry Goodenough and an LCB Line reunion—Reggie Leach, Bobby Clarke and Bill Barber.

"A lot of great memories we had as a threesome," Clarke said when the roster was announced. "I think it'll be a neat reunion. But I think it'll be just as neat to sit in the locker room with one another."

Among those from the teams that went to the Stanley Cup Final in 1985 and 1987 were Mark Howe, Brad Marsh, Dave Poulin and Rick Tocchet.

And from the more current Flyers teams were Eric Desjardins, Chris Therien, John LeClair, Mark Recchi, Jeremy Roenick and No. 88 himself, Eric Lindros.

A SECONI FIRST

When the Flyers played in the 2010 Winter Classic, the game's first goal was scored by defenseman Danny Syvret. It also marked his first NHL goal.

"I think for every NHL player their first goal is memorable," he said. "For sure I'm not going to forget this one."

Two years later, another Flyer made the first goal of the Winter Classic his first NHL goal—forward Brayden Schenn.

Like Syvret, Schenn's goal came in a losing effort.

"It's nice scoring there, but it would have been better if we got the win," Schenn said. "At the same time ... I haven't scored in the NHL before, and playing a little bit last year, and being hurt this year, it seems like it's taken forever, but it's good to get it in a game like this."

"It was probably the only time in the history of the Flyers that every generation of the team will be on the ice together," Luukko said.

Despite all the acrimony that was part of his time with the Flyers, GM Paul Holmgren wasted little time extending the invitation to Lindros, and Lindros wasted little time accepting it.

"I was very happy to receive a phone call from Paul Holmgren, who invited me down to play," Lindros told ESPN.com. "I said I would love to."

One name missing from the original roster, however, was Bernie Parent. The Hall of Fame goalie was going to take part as an off-ice ambassador, but fan outcry pushed the 66-year-old to reconsider.

"At first I said I didn't feel like it," he said, "but I thought about it, and you look at the fans, you can't be selfish on something like this. They supported us for so many years, in my case 12 years, and I said why not go out and wave to the people, maybe play for 10 minutes. That's why I made the decision."

When the players walked out of the dugouts for the game, the biggest ovation was saved for Parent, who looked like he stepped right out of 1974, wearing his trademark orange No. 1 jersey, brown pads, glove and blocker, and blank white mask. He played just 3:32, but stopped all six shots, including a penalty-shot attempt by Ron Duguay.

His teammates for a day were as impressed as the fans.

"I've been fortunate to know Bernie for a long time," Neil Little, who played the final period in net for the Flyers, said. "This meant a lot to him. To see him put on a good show, that was extra special. I was just happy. I was just like everyone else—a fan."

"It was wonderful to see Bernie," Lindros added. "I think that was fantastic. ... I think he was out there for what, six, seven minutes? That's a great feeling. That's real special for me. Nice to see that."

And like the star he is, Parent knew not to stay in the spotlight for too long.

"That was his call," Flyers alumni team coach Keith Primeau said. "He made sure we knew before we started that he was coming out five minutes in."

The game was a major success, and not just because the Flyers alums won 3–1. Fans had a wonderful, nostalgic look at the history of the franchise. But as much fun as the spectators had, the players enjoyed it even more.

"It was just incredible, the feeling that you got," Leach said. "You look around and say look at all these people, they come out here, 45,000, to see a bunch of old guys skate around the ice. At least they could see us because we were nice and slow."

"Being in the locker room, for me, that's the most fun," Clarke said. "I think a game like this will rank way up there in what I consider important moments in my hockey life."

The next day marked the first chance for the current Flyers to hit the Citizens Bank Park ice. It was a light practice as the players used the time to get acclimated to the conditions. That was followed by a family skate, annually the favorite time for the majority of the players. The family for one player got even bigger during the skate, as Claude Giroux's sister, Isabelle, accepted a marriage proposal from her boyfriend at center ice.

After practice was a bit of controversy as goalie Ilya Bryzgalov pulled the pin on a goaltending grenade, telling the gathered media: "I have great news and even better news. Okay, great news is I'm not playing tomorrow, and better news is now we have a chance to win the game tomorrow." When asked what his plan would be for sitting from the bench while backup Sergei Bobrovsky was playing, Bryzgalov said, "Make sure I don't forget my thermos with some nice tea and enjoy the bench."

That didn't go over well with his teammates. Bryzgalov had been struggling on and off the ice with his adjustment to Philadelphia, and while he had shown signs of being the Vezina Trophy finalist he had been in Phoenix, he also had struggled, to the point where after one rough outing he told reporters he felt "lost in the woods."

Added to his inconsistent play was a public display of his off-beat personality during the HBO "24/7" documentary series that followed the Flyers and Rangers in the weeks leading up to the game. Bryzgalov provided memorable insights on the universe ("The solar system is so humongous big."), the safety of tigers in the Far East ("China law, if you kill a tiger like this? Death penalty."), and how Siberian huskies are the attractive women of the dog world ("My huskie, basically she's a hot girl.").

"You saw some of the stuff Bryz said, I think it's a reflection of Bryz a little bit," Braydon Coburn said. "Bryz is a funny guy. He's got his own sense of humor. I think when somebody has the forum to really show off their different sense of humor it can be funny."

It wasn't funny the day before the game, however, but there wasn't a whole lot that could diminish the spectacle for the players.

"You're coming out of the baseball dugout and you're walking up the stairs, you're walking up to this outdoor rink, you've got all these people all over the place," Coburn said. "It was an amazing feeling."

That feeling carried over to the game, with the Flyers taking a 1–0 lead at 12:26 of the second period when Brayden Schenn scored off the rebound of a Matt Carle shot. Not a bad way to score your first NHL goal, eh?

Less than two minutes later Claude Giroux scored to make it 2–0, but that was as good as it would get for the home team. The

Rangers' Mike Rupp scored two straight goals to tie it, and then Brad Richards put the Rangers ahead at 5:21 of the third.

The Flyers pushed to tie the game, and got a golden chance with 19.6 seconds left when the Rangers' Ryan McDonagh dove into the goal crease to cover a puck that had slipped behind goalie Henrik Lundqvist. The Flyers were awarded a penalty shot, with Danny Briere given the chance for the one-on-one shot on Lundqvist.

As Briere wrote for a blog on NHL.com, his only thought was: "This game was going to overtime."

He skated in fast and hard, and as he got into the slot he attempted to snap a shot between Lundqvist's pads. However, the Rangers' goalie snapped his legs closed and made the save.

"Coming in on Lundqvist, I had beaten him once on the blocker side, once on the glove side [in shootouts]," Briere wrote. "He had stopped me a couple times before as well in shootouts, but I was still convinced I was going to score. I tried to surprise him with a quick little shot; unfortunately he was quicker than me."

The game ended in a 3–2 loss for the Flyers, who fell to 0–2 in Winter Classics, following their loss to the Bruins in 2010. However, the entire process was a winning day for the players.

"I looked around and it was pretty cool," Jakub Voracek said. "It happens maybe once in a lifetime. For some it doesn't happen at all. I'm glad I was part of it. It was a great experience."

THE BAD

1976

The Flyers' quest for a third straight Stanley Cup in 1975–76 got off to a dreadful start.

Bernie Parent, the hero of the previous two title runs, reported to training camp in 1975 complaining of neck and elbow pain. He was given massages and muscle relaxants, but even a few days in traction at a hospital did little to help heal the netminder's aching body. Further tests revealed a herniated cervical disc. Surgery was performed, sidelining Parent until late February.

Little-used Wayne Stephenson was pressed into service, but he didn't exactly get a ringing endorsement from his coach.

"Unless we get somebody better, we'll go with him," Fred Shero said.

Despite Parent's absence, the Flyers started strong, winning their first four and not losing consecutive games until the end of December. When the calendar turned from 1975 to 1976, the Flyers were 22–6–8.

By then Reggie Leach had 23 goals, Bobby Clarke had 17 goals and 36 assists, and Bill Barber had 18 goals and 23 assists.

"It's so easy," Leach told reporters. "All I have to do is get in the slot and wait for Clarkie to get me the puck."

After beating the Soviet Union's Central Red Army team on January 11, 1976, the Flyers went 24–7–8 to finish the regular season, including an NHL record-tying 23-game unbeaten streak, during which they went 17–0–6. Leach became the 13th player in league history to net 50 goals, and Barber went over 100 points.

They clinched the Patrick Division title March 21, one game after the streak ended, when Barber and Terry Crisp each scored twice in a 4–2 victory against the Toronto Maple Leafs.

The Flyers finished 51–13–16, their third straight 50-win season, and their club-record 118 points was second in the league to the Montreal Canadiens.

The Flyers led the league with 348 goals, and the high-flying LCB Line—Leach, Clarke and Barber—set records with 141 goals and 322 points. Leach established a team standard with a league-leading 61 goals. Barber added 50 goals and 62 assists for 112 points. Clarke led the league with 89 assists, finished second to Montreal's Guy Lafleur with 119 points, and won his second straight Hart Trophy as league MVP.

Despite having Parent for just 11 games, only two teams—Montreal and the New York Islanders—allowed fewer goals.

Stephenson starred in Parent's absence, winning 40 games with a 2.58 goals-against average.

The playoffs started for the second straight season with a first-round matchup with the Maple Leafs. And just like the previous season, the Flyers took the first two games at the Spectrum. Parent, getting the starting assignment ahead of Stephenson, made 23 saves to backstop a 4–1 win in Game 1. In Game 2, goals 70 seconds apart by Ross Lonsberry and Don Saleski early in the second period pushed the Flyers to a 3–1 win.

The Leafs turned up the hitting in Game 3 and lured the Flyers into giving away 16 man-advantages, which allowed Toronto to score all its goals on the power play in a 5–4 win. And despite a pair of Mel Bridgman goals, Parent played poorly in a 4–3 loss in Game 4, returning the series to Philadelphia tied 2–2.

Beside the losses, the Flyers were angry about what they viewed as mistreatment by the Toronto fans and police. During Game 3, Saleski was sitting in the penalty box when he was hit by a piece of ice thrown by a fan. Saleski turned to look into the crowd, and an overzealous police officer grabbed his stick. Joe Watson, coming to the defense of his teammate, swung his stick over the glass and smacked the cop on the shoulder. Both players were charged with crimes in the mêlée, as was Bridgman, who had decked Leafs defenseman Borje Salming.

Game 5 saw the Flyers score three times in 1:33 in the second period to blow open the game, and Saleski capped the 7–1 win with a hat trick.

The Flyers returned to Toronto with a chance to end the series, but Darryl Sittler scored a league record–tying five goals in an 8–5 Leafs win, which featured more Flyers arrests.

Dave Schultz, who took a single-game playoff record-tying 42 penalty minutes, was elbowed by a fan while leaving the ice. While Schultz was held back from attacking the 65-year-old knucklehead, Bob Kelly threw his glove into the stands, accidentally hitting an usherette in the face. Kelly and the fan who smacked Schultz were charged with assault in the fracas.

Clarke ripped his teammates after the game, saying, "We didn't play like Stanley Cup champions. We were undisciplined, unorganized."

After falling behind 2–1 after one period of Game 7 back at the Spectrum, something clicked for the Flyers. They scored four times in the first eight minutes of the second, including a pair by Bridgman, and the Flyers cruised to a series-clinching, sigh-of-relief-inducing 7–3 win.

Next were the Boston Bruins. Despite not having Bobby Orr, who was recovering from knee surgery, the Bruins got third-period goals from Dallas Smith and Gregg Sheppard against a deteriorating Parent in a 4–2 Bruins win in Game 1.

Prior to Game 2, Parent took himself out of the lineup, telling reporters, "I'm tired. I'm not in playoff shape. I don't want to cost the team a game. Let's make the move before it happens."

Saleski gave the Flyers an early 1–0 lead, and Stephenson, who hadn't played in nearly a month, held the fort until 13:17 of the third period, when Johnny Bucyk scored through a screen. In overtime, Leach knocked in the rebound of Jimmy Watson's shot off the endboards at 13:38 to give the Flyers a 2–1 win.

With Game 3 tied 2–2 after two periods, Bridgman scored off a Larry Goodenough rebound to give the Flyers the lead, and

AL HILL'S MEMORABLE DEBUT

In one day, Al Hill went from minor-league nobody to NHL record-holder.

Playing for the AHL Springfield Indians, Hill arrived home at 4:30 AM from a game in Rochester, New York. At 11:00 AM, he was told to report to Philadelphia to suit up for the Flyers. He got to the Spectrum at 5:30 PM, and was on the ice by 7:35 PM. By the time he punched out for the night, he had two goals, three assists, and a league record for a debuting NHL player.

By the time the league learned he had set a record, three scoreless games passed and Hill had been returned to the minors.

Leach and Tom Bladon added late goals for a 5–2 victory. Leach scored 23 seconds into the second period in Game 4, and Orest Kindrachuk and Joe Watson added goals in the third for a 4–2 victory.

Leach's goal in Game 4 was his 10th of the playoffs and gave him a goal in eight straight games. He wasted little time extending both numbers.

The Flyers returned home for Game 5 one win from their third straight trip to the Stanley Cup Final, but Leach nearly was absent from the party.

The team was spending a night at a hotel in Valley Forge, but Leach got into an argument with one of the coaches, left the team and drove home to South Jersey. When he didn't show up for the morning skate, teammates found him passed out in the basement of his house. When coffee and a shower didn't completely revive him, a few more beers did the trick. Teammates got Leach to the rink for the game, but Clarke had to talk Shero into letting Leach play in Game 5.

"The biggest concern was me having an argument with one of the coaches the night before," Leach said. "It all boiled down to he didn't want me to play because of the things we had said and Clarkie wanted me to play. That was it. Clarkie said let him play, he'll play well.

"Everybody says I was drunk. I wasn't drunk—I was hung over. No big deal. Not the first time anybody ever played hockey in the National Hockey League back then hung over. I remember telling Clarkie don't worry about it, just give me the puck. They're going in tonight."

They certainly were—at a record rate.

At 5:45 of the first period, he scored the game's first goal off a Barber set-up.

Sheppard beat Stephenson 59 seconds into the second, but then Leach scored the next three goals to give him a hat-trick-plus-one.

After Don Marcotte scored 6:09 into the third to cut the Flyers' lead to 4–2, Leach made it a five-goal night when he finished a Clarke feed at 8:07.

Two weeks after Sittler became the first player in more than 30 years to score five times in a playoff game, Leach turned the trick. Of his handful of goals, three came on backhanders: One to the short side, one to the wide side and one under the crossbar. He scored on forehanders to the stick side and between the pads of flustered Bruins goalie Gilles Gilbert. Three of the goals came after he crossed over from right wing to left.

"I was the type of player that when I got my confidence scoring, I could pretty well score from anywhere," Leach said.

And with nine goals in five games, Leach set a post-expansion record for goals in a series.

More importantly, the 6–3 victory sent the Flyers back to the Stanley Cup Final, against the Montreal Canadiens, where their playoff experience made them a favorite.

Leach's record output against the Bruins gave him 15 goals in the playoffs, but the Flyers that faced Montreal were a beat-up bunch. The team's top three centers were hurt or out—Clarke was slowed by strained ligaments in his knee, Rick MacLeish hadn't played since February after surgery to repair torn ligaments in his left knee and Kindrachuk was playing through a major back injury. Add to that Parent's shattered confidence, and the Flyers were far from a full team when the series started at the Montreal Forum on May 9, 1976.

Leach scored 21 seconds into Game 1 and Lonsberry added a goal later in the first, but Montreal's speed allowed them to tie the game with a pair of goals in the second period. Stephenson kept the game tied until Goodenough's power-play goal put the Flyers ahead at 5:17 of the third, but Jacques Lemaire knocked a loose puck in the slot under Stephenson at 10:02, and Guy Lapointe notched the game-winner with just 1:22 left for a 4–3 Canadiens victory.

In Game 2 Montreal's checking line of Doug Jarvis, Bob Gainey and Jimmy Roberts held the LCB Line to one shot by each player, and all the Flyers could manage was a Dave Schultz bad-angle goal with 2:25 left in the third of what ended as a 2–1 defeat.

Back in Philadelphia, home cooking helped early in Game 3. After Steve Shutt scored from 70 feet out to give Montreal the lead, Clarke fed Leach to tie the game, and Leach turned a Bill Nyrop turnover into his NHL-record 18th of the playoffs; the previous record had been 17 scored by the Montreal Canadiens' Newsy Lalonde in 1919.

Shutt scored again, knocking in his own rebound at 1:09 of the second period, but Stephenson kept the game tied, turning aside 12 of 13 Montreal shots in the second, including breakaways by Murray Wilson and Yvan Cournoyer. But at 9:16 of the third, Pierre Bouchard took a pass out of the corner from Wilson and scored through a Rick Chartraw screen. The tight-checking Canadiens limited the Flyers to just 13 shots in the final two periods, and anything that did get through, goalie Ken Dryden turned aside.

"We played our best," a pained Barber said after the game, "but there wasn't much we could do."

Down three games to none, the goal had changed to just winning one to avoid the embarrassing sweep. Kate Smith was on hand to sing "God Bless America" for the fourth time live, and she seemed to provide a good-luck charm as Leach beat Dryden from 45 feet out just 41 seconds into the game.

Shutt and Bouchard answered for Montreal, but Barber deflected a Bladon shot past Dryden with 1:40 left in the first to tie the game at 2–2.

With Lapointe off for tripping, Moose Dupont put the Flyers ahead at 13:59 of the second, and with Lemaire off for hooking at 17:20, the Flyers had a chance for an insurance goal, but Gary Dornhoefer was penalized for hooking Jarvis just 33 seconds later, negating the Flyers' last, best chance. Four seconds before Dornhoefer was set to step back on the ice, Cournoyer tied the game with 11 seconds left in the second.

With time running down in the third and the game tied, Dornhoefer hit the crossbar behind Dryden, and on the next shift Lafleur tapped in a puck in the crease with 5:42 remaining to give Montreal a 4–3 lead. Pete Mahovlich added an insurance goal 58 seconds later, and the celebration was on for the visiting team.

The Canadiens won the Cup, but Leach took home the Conn Smythe Trophy as playoff MVP. His record of 19 goals in 16 games has been matched one time, by Edmonton's Jari Kurri in 1985, but it took the Finn 18 games to do it.

The record and individual bauble was little consolation to the Flyers. They had seen their team at less than 100 percent stopped by a total of five frustrating goals.

"I thought the '76 team was loaded," Joe Watson said. "The reason we didn't win in '76 was we didn't have Bernie and we didn't have MacLeish. We go against Montreal in the Final and we lost to them before the playoffs started. Wayne Stephenson did an admirable job, but he wasn't Parent. There was nobody like Parent."

"I think the 1975–76 team was better than the two that won the Cup," team chairman Ed Snider said. "But when Bernie went out, and we had Wayne Stephenson in goal, Bernie would have won that. I think that team was better than the teams that won the Cup."

THE FOG ROLLS OUT OF PHILADELPHIA

After the Flyers were eliminated from the 1978 playoffs by the Boston Bruins, the Broad Street Bullies' days were coming to a close.

Already gone were Ed Van Impe and Bobby Taylor, who had been traded to Pittsburgh in 1976, and Dave Schultz, dealt to

Los Angeles in 1977. Barry Ashbee had passed away, and Gary Dornhoefer and Terry Crisp had retired.

And before the 1978–79 season started, Tom Bladon, Ross Lonsberry and Orest Kindrachuk were shipped to Pittsburgh, and Joe Watson was sold to Colorado.

But the Bullies' days really ended June 2, 1978. That was the day the Fog cleared in Philadelphia.

Sports experts claim that after five seasons with the same club, regardless of the sport, a coach begins to lose his effectiveness. The players have heard all the stories, all the motivational speeches; there's nothing new, and the relationship can get stale, boring and repetitive.

The end of the 1977–78 season marked Fred Shero's seventh behind the Flyers' bench. And after a disheartening five-game semifinal-round loss to the Boston Bruins—the second straight time the Bruins had ended the Flyers' season—general manager Keith Allen was pondering whether a coaching change was needed.

"I'm sort of a believer that you have to change coaches every once in a while, and I did wonder if [the players] were still getting Freddie's message," Allen said in *Full Spectrum*.

Shero had a year left on his contract, and Allen was content to let it run its course, knowing Bob McCammon was gaining experience with the franchise's American Hockey League affiliate in Maine after being hired in 1977. But a week after the 1978 playoffs ended, Allen found an envelope waiting for him from Shero. Enclosed was the coach's letter of resignation.

Two days later, Shero and his agent met with Sonny Werblin, the new president of Madison Square Garden, at Pimlico Racetrack in Baltimore, the site of the Preakness Stakes. Owner Ed Snider learned of the meeting after it happened, and suspected Mark Stewart, Shero's agent, of trying to orchestrate Shero's move from Philadelphia to the New York Rangers; the Rangers had been rumored during the 1978 playoffs to have interest in hiring Shero.

Snider told scouting director John Brogan to write a reply to Shero, stating that his resignation would not be accepted, and that the coach would be expected to honor the final year of his contract.

SHERO JOINS THE HALL—FINALLY

More than 30 years after he coached his final game, and more than 20 years after his death, Fred Shero finally earned his place in the Hockey Hall of Fame, elected into the builder's category as part of the 2013 class.

Shero went 308–151–95 in seven seasons with the Flyers. His teams finished first in the league four times and won the only two Stanley Cups in club history.

In addition, Shero was an innovator. He was the first coach to have a full-time assistant on his staff; among the first to use morning skates; an early proponent of studying game film; and immersed himself in the Soviet style of play, which he used to lead the Flyers to Cups in 1974 and '75.

"Other than [general manager] Keith Allen, Freddie Shero was the person who should have gone into the Hall of Fame ahead of myself, Bernie Parent, Billy Barber, any of us who have gone in," Bobby Clarke told the Flyers' website. "He was that important to the success of the Flyers."

"No one deserves it more than Fred Shero, in my opinion," Flyers chairman Ed Snider said. "He was the guy that put it all together. We gave him the parts and he made it work."

Shero took his case to the press, saying: "I feel my effectiveness to motivate the players has been exhausted. The organization needs a change, whether they realize it or not. Most of the players have been with me too long and I've been with them too long."

He then added: "I really believe I don't want to coach anymore. Coaching anywhere else would be a demotion."

The next week, Snider took a phone call from Werblin, who said he had read about the Flyers' coaching situation and asked if he could talk to Shero about coaching the Rangers. Snider's reply was for Werblin and the Rangers to stay away because Shero was Flyers property.

Snider hung up from Werblin, called Rangers president Bill Jennings and asked him to help set up a deal that worked for both teams. Snider asked for $100,000 and the Rangers' first-round choice in the 1978 draft, the seventh overall selection. He settled for $50,000 and the pick, which was used to select Ken Linseman.

Years later, Snider said dealing away the only coach to lead his team to a Stanley Cup was a good move.

"The time had come to make a change," Snider told Jim Jackson in *Walking Together Forever*. "Everything worked out beautifully for us. We basically suckered the Rangers. We ended up with a first-round pick for a coach we probably were going to fire anyway."

So the Flyers got what they wanted, and so did Shero. Shero had played parts of three seasons for the Rangers in the 1940s and was coaching their minor-league affiliate in Omaha when he was hired by the Flyers.

"My heart has always been here," Shero told reporters the day he was hired by New York.

"He said he had enough of coaching and he obviously wasn't telling the truth," a disappointed Bobby Clarke told reporters. "It's fairly obvious he had an idea of where he was going all along. He probably knew during the playoffs. You wonder how much he could concentrate on what we were doing."

Shero's first trip back to the Spectrum was for a preseason game. The Flyers ripped Shero's Rangers 8–2, and the fans ripped their old coach, hanging signs reading, "Rangers: Beware, He Lies," and, "Win Today and Renegotiate Forever."

Meanwhile McCammon, tabbed as Shero's replacement, was himself replaced after 50 games, by Maine coach Pat Quinn. Quinn had been Shero's assistant during the coach's final Flyers season, and then sent to the AHL club when McCammon was promoted. Ironically, McCammon returned to Maine to fill Quinn's spot.

Quinn led the Flyers to an 18–8–4 finish and a three-game preliminary-round playoff-series win against the Vancouver Canucks.

But that was as far as the 1978–79 Flyers would go, as Shero's Rangers knocked them off in five games, outscoring them 28–8, thanks in part to John Davidson's magnificence in the Rangers' net and the Flyers missing Bernie Parent from theirs.

Shero guided the Rangers past the New York Islanders and into the Stanley Cup Final, where they lost to the Montreal Canadiens.

The following season, the Flyers eliminated the Rangers in five games in the 1980 quarterfinals. That would be the old coach's last hurrah—the Rangers fired Shero 20 games into the 1980–81 season.

Though there were hard feelings at the time of his departure from the Flyers, Shero's son Ray said his father held no bitterness toward his former team.

"There was no sense of revenge or anything like that," he said in *Walking Together Forever.* "My dad was just trying to do the best he could for the Rangers at the time. We all wish the parting with the Flyers could have been handled a little better, but it was in the past. Everybody had agreed it was time to move on."

Fred Shero was diagnosed with stomach cancer in 1983, but recovered enough to work as a radio color analyst for New Jersey Devils broadcasts, and felt well enough to coach a team in Holland in 1987.

On March 22, 1990, Shero was inducted into the Flyers' Hall of Fame.

"Once a Flyer, always a Flyer," he said that night. "I knew the day I left here [in 1978] that I had made a mistake." Shero's words struck a chord, and he was hired by the team as a senior adviser.

His health took a turn for the worse months later; the cancer had spread to other parts of his body, and on Saturday, November 24, 1990, the greatest coach in team history died.

Fred Shero is remembered for many things, but it was his words from that memorable 1974 playoff run—"Win together today and we will walk together forever"—that blinked back into focus at his funeral.

"Forever didn't stop Saturday," Clarke said in his eulogy. "Freddie left a piece of himself with every one of us."

LEON STICKLE

Mention it to any Flyers fan, and the name Leon Stickle still brings dirty looks and dirtier words.

The 1979–80 season was Stickle's 11th as an NHL linesman, and he drew the assignment to work Game 6 of the Stanley Cup

Final between the Flyers and the New York Islanders at Nassau Veterans Memorial Coliseum on May 24, 1980.

Up to that point, the Flyers looked like they had an outstanding chance to win the franchise's third Stanley Cup.

Powered by their record-setting 35-game unbeaten streak, they had finished 48–12–20, and their 116 points were the most in the league. A reinvigorated Reggie Leach scored 50 goals, Bill Barber had 40 and Ken Linseman had team highs of 57 assists and 79 points.

The Flyers swept a young Wayne Gretzky and the Edmonton Oilers in a best-of-five preliminary-round series, and then won the first three games in the best-of-seven quarterfinals against the New York Rangers, including a 29-save Game 3 shutout by goalie Pete Peeters. The Rangers won Game 4, but the Flyers clinched the series two days later. Against the Minnesota North Stars in the semifinals, the Flyers lost Game 1 but won the next four to set up a Stanley Cup Final series between the Flyers and Islanders.

In Game 1 the teams traded goals through the first two periods, and were tied 2–2 when Rick MacLeish scored off a Paul Holmgren pass at 13:10 of the third. The Flyers were just 3:42 from a win when the Islanders took advantage of a hooking penalty on Al Hill. Mike Bossy sent the puck into the slot where Stefan Persson beat Peeters for the tying goal.

Jimmy Watson was whistled for holding 2:08 into overtime when he grabbed John Tonelli around the shoulders. In those days overtime penalties were rare, and fans were unhappy despite the clear infraction. Just one second before Watson could get back on the ice, Tonelli fed a pass to Denis Potvin, who scored the NHL's first overtime power-play goal to give the Isles a 4–3 win.

The Flyers came back in Game 2. Trailing 1–0 early, they went ahead when Holmgren and Bob Kelly scored 1:15 apart, and Bobby Clarke added a goal before the period's end to make it 3–1. Keyed by Holmgren's hat trick—the first American-born player to score three in a playoff game—the Flyers tied the series with an 8–3 knockout.

Coach Pat Quinn surprisingly tabbed Phil Myre for Game 3 ahead of Peeters, but the move didn't work as Myre was ripped for six goals, including five on the power play, as the Flyers fell 6–2.

TERRY GREGSON

A persecution complex has seemed to exist in the minds of members of the organization since the Broad Street Bullies days.

Many of the conspiracy buffs point to referee Terry Gregson and May 2, 1999.

With 2:54 left in a scoreless playoff game with the Toronto Maple Leafs, John LeClair got his left elbow up on the Leafs' Mike Johnson. Gregson's arm went up, and the Flyers' season went down—with Toronto up a man, they got the game's only goal with 59.2 seconds left.

An enraged Mount Snider erupted, calling Gregson "a coward."

"As far as I'm concerned, I'm sick of this crap," the chairman added. "When an official decides to decide the game, when the players are playing their hearts out, that's a disgrace to this team and to this league, and I won't put up with it anymore.

"They call this chicken you-know-what on John LeClair, one of the cleanest players in the league. It's a disgrace. ... Gregson, I hope he can sleep well tonight, because he knows damn well what he did."

Peeters was back in goal for Game 4, but it didn't change much. Game 3 injuries sidelined Watson (broken collarbone) and Holmgren (torn knee cartilage). John Paddock and Linseman scored to keep the game close, but Bob Bourne blocked a Bob Dailey shot and fed Bobby Nystrom, who finished a two-on-one break, and Clark Gillies scored to finish the 5–2 Islanders win.

Down three games to one, the Flyers returned home with their season on the line. All the good they had accomplished during the 35-game unbeaten streak was 60 minutes away from going out the window.

"We knew if they don't win the Cup they either would be the streak team or the Cup winner," longtime Philadelphia media member Al Morganti, who covered the team for the *Philadelphia Inquirer*, recalled.

Holmgren, wearing a bulky knee brace, returned for Game 5, as did Watson. But when Holmgren went to the penalty box for slashing, followed by Moose Dupont 1:37 later for holding, Persson scored off a Bossy pass on the two-man advantage for the lone goal of the first period.

The Flyers had just six shots in the period and went 16 minutes without any, but a different team took the ice in the second period. Clarke one-timed a Behn Wilson pass 1:35 in to tie the game, and MacLeish beat Isles goalie Billy Smith over his glove to put the Flyers ahead. Bryan Trottier scored to tie the game, but just 48 seconds later Mike Busniuk popped out from behind the Islanders' net to give the Flyers a 3–2 lead heading into the third period.

MacLeish and Brian Propp scored to push the lead to 5–2, and after Persson scored again, a one-legged Holmgren answered with his 10th goal of the postseason to finish the 6–3 win and send the series back to Long Island.

The Flyers felt the momentum swing heading into Game 6. Their smiles got even bigger when Nystrom was given an extra roughing minor after fighting Kelly, and Potvin was whistled for cross-checking 34 seconds later. Leach scored on the five-on-three advantage, and the Flyers looked like they were on the way to forcing a Game 7 back in Philadelphia.

Their smiles would be wiped away four and a half minutes later. Peeters stopped a Bossy shot, but the rebound popped into the air and Potvin smacked it into the net. The Flyers claimed Potvin's stick was above his shoulders when he made contact with the puck, which would have nullified the goal. The officials disagreed and the goal stood.

It only would get worse for the Flyers.

Just 2:12 after the Potvin goal, Gillies skated the puck into the Flyers' end and dropped a pass that drifted about two feet beyond the blue line and into neutral ice, where Butch Goring grabbed it and skated over the blue line into the Flyers' end. Gillies had never left the zone, so when Goring crossed the blue line, the whistle should have blown for offside. Dupont pointed at the line, assuming play was about to be stopped. Propp, who was backchecking Duane Sutter, slowed down, assuming play was about to be stopped.

ARVEDSON HITS THE WALL

One of the more gruesome injuries in Flyers history occurred January 20, 2000, when Flyers forward Marc Bureau checked Ottawa Senators winger Magnus Arvedson into the frame of the bench door.

Arvedson was rushed to Pennsylvania Hospital, where he had three inches of his bowel removed to repair a hole in his small intestine. He spent a week in the hospital and lost 20 pounds, but was able to return two and a half months later for the playoffs.

"I definitely know the offside one was way offside," Propp said. "It was so obvious that I slowed down for a second."

Linesman Leon Stickle, though, never blew his whistle. Play never stopped.

Goring sent a pass past Dupont and Propp to Sutter, who beat a stunned Peeters under the crossbar.

The Flyers, incredulous about the non-call, composed themselves, and Propp scored with 1:22 left in the first to tie the game.

Between periods, a fuming Ed Snider stormed into the officials' room and confronted Frank Udvari, the supervisor of officials, and spoke to him in what Snider called, "A very strong manner."

"Udvari said the officials felt the puck, when he [Potvin] hit it, hit our player first before it went in," Snider said. "I said it's still a high stick, and the whistle should have blown. He said our player touched it and we had control and then it went in. The film showed that didn't happen, and the officials changed their tune. They said it wasn't a high stick when he made contact, it was below the crossbar. That's bullshit. It was pure BS. ... Every time a guy raised his stick and hit the puck, it was a high stick. There was no technology, there was no replay. Anytime a player had his stick up and smacked the puck, nobody tried to gauge where he hit it—it was a high stick.

"We got screwed out of two goals in that game."

Bossy gave the Islanders the lead with a power-play goal 7:34 into the second, and with 14 seconds left, Tonelli got past Clarke

AN AWFUL ACCIDENT

The Flyers nearly were witness to an on-ice fatality January 23, 2000.

In a game at the Molson Centre in Montreal, Canadiens forward Trent McCleary dropped to block a Chris Therien slap shot. The puck hit the winger in the throat, fracturing his larynx and causing massive bleeding that led to a collapsed lung. A tracheotomy was performed to keep McCleary alive. He later needed his larynx and windpipe reconstructed.

"He was making a sound like a muffler on a car," Therien said the next day.

David Mulder, a Canadiens team doctor, said, "Until we performed the tracheotomy, he was in great danger. It was as close [to death] as I think you could come. It was a matter of seconds."

and fed a pass to Nystrom, who got behind Leach and scored to give the Islanders a 4–2 lead with one period to play.

Summoning one last bit of strength, Dailey scored from the point 1:47 into the third, and then Dupont's slap shot hit off MacLeish and then Paddock before finding its way behind Smith at the 6:02 mark to tie the game.

The teams played into overtime, with Linseman and Al Hill having chances to win it for the Flyers, but Smith denied both. Just over seven minutes into the extra session, Hill's soft clear out of the zone was picked up by Lorne Henning, who backtracked and then sent a pass to Tonelli that trapped the line of Hill, Mel Bridgman and MacLeish too far up ice. Dailey skated after Tonelli, missing Nystrom, who cut down the backside. Dailey tried to recover and get back to Nystrom, but Tonelli sent a pass over Dupont's stick right to Nystrom, who had a stride on Dailey and tipped the puck with his backhand over a sliding Peeters.

The Islanders had won the first of their four straight Stanley Cups.

Snider went on the warpath after the game, telling the *Philadelphia Bulletin*'s Ray Didinger: "It was an absolute, total [expletive] disgrace. Anybody who's impartial knows we took a screwing today. I believe the [officials] who come out of Montreal and Toronto don't want [us] to win. I believe that right down to the pit of my stomach. ... The problem with this league is [referee-in-chief] Scotty Morrison. He should be shot."

General manager Keith Allen was just as bitter, but slightly calmer, than his boss: "You can say they [referees] are human and they make mistakes, but this was the Stanley Cup Final, and [the offside goal] wasn't even close. I know people think we cry a lot about the officials, but just look at it. You can see it."

For his part, Stickle admitted the Flyers had a legitimate gripe. "I guess I blew it," he said that night. "Maybe I was too close to the play. Maybe there was tape on the stick and it confused me."

Today, Snider is a bit calmer when he looks back on the events of May 24, 1980, but his opinion remains the same.

"We had the Cup taken away from us that year," he said. "That team would have won the Cup."

Dating back to the prime days of the Broad Street Bullies, the Flyers always have felt a bit of a persecution complex. Most hockey people, including the media, always have ignored it as whining. But this time, though, they had a point.

"That wasn't a case of crying," Morganti said. "They got screwed—they really did get screwed. They legitimately got screwed."

"A CHOKING SITUATION"

The 1997 Stanley Cup Final was supposed to be the crowning achievement for the Legion of Doom–led Philadelphia Flyers.

The threesome of Eric Lindros, John LeClair and Mikael Renberg had used their abundant size and skill to run roughshod over the rest of the NHL.

The Legion had meant doom for Eastern Conference competition, as the Flyers walked through their postseason battles with the Pittsburgh Penguins, Buffalo Sabres and New York Rangers in five games each. In the first three rounds of the playoffs, Lindros had racked up 11 goals and 12 assists; LeClair had seven goals and 11 assists, and Renberg had five goals and five assists.

And with players like Rod Brind'Amour, Joel Otto, Dale Hawerchuk and rookie Dainius Zubrus, the Flyers had ample size, strength and scoring depth up front. Eric Desjardins, Chris Therien and Paul Coffey, acquired in December to add mobility to the defense, anchored the back end.

The Flyers' only weak spot looked to be in goal, but coach Terry Murray had pushed all the right buttons in alternating Ron Hextall and Garth Snow.

"The Flyers had that big question in goal," Chuck Gormley, longtime Flyers beat writer for the *Courier Post*, said. "It was like [spinning] the roulette wheel and every time you'd get the right number. Terry Murray, for the criticism he received, he played that [perfectly]. How he got that team to the Final with that kind of goaltending situation was amazing. He knew the call to make each time."

The Detroit Red Wings, the Flyers' foe in the championship series, were seen as just another speed bump on the road to the Cup.

The common belief was the Red Wings didn't have the size or strength to handle the Flyers, especially down low in their zone, and over time the Flyers would push the Wings off the ice.

With the left-wing lock trapping system, the Grind Line of Darren McCarty, Kris Draper and Joey Kocur, and high-skill defensemen Nicklas Lidstrom and Larry Murphy, the Red Wings needed only the first period of the first game to make that view seem as erroneous as someone who believed the sky was orange.

On a Flyers power play 6:38 into the game, Draper stripped Lindros of the puck and started a two-on-one break with Kirk Maltby, who scored over a flopping Hextall.

The Flyers answered 59 seconds later when Lindros slid the rebound of a Janne Niinimaa shot to Brind'Amour, who tied the game.

Another turnover by the Flyers, this time by Kjell Samuelsson, allowed Kocur to score with 4:04 left in the first. Then Coffey fumbled the puck away to Murphy, and Sergei Fedorov finished a three-on-one to put the Wings ahead 3–1.

LeClair scored between goalie Mike Vernon's pads late in the second to cut the deficit to 3–2, but 56 seconds into the third period Steve Yzerman beat Hextall from long distance to finish the Wings' 4–2 victory.

NIINIMAA-METALLICA

One of the urban legends surrounding the Flyers is how Metallica got a Flyers defenseman benched.

Prior to a game against the Ottawa Senators on October 11, 1997, defenseman Janne Niinimaa was seen rocking in the CoreStates Center parking lot as the heavy metal band played a free pregame concert.

That night, Niinimaa took a seat in the press box, and the assumption was coach Wayne Cashman benched the blueliner as punishment. Niinimaa said he only went to the show because Cashman previously had informed him that he wouldn't be playing that night.

Murray opted for Snow in Game 2, but it made no difference as more poor Flyers decisions put the Wings up 2–0 before the game was 10 minutes old. First, Brendan Shanahan picked off a Samuelsson pass, and with Coffey backpedaling, fired a shot from about 50 feet out that ticked off the defenseman's skate and went behind Snow just 97 seconds into the game. Later, with Coffey off for hooking, Yzerman smacked a puck from between Samuelsson's skates and past Snow to make it 2–0.

The Flyers woke up late in the first when consecutive Red Wings penalties allowed Brind'Amour to score a pair of power-play goals 1:09 apart.

Rather than build on the momentum, though, the Flyers allowed the Wings to come back. Snow blocked an Yzerman shot, but the long rebound went to Maltby. With Coffey again giving too much ground, Maltby's 50-footer got behind Snow, giving Detroit a 3–2 lead just 2:39 into the period. Shanahan scored again in the third, and the visitors' stifling defense allowed them to go home up two games to none.

"I saw this team really struggling to break through the pressure of the event," Murray said. "It wasn't just the spotlight of the Stanley Cup Final, it was a heat lamp. We started off here in Philadelphia, and for two or three days before the first game, this is where all the media was because Detroit was coming here.

They [Detroit] came the day before the game, had their press conference and played Game 1. We had three days of intense pressure."

Murray believed in the hope of a comeback of historic proportions—at that time, only two teams had ever lost the first two Cup Final games at home and won the series—and that getting away from home would help his team.

It seemed to work early in Game 3, as LeClair banged in the rebound of a Desjardins shot at 7:03 of the first to open the scoring. It was the Flyers' first lead of the series. And it lasted exactly two minutes.

Another awful turnover, this time by Karl Dykhuis, led to an Yzerman power-play goal. And just 2:02 later, Dykhuis coughed the puck up to Fedorov, who sped past Dykhuis and Samuelsson and beat Hextall.

The Flyers had a chance to answer, as back-to-back Detroit penalties gave the Flyers a 90-second five-on-three advantage, but they could muster just one shot. The Flyers got another power play moments later when Martin Lapointe was sent off, but again they came up empty. To add insult to the injury of missed opportunity, Lapointe jumped out of the penalty box and scored with 60 seconds left in the period to give the Wings a 3–1 advantage.

Things only got worse as Detroit sucked all the life out of the Flyers, holding them to just 14 shots in the final 40 minutes of hockey and skated away with a 6–1 win.

"We got beat very soundly," Murray said. "We didn't really have any kind of a game going. It was very frustrating for the team, for the whole organization, because we had put every part of our game in place in the other three series. We weren't able to get a forecheck going, we weren't generating any offensive-zone time, we weren't generating chances. There were a lot of things building and it didn't look like it was going to clear up."

Reaching into his bag of coaching tricks, Murray recalled watching Wings coach Scotty Bowman during the 1995 Stanley Cup Final, when the Wings were en route to being swept by the New Jersey Devils.

"I remember very clearly when Detroit played the New Jersey Devils," Murray said. "And [the Devils] killed them, they shut them down. As great a team as Detroit was, they [New Jersey] gave them no sniff whatsoever. And Scotty Bowman, in the media press conference following that series, went after his team and his players big-time. But it was a learning process and they broke through. A lot of the players that were key players on that hockey team, over the next several years, [scored] a lot less points, [had] a lot less individual statistics, became more of a team, and look where they ended up. They became a great franchise."

Following Bowman's lead, Murray tore into his team in a meeting the day after Game 3. Then, in an interview session with the press, Murray was asked about his team's confidence. His attempt at psychoanalysis failed miserably.

"Many teams have been through this problem before, and it is basically a choking situation that I call it for our team right now," he said that day.

Go ahead and re-read that last paragraph. In public, a coach had just called his players chokers. Jaws could be heard dropping like anvils.

"All of us couldn't believe those words would come out of a coach's mouth," Gormley said.

Murray's players equally were stunned, leading to a classic reaction by Desjardins—"Aye-yi-yi-yi-yi-yi-yi"—to which the written word truly can't give justice.

Forward Daniel Lacroix, told by a reporter that he was shocked by the statement, replied, "You think you're [expletive] shocked!"

Desjardins was left to answer the horde of questions following Murray's statement, since Lindros, the team's captain and supposed point man for media inquiries, had left the building through an exit under the Joe Louis Arena stands after the initial team meeting broke up.

"Nobody likes to be called that," Desjardins said of the choker label. "I don't want to start a big war in the paper, but of course it hurts. It hurts to hear that."

"I don't think anybody liked it," Hextall said. "The media made a bigger deal and twisted it more than it was meant to be. I

John LeClair and the high-powered Flyers were left searching for answers after losing in a sweep against the Red Wings in the 1997 Stanley Cup Finals.

remember Murph [Murray] coming to me shortly after that and he asked me if he needed to address the team and I said, 'What's the big deal?' We're playing in the Final, and to me, I didn't care. That didn't bother me, it didn't affect me. It was something Murph said that he didn't mean the way it came out. Not a big issue to me."

"I didn't care," Brind'Amour said. "I don't believe he meant we were chokers. He meant we weren't playing the way we're capable of because we hadn't hit that adversity. I don't think he meant we were choking. But of course everything gets turned into a big deal. That's just an unfortunate choice of words. I didn't care. It didn't bother me."

"We're trying to get one win," Murray said a decade later in explaining his choice of words. "We went out the next game in

Game 4, and I said we're not trying to win the Stanley Cup right now, we're trying to win the first game. It was trying to find a way to win the first game, to try to kick-start our team again and start to play the way we had, [the way] I knew that we could play."

Regardless of what he meant, all the goodwill Murray had built with his team had been thrown away. And any kind of motivation he hoped would come from an angry bunch of players never materialized. Although the Flyers came out hard and fast in the first period of Game 4, all the energy got sucked out when Lidstrom's long shot eluded Hextall with 33 seconds left in the first.

The second period capped the series when McCarty scored one of the more memorable goals in playoff history. Taking a pass from Tomas Sandstrom, McCarty turned Niinimaa inside-out and then finished by pulling the puck away from a diving Hextall and scoring into an open net 13:02 into the period.

The Flyers continued to attack, but all they could manage was Lindros' only goal of the series, with 15 seconds left in the game and with Hextall pulled for an extra attacker. The game ended in a 2–1 loss for the Flyers, and the Red Wings winning the franchise's first Stanley Cup since 1955.

"That was a negative, no doubt about that," Murray said of his "choking" comment. "Some of the players, they did bring it up. They felt it did have an impact on their performances. We were a little bit better in Game 4 than we were in Game 3, [but] it didn't have the effect because we didn't win the game and the series was over."

In reality, there were a number of reasons the Flyers lost to the Red Wings, with Murray's caustic remarks ranking far down the list.

"I don't think people knew how good that team was," Hextall said of the Red Wings. "I look back and there's a lot of us who didn't play up to expectations, but I think a big part of that was how good that team was." The core of that Red Wings group went on to win Cups in 1998 and 2002.

At even-strength the Flyers were outscored 11–2 in the series. The goaltending was bad, the defense committed far too many turnovers and the power play went 1-for–10 in the final two games. And the Legion of Doom, which scored at ease during the first three rounds of the playoffs, was rendered pointless in the Final—figuratively and almost literally, with Lindros, LeClair and Renberg combining for three goals, seven points and a minus-12 rating.

When the team met in Voorhees for breakdown day, Murray made what became his final statement to his team.

"I stood in front of the team and I apologized to the team for saying it [choking]," he said. "I tried to explain what my position was in the moment that I said it. Players came up to me afterward and said, 'We appreciate you explaining it and we understand. Let's just move on.'"

But it was Murray who would do the moving. Six days after the series ended, general manager Bob Clarke told Murray his contract would not be renewed. Clarke never gave a reason, but it was easy for Murray to figure what led to his demise.

"It was assumed on my part," he said. "How can you get fired after going to the Stanley Cup Final? You lose four straight? Detroit had just lost four straight to New Jersey two years before that and they weren't making the change. In fact, Scotty got extended. Absolutely that ['choking' statement] entered into it, but I was never told that at the time."

Murray spent two and a half seasons as the head coach of the Florida Panthers, but his brother, Bryan, was the GM who hired him. Both were fired during the 2000–2001 season. He returned to the Flyers in 2001 and worked as a pro scout and assistant coach under Ken Hitchcock and John Stevens, but as numerous head coaching positions came open over the next decade, he rarely, if ever, was considered. The drought ended when the Los Angeles Kings hired him as their head coach in July 2008. He guided the Kings to the playoffs twice in his three full seasons and put the defensive system in place that helped the Kings win the Stanley Cup in 2012. He returned to the Flyers' organization as coach of the team's AHL affiliate, the Adirondack Phantoms, in 2012. However, he believes his words from that 1997 press conference always will be part of his biography.

"It always will [follow me]," he said. "It was the wrong thing to say. Maybe it was a deer-in-the-headlights kind of effect. Maybe that statement would have been more appropriate. But it was the reality of the situation."

FIGHT NIGHT IN PHILLY

Old-style, bench-clearing brawls don't happen very often anymore, but on March 5, 2004, fans got a memorable throwback affair.

The Ottawa Senators were in Philadelphia for the first time since Martin Havlat cross-checked Mark Recchi in the face a few weeks earlier. Havlat was suspended for his stick work, but the Flyers believed that wasn't nearly enough punishment.

Days before Ottawa came to town, coach Ken Hitchcock said someone was going to make Havlat "eat his lunch."

Serving as waiter would be the Flyers' chief enforcer, Donald Brashear. He, as well as his partner in fisticuffs, Todd Fedoruk, had missed the previous Flyers-Senators game with knee injuries, which allowed the Senators to hit the Flyers with impunity.

"Guys get a little braver and play a little chippier when Brash and me aren't in the lineup," Fedoruk told reporters the day before the game. "You'll see how some guys shy away and are quiet."

There was little quiet on this night. In the first period Ottawa's Shaun Van Allen drove Flyers rookie defenseman Joni Pitkanen into the boards, knocking him out with a concussion. Later in the first, the Sens' Marian Hossa rode the Flyers' Chris Therien hard into the boards, knocking the defenseman out of the game with a strained left shoulder.

While the Flyers may have been losing the war of attrition, they were in firm control on the scoreboard, and when Alexei Zhamnov scored with 6:54 left in the third period, they held a 5–2 advantage.

But with 1:45 left in regulation, a time warp hit Philadelphia, and suddenly the game turned into a typical Broad Street Bullies donnybrook.

The brawling started with the teams' two veteran enforcers, Brashear and Rob Ray, tangling in front of the Flyers' net. Brashear shoved Ray, who at first seemed uninterested, but then elbowed

Brashear in the head. That set off Brashear, who began raining left hands on Ray's face, and then a nasty right cross opened a vicious gash over Ray's right eye.

While Brashear watched Ray skate off, two Senators—Todd Simpson and Brian Pothier—jumped Brashear from behind, with Pothier throwing punches over a linesman. When Patrick Sharp tried to intervene, Simpson knocked him down and began pounding him. Danny Markov jumped in and began scrapping with Simpson.

While this was going on, Senators goalie Patrick Lalime began shedding his gear and skated into the fray, heading right for Flyers netminder Robert Esche, who provided a more than willing combatant. Lalime tore Esche's jersey off, but Esche kept throwing punches.

Meanwhile, Branko Radivojevic was tossing Van Allen around. The Flyers forward lost his sweater but won the battle. With Markov and Brashear already off the ice, the 6'3", 220-pound Simpson showed his courage by taking pokes at the Flyers' 5'10", 185-pound Sami Kapanen, who had been forced back onto defense following the injuries to Pitkanen and Theiren.

When officials finally got things settled down and the players were sent off the ice, Brashear, Markov, Esche and Radivojevic stood in the tunnel leading to the locker room, watching the replays on the center-ice scoreboard, and Brashear continued to jaw at the Senators as they skated off.

Round 2 began at the drop of the next puck, when Senators tough guy Chris Neil first speared Radovan Somik, then began throwing punches at the Flyers' soft second-year Czech forward. Neil easily buried Somik, who at least got in one good punch, while Neil landed at least one cheap shot after he knocked Somik down.

Meanwhile, Sens gargantuan defenseman Zdeno Chara, all 6'9" of him, made a bee-line for another non-fighting Flyer, 6'1" defenseman Mattias Timander. Chara rag-dolled Timander for a bit before officials broke it up.

Only three seconds had dripped off the game clock.

The chippiness between the Senators and Flyers boiled over into a vintage hockey brawl in March 2004. *Photo courtesy AP Images.*

Once that was settled, another brawl broke out on the ensuing faceoff, between centers Michal Handzus and Mike Fisher. The bigger Handzus, though, got a little overzealous and allowed Fisher to use his leverage to flip Handzus down onto his back in what could have been a scary scene. Instead, the Flyers' Czech ironman skated off as part of the seventh fighting major of the night.

After all that, another three seconds had dribbled away.

Finally, a hockey game interrupted the fights, which caused the fans to boo lustily. Only in Philadelphia. But they wouldn't have to wait long for Round 4.

After a Flyers dump-in, Recchi laid a solid hit on Senators defenseman Wade Redden, who responded by grabbing the nearest Flyer, who happened to be John LeClair.

While the two big bulls wrestled around in the Ottawa end, back at center ice Recchi and Bryan Smolinski threw down their gloves and went at it, with the tenacious Recchi pounding Smolinski with right hands before Smolinski landed a right cross and both players ran out of gas. This time, 24 seconds had elapsed, leaving 1:15 of game action remaining, which was just enough time for one more throwdown.

At the next drop of the puck, Ottawa center Jason Spezza went after Sharp, which ended badly for Spezza. As Spezza came forward, Sharp caught him and threw a few right-hands, and when Spezza went down, Sharp landed on top of him and got in another shot before the officials could separate them.

After Sharp and Spezza were sent off and the teams lined up for the faceoff, there were as many players—Zhamnov, John Slaney and Tony Amonte—left on the Flyers' bench as there were coaches. There were just two players left on the Ottawa bench— Hossa and Antoine Vermette.

Throughout all the brawling, the player around whom all the venom centered, Havlat, sat safely in the penalty box, sent there by coach Jacques Martin to serve a penalty.

The night the Wachovia Center became the Blue Horizon turned into a record-setter. In all, there were an NHL-record 413 penalty minutes assessed, breaking the former league record of 406 from a 1981 game between Boston and Minnesota. The 409 penalty minutes in the third period also was a record, as was the 213 penalty minutes given to the Flyers for the game, and the 209 given them in the third period alone.

The most penalty minutes in any Flyers game prior had been 380, against the Los Angeles Kings on March 11, 1979. Of that 380, 194 of them were whistled on the Flyers.

There were 21 fighting majors called, including two on Brashear. The Flyers' enforcer ended the night with 34 minutes in penalties to lead the home team, but his total was topped by Spezza, who not only got pounded by Sharp, but was flagged for a 10-minute misconduct as well as a double game misconduct, and finished with 35 PIM.

Oddly enough, there were non-fighting related milestones as well that night. Markov's first-period goal was the 10,000th in Flyers history, making the club the fifth in league history—and the first expansion team—to reach that mark. Also, the game was the 1,000th of Amonte's career.

There nearly was one more brawl after the game. Flyers general manager Bob Clarke, who was part of similar full-scale fracases as a player, attempted to get into the Ottawa dressing room to get a piece of Martin, but was restrained by Flyers staffers.

"I would not have hit him. I am not that stupid," Clarke said a day later. "But I would have confronted him. I understand Rob Ray fighting Donald Brashear. That's okay. Even Mark Recchi and Patrick Sharp, they can fight. But don't go after guys who don't know how to defend themselves like Somik and Timander.

"I don't think a guy like that [Martin] should send players out to beat the crap out of players who can't fight. I wanted to say something. It's not like [Martin] is a big, tough bugger whose teams play that way and stuff.

"What Neil did is not something to be proud of. ... I'm ticked off that a player like Neil would go after a player like Somik. ... If Martin says it's not his responsibility, then he doesn't have control of his bench."

Days later, Comcast SportsNet showed a replay of the game, which drew a 1.0 rating—higher than many regular Flyers telecasts. The NHL, unhappy with the right hook to its public image, demanded CSN never replay the game again.

And for the record, the only player fined or suspended was Markov, who got a one-game ban for being hit with his third game misconduct of the season.

PRIMEAU BOWS OUT

The Flyers led the league in games lost to injury in 2005–06, but no ache or pain hurt worse than the loss of captain Keith Primeau.

Primeau finally was feeling better after suffering as many as three concussions between February and June in 2004. He missed 21 games after a nasty collision with the New York Rangers' Bobby Holik in February, and suffered possibly two more head injuries, against Toronto and Tampa Bay, during his amazing playoff run.

The lockout that saw the cancellation of the 2004–05 season gave him time to recover at his own pace, and by October 2005 Primeau felt like any remaining fogginess in his head had cleared.

That all changed, however, Tuesday, October 25, 2005, in Montreal, when Primeau was leveled by a high, vicious elbow to the head by the Canadiens' Alexander Perezhogin.

"All I remember is we were killing a penalty and a shot comes off the boards and the rebound comes into the slot and I turned," Primeau said. "The puck comes to my left side, so I turned to the right. I'm going to try and find the puck, so I'm not looking at who's coming, and I turn right into Perezhogin and I go down."

Primeau was encouraged by how he felt in the immediate aftermath of the hit. "I'm actually excited because I was leery of when the first hit I was going to take, when it was coming and how I would react," he said. "I was excited because I thought I got through it. After the game I got on the bus, I called my wife, I called my parents, and said I feel good, I'm fine. I think it was a good thing. I got hit hard and I'm okay."

The good feelings wouldn't last.

"The next day wasn't too bad," he said. "The following day was a game day, Thursday. We were at home against Florida, and in the game I was in a daze. I was sluggish. I remember Hitch [coach Ken Hitchcock] hollering at me to get into it, get involved, and I just couldn't. I thought it was because we had been off for a year."

That night the Flyers flew from Philadelphia to North Carolina for a game the next day against the Carolina Hurricanes, but Primeau said, "I wasn't good."

He played that Friday night in Carolina, but registered just one shot and was an uncharacteristic minus-3 in 17:26 of ice time in an 8–6 loss.

The team had a day off before a game in Ottawa on Sunday, October 30. When Primeau woke up that morning, he knew something was wrong.

"That morning I went to Hitch and said, 'I don't feel right,'" Primeau said.

He sat out that game, but thought it wouldn't be long before he was back in the lineup.

"I literally thought it would be a game or two," he said, "but after I removed myself and started paying attention to the symptoms, I knew I was in trouble."

That day in Ottawa started a nine-month odyssey of trips to doctors throughout North America in a quest to find some way, somehow, to continue his career.

"It was torture because I continued to expect to get better," he said. "That year was a very frustrating time because I continued to hold out hope I would heal and I would be back in the lineup."

Months of work culminated in an ordinary early April day when he shockingly took the ice with teammates. That one, hour-long appearance began fueling rumors of a playoff return for a team that by the spring of 2006 looked to be running out of gas.

Primeau advised people not to take it too seriously, but that didn't stop the spread of rumors of an impending return—Suprimeau stepping out of the phone booth to rescue his troubled teammates from impending playoff doom.

It never happened. Days later, Primeau gathered the media in a closed locker room and unleashed his anger in a post-practice rant at a press corps that he thought was being unfair to the fans and causing a distraction to his teammates. As he spoke passionately, he clenched and unclenched his long fingers around a Powerade bottle, nearly choking the fluid out of it.

"I said to everyone, I'm not better," he said, although that day he used much saltier language. "There's no ulterior motive here. I'm just trying to put myself in a position to be ready if I'm healed. Everybody kept saying, 'He's coming back, he's coming back,' and it became a distraction, and that's not what I wanted. Not at all."

Primeau went back into hiding during the Flyers' aborted playoff run. He would arrive early in the morning, before the press and most of his teammates, work out alone and leave before anyone could talk to him.

This continued into the summer, when Primeau retreated to his cottage outside Toronto. His workouts continued, with a return targeted for the 2006–07 season.

"I really thought I was turning the corner [over that summer], and I took a few days off to spend with my family [at home in Canada], and I figured when I get up north, I'll be up there, it'll be quiet, the environment will be good, I can put my work in and get myself ready."

Like most people who go the gym for the first time after a long layoff, though, Primeau did too much too fast.

"The first day I worked out," he said, "I pushed it too hard, like I was trying to get my conditioning back in one day, and it laid me up for a week."

Too much work, combined with a summer flu bug, led to a return of all the bad, old feelings: Pressure in his head, dizziness, nausea, exhaustion.

It was so bad, a planned trip in August to Finland, where he was going to work out with a professional team part-owned by teammate and close friend Sami Kapanen, was scrapped. Instead, he returned to South Jersey to meet with team neurologist Gary Dorshimer. Dorshimer explained to Primeau that the concussions had left an open door into his body; since his brain was his most vulnerable part, it was the first place any virus would attack.

Dorshimer instructed Primeau to take a week off, but after seven days, "He [Dorshimer] checked with me, and I said I'm just not there."

Dorshimer took that message to GM Bob Clarke, who confronted Primeau about his health.

"Clarkie called me and said, 'Keith, I hear you're not doing well.' I said I don't think I'm going to be able to do this. I said I'm going to keep working out, my intentions haven't changed, I'm still coming back in August," Primeau said. "I'm not going to Finland, but I'm going to try and skate. So I did, I came back and skated again. I was out there practicing with the guys, trying different treatments again."

Watching was Jim McCrossin, and it was the trainer, who had traveled with Primeau to doctor's appointments, who had helped him through the worst of the dizziness and the headaches, who helped him with all the experiments—from different-colored visors to massages—who finally told Primeau the cold, hard truth.

"I remember Jimmy calling me into his office and saying, 'Keith, it's been a valiant effort, but even if you got yourself in a

HI, MY NAME IS ...

Injuries and poor play led the 2006–07 Flyers to dress 49 different players, obliterating the previous team record.

Among that group were five different goalies—Robert Esche, Antero Niittymaki, Martin Houle, Michael Leighton, and Martin Biron—and 14 rookies.

position to play, I could never personally give you permission to go back out on the ice,'" Primeau said.

A gamer, a warrior in every sense of the word, Primeau could have thrown a tantrum and trashed the training room; instead, he listened. And understood.

McCrossin was right. It was over.

"I think it was relief," Primeau said of his feelings that day. "I needed somebody to make the decision for me. I was going to keep going and going until they said stop. That's what I needed. As much as it hurt, it was the right decision. I guess for the first time it was the first cold, hard slap of reality. I needed someone to give me the finality of it. Because everyone's saying, 'Okay, Keith, you can do it. Way to go.' I was kind of embarrassed by it, because I thought maybe I was being naïve and everybody felt bad for me, and I didn't want that."

Instead, he got the truth, from McCrossin and then from Clarke. And days later, on the eve of training camp, Primeau said the words himself: He was done, retiring at the age of 34.

2007: A DISASTER OF HISTORIC PROPORTIONS

The 2006–07 season marked the 40th anniversary of the birth of the Philadelphia Flyers. It was to be a campaign of great celebration, bracketed by the release of a pair of momentous DVDs, one highlighting the 10 greatest games in the franchise's history, another the definitive 40th anniversary DVD, showcasing the greatest moments in the club's illustrious history.

The 40th season of Flyers hockey would go down in history, but not in the way anyone would have hoped.

The seeds for the disastrous 2006–07 season had been planted in the days following the lockout that caused the cancellation of the 2004–05 season. The settlement of the labor dispute saw the implementation of a salary cap for the first time. That meant GM Bob Clarke had to pare a payroll that hovered around $60 million to the new cap ceiling of $39 million. To do so he bought out veterans John LeClair and Tony Amonte, chose not to re-sign productive players like Mark Recchi and Vladimir Malakhov, and traded Danny Markov and Jeremy Roenick.

As teams struggled to get under the cap, Clarke jumped head-first into one of the deepest pools of unrestricted free agents ever and emerged with three giant catches.

First came defensemen Derian Hatcher, signed after he was bought out by the Detroit Red Wings to a four-year, $14 million contract, and fellow blueliner Mike Rathje, signed away from the San Jose Sharks to a five-year, $17.5 million deal.

A day later came the biggest prize, all-world center Peter Forsberg, who left the Colorado Avalanche for a two-year, $11.5 million pact.

The moves were swift, stunning and thought not to be possible in a salary-cap world. In a matter of days, Clarke had cut a third of his payroll while improving a team 14 months removed from the Eastern Conference Finals.

He also re-signed Keith Primeau, Robert Esche, Eric Desjardins, Kim Johnsson and Simon Gagne, and was poised to add highly regarded rookies Jeff Carter and Mike Richards to the mix, as well as jumbo-size free-agent forwards Mike Knuble and Turner Stevenson, signed before the lockout.

The Flyers were installed as an early favorite for the 2006 Stanley Cup. Clarke, however, tried to downplay the hype surrounding his new and improved team, saying in the summer of 2005, "I think starting this year we're a pretty good team. I'd say we're one of the teams that can compete for it. But so much can happen along the road that I can't say we're closer to a Stanley Cup than anybody else right now."

The financial landscape wasn't the only thing to change coming out of the lockout. The game on the ice underwent a massive transformation. Referees were empowered to crack down on obstruction-type penalties. No longer would defensemen be able to hook, hold or impede an offensive player, so skaters now would be allowed to use their speed and skill.

The days of the large, immobile defensemen who could hack, whack and maul opposing forwards into submission were gone. The winning formula—seemingly overnight—had become speed and skill over size and strength.

Teams like the Buffalo Sabres got the message; the Flyers did not. Hatcher and Rathje quickly were exposed as 6'5", 235-pound twin towers of immobility, and quickly began to resemble the NHL's most expensive traffic cones.

On top of that was a seemingly non-stop injury soap opera that started before training camp, when Sami Kapanen injured his shoulder and needed surgery that sidelined him until Thanksgiving. Hatcher missed the early part of the preseason with a knee injury, and Forsberg missed time having a bursa sac removed from his ankle. Carter struggled early while recovering from a summer-long bout of mononucleosis and a position change from center to wing on the team's top line.

Real devastation hit October 25, 2005 in Montreal, when Primeau was leveled by an elbow to the head by the Canadiens' Alexander Perezhogin. Primeau played twice more, but just nine games into the season, the captain stepped out of the lineup with another concussion, his second documented [and possibly his fourth] in 20 months.

That left three of the Flyers' four lines being centered by rookies—Carter, Richards and R.J. Umberger, who was recalled from the minors when Primeau went out. Off the ice, the players were left without their emotional leader, as well as the buffer between themselves and their ultra-abrasive coach, Ken Hitchcock.

The Flyers muddled on, and despite the rash of injuries, embarked on the franchise's longest-ever road trip, an 11-game odyssey that bridged the end of December and early January.

Wins in their first four games sparked an 8–2–1 trip, which pushed the Flyers to the top of the league standings with a 28–10–6 record.

But just when the Flyers hit the top, the floor dropped out from under them.

With Esche missing the entire trip with a groin injury, it meant rookie Antero Niittymaki was forced to start 18 straight games in goal, including all 11 on the road trip, leaving him out of gas once the team returned home.

And there were a slew of injuries that decimated the defense corps: A concussion suffered by Johnsson, sports hernia surgery for Joni Pitkanen and shoulder surgery for Desjardins. In addition, Hatcher played through knee pain and Rathje tried to skate through a nerve problem in his back.

Up front, Forsberg missed the final eight games before the Olympic break, Stevenson was out with a degenerative hip condition, Branko Radivojevic seriously injured his ankle and Gagne had a sore hip.

It got no better after the Olympics as the club's ironman, Michal Handzus, missed the first two weeks after the break with a torn rotator cuff.

"That's when we went from being the top dog into complete survival mode," Hitchcock said. "That's the way we played the rest of the season and playoffs. We were wondering every day who could play and who couldn't."

The Flyers barely survived, going just 17–16–5 after the road trip and earned the fifth seed in the playoffs, where they met the Buffalo Sabres in a worst-case scenario matchup.

The Sabres were the poster boys for the New NHL. Their game was based on skill and speed. Their forwards attacked in waves; their defense, while not physically imposing, made smart decisions; and they were backed by an emerging star in goaltender Ryan Miller.

The Flyers had beaten the Sabres just once in four regular-season games, but the one win was in Buffalo, providing a glimmer of hope. Game 1 of the playoffs had a chance to be number two. The Flyers fell behind 2–0 early in the second period, but Knuble got a goal back late in the second period, and Gagne tied the game with 1:51 left to force overtime.

Esche was nothing short of brilliant, stopping 55 of the first 57 shots he faced, but he couldn't stop the last one, when Danny Briere tapped in a Jochen Hecht pass 7:31 into the second overtime.

Game 2 was a disaster. The Sabers scored five times on 10 shots in the first period and completely outclassed the Flyers in an 8–2 rout. The Flyers didn't help themselves, handing the Sabres 12 power plays, more than half of which came on obstruction-type calls—lazy penalties that left an apoplectic Hitchcock to say: "Our team was embarrassed tonight. We were embarrassed for our fans and we were embarrassed for the city of Philadelphia at the way we played. We've got to make amends when we go home."

Forsberg, a non-factor in the first two games, was the best player on the ice in Game 3, scoring a pair of goals and setting up Gagne's empty-netter. He also threw his body around with reckless abandon, including a head-high shot on Briere in the first period that set the tone in a 4–2 win.

They tied the series with a gut-wrenching 5–4 victory in Game 4. Umberger, knocked senseless by a massive Brian Campbell hit in the first overtime of Game 1, notched the game-winner, scoring off a two-on-one break with Carter. Forsberg scored twice more and had an assist, and the Flyers packed the series momentum with them for the return to Buffalo for Game 5.

All the good, though, went out the window in the initial 20 minutes, as the Sabres held them to just three first-period shots. Miller made 24 saves in all to record a 3–0 shutout that sucked all the life out of the Flyers.

"The way we showed up today, we might as well have just gone home after warm-ups," defenseman Denis Gauthier told reporters.

Game 6 in Philadelphia was the coup de grace, and a harbinger of the disasters to come. The Sabres scored three times in the final 8:44 of the first period, and the 7–1 humiliation matched the worst home playoff loss in Flyers history.

It was so bad Esche received a mercy ovation when he was pulled from the game in the second period. Philadelphia fans understood the netminder had no chance on the five goals he allowed due to a lack of support from his teammates.

Despite the way the series ended, Hitchcock believes his team lost more because of injuries than the Sabres' superior skill.

"We made the decision, rather than operate [on injured players] and be done, we opted to rehab players and continue to play," he said. "Those players weren't able to perform near their capabilities during the playoffs. They gave us what they had the first four games, and Buffalo took advantage in Games 5 and 6. Buffalo was a better team, but health-wise they were better than us."

Clarke must have agreed, because he did little to upgrade the team in the summer of 2006. Even with Primeau's retirement, Clarke felt he had enough depth at center that he could trade the versatile, valuable Handzus to the Chicago Blackhawks for foward Kyle Calder. On defense, Desjardins retired, and Johnsson signed with Minnesota; to replace them Clarke signed Lars Jonsson, a 2000 first-round pick of the Boston Bruins who had been playing in Sweden the previous six years, and Nolan Baumgartner, who had just played his first full NHL season in his 11th professional campaign. The previous summer's Neiman Marcus–like shopping spree became a visit to Wal-Mart that saw Clarke add low-cost fringe players like forwards Marty Murray, Randy Robitaille, Mark Cullen and Geoff Sanderson.

Most of the nine new players Clarke brought in came on the cheap, and early in the 2006–07 season, the club looked to have gotten what it paid for.

Four losses in five games to start the season was the prelude to a return to Buffalo on October 17. It turned out to be one of the blackest days in club history, as the Sabres eviscerated the Flyers 9–1.

"The character on this team is not showing right now," Richards told reporters. "We're getting behind in games and we seem to implode."

Changes were needed, so Clarke waived three players—Baumgartner, veteran center Petr Nedved and fringe forward Niko Dimitrakos all were sent to the minors. It didn't help as two more losses on a swing through Florida followed. The Flyers staggered home with a 1–6–1 record.

Watching the Buffalo game from home, team chairman Ed Snider had seen enough, and wanted to make even more changes. He waited until the team returned home, and early on a Sunday morning, October 22, 2006, Snider accepted Clarke's resignation as GM, something he initially had offered two weeks earlier. Assistant GM Paul Holmgren replaced Clarke, and his first move, with Snider's approval, was to fire Hitchcock.

"Homer called me into his office and said he was making a change," Hitchcock said. "When you're not winning, the pressure starts and then the evaluation has to start—how good is the team, and can it play better for another coach. The Flyers thought they could play better for another coach."

That other coach was John Stevens, eight games into his first NHL coaching stint as Hitchcock's assistant after spending the previous six years coaching the club's AHL team, the Philadelphia Phantoms.

"We're very confident we can turn this thing around," Stevens said then. "I'm very good at getting players to relax and play."

More changes came, as separate deals with the Islanders saw young defenseman Freddy Meyer go for veteran blueliner Alexei Zhitnik, and Robitaille was dealt for forward Mike York. Zhitnik did little to help, and York was a complete bust, arriving overweight and undermotivated.

The team's stock tumbled faster than Enron's. Injuries, poor play and the seemingly non-stop saga surrounding Forsberg's right foot—mostly, his inability to find a skate to fit his surgically repaired appendage—sent the club to never-before-seen depths. The season turned into a slow-speed, 82-car accident.

As the losses piled up like cordwood, the feeling in the locker room was one of a distinct lack of leadership or direction. Some of that is directly attributable to Forsberg. Named captain during the summer, the talented Swede wore the C like a scarlet A.

"It can be a burden," Primeau said of being a captain. "It's a big responsibility, and not everyone is cut out to carry that responsibility." The foot issues limited Forsberg to cameo appearances in the lineup, and combined with his impending free agency—the two-year deal he signed coming out of the lockout was due to expire at season's end—Forsberg became more of a story off the ice.

History, seemingly ever-repeating in Philadelphia, once again meant teammates were left to answer questions about another injured captain. Kapanen went so far as to tape off his dressing stall at the team's practice facility as a media "no-fly zone."

Despite flying Forsberg all over North America in search of the perfect skate, and despite all the losing, the Flyers wanted him to sign a new contract. Frustrated with his foot and his play, Forsberg said he didn't know what his future held and wouldn't make any long-term commitments.

Snider took one last stab at signing him to a new contract in late January, but not even that went right. Hours after a Saturday night game, Forsberg confirmed he had a meeting scheduled with Snider for the next morning, but the team chairman called reporters in the press box to claim no get-together was planned.

The pair did, indeed, meet the next day, a Sunday morning, at Snider's office at the Wachovia Center. Snider pressed Forsberg to agree to a new deal, while Forsberg stubbornly held his ground, repeating that he wouldn't make a decision on his future until the summer, at the earliest.

After that meeting, Holmgren asked Forsberg for a list of teams to which he would accept a trade; the Nashville Predators were at the top of the list.

At noon on Thursday, February 15, hours before the Flyers were to play the Toronto Maple Leafs and two weeks before the trade deadline, Snider made one final plea to Forsberg to sign a new deal. When the All-Star again refused to change his mind, Forsberg volunteered to waive his no-trade clause, and Snider told Holmgren to make the best trade possible.

When the players came off the ice after warm-ups a little before 7:00 PM, Holmgren walked into the locker room and informed Forsberg he had been dealt to Nashville in return for forward Scottie Upshall, defense prospect Ryan Parent, and first- and third-round picks in the 2007 draft.

"It was literally five, seven minutes before the game," Knuble, Forsberg's linemate, told reporters. "I've never seen that, a guy getting yanked out of the locker room as you're tightening up your skates."

Those weren't the only trades before the deadline, as Holmgren set his sights on shedding salary and making the club younger and faster. Zhitnik was sent to the Atlanta Thrashers for young defenseman Braydon Coburn. The disgracefully disappointing Calder was jettisoned to Detroit in a three-way deal that netted the club defenseman Lasse Kukkonen. And in a move to shore up the future, a second-round pick was traded to Buffalo for goalie Martin Biron.

The Flyers lost the night Forsberg left, as they did most nights during the 2006–07 season. The team won back-to-back games only four times all season, and their longest win streak was just three games.

They set a number of club records during the season. Their 56 points were the fewest in franchise history, and also were the fewest in the league, the first time the Flyers finished at the bottom of the standings.

Their 48 losses were the most in club history, and their 22 wins were the fewest since the 1969–70 season. They posted six winless streaks of five games or more, topped by a club-record 10-game slide from December 8 through December 27.

They won just 10 times on home ice, their fewest ever in a season. Among their 31 home defeats were winless streaks of six and 13 consecutive games, shattering the previous club record of five straight. Between November 2 and February 8, the Flyers went 1–16–3 at home, with the lone win coming against the Columbus Blue Jackets on November 24—ironically, in Hitchcock's first game as Blue Jackets coach.

The 2006–07 season was a historical one, for sure.

MEET BOB-BOOSH-TON

Coming off their surprise run to the 2010 Stanley Cup Final, one of the Flyers' first orders of offseason business was re-signing goaltender Michael Leighton. Even though he struggled against the Chicago Blackhawks in the championship series, they likely would not have gotten there without him.

However, a bulging disc that first affected Leighton during the previous spring's playoff run came back worse during a pre-season game in Toronto.

"I don't know what kind of move I did, but all of a sudden my left foot just started going numb, my toes went numb," Leighton said. "My ankle was rolling over—I had no control over my ankle. And I started getting a sharp pain down my left [gluteus]. ... After the game I got an MRI and they said that bulging disc had herniated [and] it was pushing on the nerve, which was causing the pain, but also blocking the nerve, which was causing the numbness and the weakness."

Leighton had surgery in October, putting him on the shelf and leaving the crease to veteran Brian Boucher, and putting three youngsters in a competition for the second spot—Johan Backlund, who had played one NHL game; Joacim Eriksson, a 2008 seventh-round pick; and an unknown, undrafted goalie from the middle of Russia named Sergei Bobrovsky.

"He's got a lot of athleticism," Flyers director of player development Don Luce said of Bobrovsky during the Flyers' rookie camp in July 2010. "He's very mobile in net. He's got a great personality. Upbeat kid, wants to learn. He's got some good technique."

He also had far more skill and competitiveness than the Flyers realized.

"I will do everything I need to do to make management see me as a goalkeeper for the [NHL] team and I will put in the work for it," Bobrovsky—who spoke no English—said via translator over the summer.

It didn't take long for Bobrovsky to make an impression on coach Peter Laviolette and the rest of the Flyers' decision-makers. As training camp wore on, Backlund—the favorite to win the No. 2 job—was sent to the AHL, and Eriksson was returned to his Swedish club.

On opening night in Pittsburgh—against the Flyers' biggest rival and their galaxy of stars celebrating the opening of their new home, Consol Energy Center—Laviolette made the stunning decision to start Bobrovsky. The rookie made the coach look smart, though, stopping 29 of 31 shots as the Flyers skated off with a 3–2 win.

"He had a good 30 days … a solid body of work from the time we started watching him to the time we picked him as our goalie," Laviolette said that night. "Bob went in there and did his job."

Bobrovsky had an outstanding start to the season, winning eight of his first 10 starts, including a run in November that saw him go 7–1–2 with a 2.02 goals-against average and .931 save percentage to earn NHL Rookie of the Month honors.

As with most rookies, he hit a bit of a wall in December, but Boucher was there to pick up the slack, winning four of his five December starts.

The Flyers had the second-most points in the Eastern Conference heading into their December 30 game against the Los Angeles Kings, which featured the return of Leighton, two months removed from back surgery and after two rehabilitation stints in the AHL. However, he allowed two goals in each of the first two periods and needed his offense to save him in a 7–4 victory.

Days later Leighton went back to the AHL, and the Flyers' net went from a trio back to a duo.

Bobrovsky and Boucher alternated the rest of the season, helping the Flyers win the Atlantic Division and earn the second seed. Bobrovsky finished the regular season 28–13–8 with a 2.59 goals-against average and .915 save percentage in 54 games, while Boucher went 18–10–4 with a 2.42 GAA and .916 save percentage in 34 games.

They opened the playoffs against the seventh-seeded Buffalo Sabres, and Bobrovsky was solid in Game 1, stopping 24 of 25 shots, but the offense wasn't there and the Sabres won 1–0. Game 2, however, went south in a hurry. After Claude Giroux gave the Flyers a 1–0 lead four minutes into the first period, Bobrovsky allowed three goals in a 5:47 span and was yanked with 7:30 left in the period. Boucher replaced him and stopped 20 of 21 shots as the Flyers held on for a 5–4 win that evened the series.

Boucher started Game 3 and made 35 saves—including a few during 2:45 straight of shorthanded time in the third period, 1:15

of it two men down—in the Flyers' 4–2 win. However, his backup drew more attention—Leighton, as Bobrovsky was made a healthy scratch for the first time all season.

"I was surprised," Leighton said of his addition to the active roster. "I had played half the season in the minors and Bob proved himself that year that he can handle the load. They gave him a chance the first couple games and things didn't work out so they switched to Boosh. Maybe they were looking for a different person in the locker room to give confidence to the guys and stuff, I don't know. It was good just to get back on the bench and back into the NHL again."

Laviolette stuck with the Boucher-Leighton pairing for Game 4, and while Boucher was solid with 28 saves on 29 shots, the offense again was absent and the Sabres tied the series with their second 1–0 victory.

The third time with the same goalie tandem wasn't the charm, however, as the Sabres blitzed Boucher for three goals on 11 shots and he was pulled 15:36 into the game. Leighton replaced him and did better than his previous NHL appearance, making 20 saves through the end of regulation. But 5:31 into overtime, Mike Weber's shot banged off his pads and went right to Tyler Ennis, who deposited the puck behind Leighton to give the Sabres a 4–3 win and a 3–2 series lead.

The day before a crucial Game 6, Laviolette had all three goalies on the ice for practice, and revealed nothing as to who his starter might be.

"Certainly where we're at right now, how the playoffs have gone, that will factor into it probably more than how somebody played halfway through the year or the beginning of the year or last year," Laviolette said that day. "I think it'll be more current than anything, but the overall picture, as well."

When the team came out for Game 6, it was Leighton in net. However, the move nearly backfired as Leighton allowed three goals on eight shots in the first period.

"They said all right, you've done it for us before, and they threw me in," Leighton said. "That was a game where things weren't going good for me. I didn't feel good, didn't play good. For me it was very disappointing because it was a chance to really get back into it and do something again and it didn't work out. That was disappointing."

Boucher replaced him to start the second and stopped 23 of 24 shots over the final two periods as the Flyers rallied to tie the game, and then Ville Leino scored 4:43 into overtime to force a Game 7.

Laviolette tried to defend his goaltending decision after the game, saying: "The way [Leighton] looked when he came up here in practice, he looked good. We had him on the bench, he came in in a relief opportunity and he continued to look good. Decisions are tough and it didn't go that way tonight for him."

Instead of again delaying his decision, Laviolette wasted no time naming his Game 7 starter, announcing immediately after Game 6 that Boucher would start Game 7. Bobrovsky was designated to be the backup, and Leighton would spend the remainder of the playoffs as a healthy scratch.

After all the goaltending issues the Flyers faced, it was the Sabres who had a crease conundrum in Game 7, as the Flyers took a 4–0 lead 1:59 into the third period, chasing Miller, and Boucher stopped 26 of 28 shots as the Flyers advanced to the second round with a 5–2 win.

While others criticized the Flyers and their goaltending carousel—the Buffalo News called the Flyers' three-headed goalie monster the Three Stooges—Boucher said he blocked it all out.

"I didn't pay much attention to that [goalie talk], to be honest," he said after Game 7. "I felt pretty good about myself. Aside from three minutes [in Game 5], I felt like I was doing a pretty good job. For me, I just try to focus on myself, knowing where I'm at and how I'm preparing. Not worry about the outside stuff."

The Flyers were the first team since the 2004 Vancouver Canucks to start three goalies in one playoffs series, and the first team since the 1988 Detroit Red Wings to win a playoff series while starting three different goaltenders.

It was no surprise to see Boucher in net to start Game 1 of the second round against the Boston Bruins, but he wasn't there long.

It was a 1–1 game with 35 seconds left in the first when Boucher juggled a Nathan Horton shot and it fell into the net to give Boston a 2–1 lead. Then 2:34 into the second Mark Recchi scored, which opened the floodgates. Boston scored twice more in the second, chasing Boucher after Brad Marchand's goal with 2:46 left.

Bobrovsky allowed two goals on 10 shots in relief of what became a 7–3 loss, which made it easy for Laviolette to go back to Boucher for Game 2. Boucher was far better, shaking off an arm injury that sidelined him for the final 8:59 of the second period to make 30 saves in regulation. However, he was left helpless with six minutes left in overtime when Braydon Coburn's pass around the boards hopped over Kimmo Timonen's stick and went to Nathan Horton, who found David Krejci for a one-timer from the hash marks to give the Bruins a 2–0 series lead.

The series shifted to Boston for Game 3, but Boucher left his game in Philadelphia. He gave up a pair of goals 1:03 into the game, and was pulled after allowing his fourth goal on 20 shots with 4:46 left in the second period. Bobrovsky again came on in relief—the sixth time in 10 games the Flyers had a mid-game goalie change—and stopped seven of eight shots, but the Flyers lost 5–1.

By the time Game 4 rolled around, the players had become sick of the goalie talk.

"We haven't cared all year long," Danny Briere said. "Both of them [Boucher and Bobrovsky], they've been good for the most part. Like everybody else they've had some tougher games, like we all have. But it never mattered and it's not going to start at this point."

Briere was right in that it didn't matter who started Game 4, because the Bruins—who would go on to win the Stanley Cup— were just too good. Bobrovsky, starting for the first time since the playoff opener, allowed three goals on 25 shots, and a pair of Boston empty-net goals saw the Flyers' season finished with a 5–1 loss.

Goaltending wasn't the sole reason the Flyers' season ended prematurely, but a lack of a solid performance in net was just too much to overcome. It also set the wheels in motion for the seismic changes that would come months later.

"I think that's where Paul [Holmgren] saw that we needed to do something," team president Peter Luukko said.

LAPPY

Ian Laperriere played just 95 of his 1,150 NHL regular-season and playoff games with the Philadelphia Flyers, but few who watched him during the 2009–10 season will forget his impact.

Nor will the impact of his one season with the Flyers ever leave Laperriere—literally or figuratively.

The Flyers signed Laperriere to a three-year contract July 1, 2009. Known as one of the most-respected players in the league, he immediately ingratiated himself as a leader in the Flyers' locker room.

"He's one of the best team guys I've ever been around," Arron Asham said.

"He's an example for everybody," added forward Ville Leino. "He's an ultimate warrior. Guys love him. He's a great guy. ... He eats, sleeps and breathes hockey. He's a motivator to every one of us."

Laperriere had 20 points in 82 games in his first season. He also blocked 74 shots, and is best remembered for two in particular—because he stopped them with his face.

Killing a penalty late in the first period of a game against the Buffalo Sabres on November 27, 2009, Laperriere dropped to his knees to block a Jason Pominville shot, and the rising puck hit him in the mouth.

"What I did was stupid," Laperriere said after the fact. "I was in the slot and went on my knees thinking he was closer and took it right in the face. It was the first time I was ever seriously injured blocking a shot."

The puck knocked out seven teeth—five real, two fake—and caused a cut that needed 80 stitches to close. Remarkably, Laperriere returned to the game in the third period, stunning even his own teammates.

"It was up there as one of the most shocking things you'd ever seen," James van Riemsdyk said. "It was a pretty gruesome sight with all the blood. ... To see him basically pop up, go get stitched up and come back out was pretty amazing."

Laperriere could barely speak the next day because much of his mouth was stitched up, but he still attended the optional morning skate and played that night against the Atlanta Thrashers.

He avoided any more damage the rest of the regular season, but that changed in a drastic way on April 22, 2010, Game 5 of the Flyers' first-round playoff series against the New Jersey Devils. They were up 3–0 3:56 into the third period when Laperriere came out to kill a penalty. When Devils defenseman Paul Martin wound up for a shot, Laperriere slid down to block the shot. He laid out a few feet in front of Martin, but his angle was off and the puck slammed into Laperriere's face, just above his right eye.

The lasting memory of the moment is Laperriere jumping to his feet, a spray of blood trailing him, as he tried to get off the ice.

"I didn't get knocked out and I do remember everything," Laperriere said on the one-year anniversary of the injury. "I remember a big sting on my face and the fear of losing my eye. That was the first thing that came to my head. I couldn't see anything out of my right eye. I didn't panic, but I was close to it. Jimmy [McCrossin, trainer] came on the ice and that was the first question I asked him, is my eyeball still there? I don't care if I lose my sight but at least I'll have an eyeball in there. I know it sounds gross, but that's what I felt."

The eyeball was still there, but he needed 70 stitches to close a gash on his face. He also suffered a non-displaced orbital bone fracture and—most seriously—a brain contusion. It was assumed that Laperriere's season, and possibly his career, would be over.

When the Flyers returned home for Game 3 of the conference semifinals against the Boston Bruins, the team showed a commercial based on the NHL's "History Will Be Made" series on the center-ice scoreboard, with the tagline reading, "What if Ian didn't believe in sacrifice?" He then was shown standing in the Zamboni entrance and received a prolonged standing ovation from fans and players from both teams.

"He epitomizes the spirit of Philadelphia," van Riemsdyk said. "They have some passionate sports fans in Philadelphia. To see

THE FLYERS' IRONMAN

Ian Laperriere's playing career may have ended in 2012, but his days as an athlete didn't stop.

"Even if I'm not playing hockey I'm going to be an athlete the rest of my life," Laperriere said. "You always try to challenge yourself."

The first challenge was running a marathon, which he did when he ran the Philadelphia Marathon in November 2012. That wasn't enough, however, and he spent more than six months training for an Ironman triathlon—a 2.4-mile swim followed by a 112-mile bike ride and capped by a 26.2-mile run.

In August 2013, Laperriere completed the Ironman North American Championship at Mont-Tremblant, Quebec, in 12 hours, 11 minutes, 55 seconds.

Laperriere said he didn't have a time goal in mind, but said prior to the race that anything in the 12-hour range would be good.

"Around 12 hours would be something I'd be happy with," he said. "But at the end of the day, it's a crazy distance. You never know what can happen, in training and the race, and you just have to be happy to finish it."

him lay it on the line for their team, they obviously were very proud to have him be a Flyer."

They were able to show their pride again exactly one month after the injury, as Laperriere was a stunning addition to the lineup for Game 4 of the Eastern Conference Finals against the Montreal Canadiens.

"We beat Boston, we go to Montreal, I'm starting to feel better," Laperriere said. "The first two weeks I had positional vertigo and that's the scariest thing I've had in my life. I really felt like I was going to be like that for the rest of my life, until the doctors figured out what it was. In the beginning we thought it was coming from my head, which it is, but it's behind my ears. It took two weeks before the doctors figured that out. And when they fixed me, after that I felt 200 times better. I didn't have the

MISSING: 7 TEETH. IF FOUND, PLEASE RETURN TO IAN LAPERRIERE

Ian Laperriere lost seven teeth and needed 80 stitches to close a cut to his mouth when he was hit in the face blocking a shot in a game against the Buffalo Sabres in November 2009.

Once the scars healed, he had a dentist fit him for a bridge and replacement teeth. The mold was sent out, but when it was returned to the Flyers, there was a problem—no teeth in the box.

Someone stole Laperriere's bridge and teeth, leaving Laperriere more upset than when he got hurt.

"I'm so angry," he told CSNPhilly.com. "The box came and it was empty. When you're 20 years old and you lose some teeth, it's okay, now you look like a hockey player. But when you are 36, it's not so cool. Who's going to wear them? They're not going to fit anyone except me."

dizziness, I didn't have that vertigo feeling, which is the worst feeling in the world. All of a sudden you're feeling better. I still had headaches, but if you play in the NHL you play through headaches. ... I've played with headaches before. I said I can do that, I feel pretty good. Start skating by myself, no dizziness, not too bad headaches, and all of a sudden you're talking to yourself and the little person on your shoulder is convincing the big person that you're okay. I won't play 20 minutes, but I might hit seven minutes; I know I can help. I want to be part of it."

"It was one of the most inspirational things I've seen in all my years in the game," Flyers GM Paul Holmgren said of Laperriere's playoff return. "It's right up there, if not at the top of the list."

"It gave our team a boost," van Riemsdyk said. "We came out guns blazing in that series and I think a lot of that was the boost of having him in the lineup. ... To see him out there was pretty uplifting for all of us."

However, Laperriere admits now that he lied his way into the lineup.

"Did I lie? Yes," he said. "I lied to myself first of all. I convinced myself first I was okay. I passed all the tests—every test they had me pass, I passed them. ... Yes, I did lie to them. I'm sorry if they take it personal, but I don't regret it."

At age 36, Laperriere saw that Flyers team as his best—and possibly last—chance to get his name on the Stanley Cup.

"I played in this League for a long time, never been close to anything like the Cup or semifinals or anything like that," he said. "Do I regret it? Not a chance. I don't regret anything. When I'm 60 years old am I going to suffer the consequences? Who knows? Same with the guy who took drugs when they were younger—is he going to suffer when he's 60? He doesn't know, either. For me, it was my rush, my dream. I didn't want to miss the chance to be part of something special."

Laperriere played Games 4 and 5 against Montreal and all six games in the Cup Final against the Chicago Blackhawks, averaging just about seven-and-a-half minutes per game, and he had 13 hits and five blocked shots.

The end wasn't the one Laperriere or the Flyers wanted, as they lost the Cup to the Blackhawks in six games, but Laperriere felt with a summer of rest he would be able to return to full health for the 2010–11 season. But he never felt right during his summer workouts, and after one preseason game, he knew it wasn't going to happen.

"I played one preseason game and I felt like things were going 100 miles an hour next to me," he said. "After that New Jersey game, we flew to Toronto, I didn't play that night, and the next morning we flew to Minnesota and that's when I couldn't bear the headaches any more. I called Jimmy, said I want to meet you at the rink. [Team president] Peter Luukko was there, Paul Holmgren was on the road. I was nervous, because I lied to them all along, and I was nervous for their reaction."

His concerns were put to rest immediately, as he was assured his health was the only thing the organization cared about.

"Lappy had laid a lot on the line for the organization," Holmgren said. "The way he came back in the playoffs ... we felt that if he was still suffering issues, let's get this fixed."

As the end of his hockey career became a reality, Laperriere began to shift his focus on other areas of the Flyers' organization,

THE MOVIE STARS

The Flyers' fervent following also reaches Hollywood. That's how four players—Ian Laperriere, Scott Hartnell, Matt Carle, and James van Riemsdyk—were cast for the 2012 film, *This Is 40*.

The four Flyers play hockey players—not much of a stretch—who party with the film's two female leads, Leslie Mann and Megan Fox, at a nightclub. In the scene, Fox puts Laperriere's fake teeth in her mouth.

"I thought it would always be a little bit of a fake," van Riemsdyk said. "But I can attest that they were ... it was his backup set, but they were his teeth in her mouth."

"That was something," Laperriere said in a Q&A session promoting the film. "I can brag about that. Not too many guys can say that."

making scouting trips to watch current and future prospects, as well as working with players at the AHL level.

He also continued to skate and work out, and for his perseverance was awarded the 2011 Bill Masterton Trophy for dedication to the game. He's the only player in the award's history to win it without playing a game.

"It's the only way I could have ever won a trophy in the NHL," Laperriere joked in his acceptance speech. "Take two pucks to the face."

He finally announced his retirement in June 2012, and immediately was named the team's director of player development, where he has a major role in working with current and future Flyers prospects.

"He's been a solid role model for our young prospects," Flyers director of scouting Chris Pryor said. "He can relate to them because he just got done playing and they respect the sacrifice and commitment he made when he played the game."

"Lappy truly is a special individual," Flyers chairman Ed Snider told the Philadelphia Daily News. "He represents everything that the Flyers are, and I am very proud of him."

THE UGLY

BARRY ASHBEE

Barry Ashbee didn't need a nickname. He could have been called "Blood and Guts," but even that didn't quite describe just how truly strong and tough a man and a player the Flyers defenseman was.

Ashbee toiled in various low-level hockey outposts before signing with the Hershey Bears of the American Hockey League in 1962. He spent four seasons in Hershey before finally making the NHL with the Boston Bruins in the 1965–66 season, for a whopping 14 games.

With expansion coming, the blueliner's full-time NHL future seemed a reality, but a back injury led to surgery that sidelined him for the entire 1966–67 season, and he went unselected by the six new teams in the expansion draft.

"There was some disappointment when he didn't get picked in 1967," Donna Ashbee, Barry's widow, told Jim Jackson in his 2004 book *Walking Together Forever*. "However, especially after the back surgery, he was just determined to play again. ... He came to the conclusion that he still wanted to play hockey, and if it was going to be in the minors, we were in a good spot because Hershey was a great place to be."

The minor leagues was just where the Bruins, Hershey's parent club, saw him, and that's where he spent the next three seasons.

On May 22, 1970, shortly after being named general manager of the Flyers, Keith Allen made one of the most important trades in franchise history, sending Darryl Edestrand and Larry McKillop to the Bruins in exchange for the 31-year-old Ashbee.

The *Philadelphia Bulletin*, in an unbylined story, termed the move "small and puzzling," but it didn't take long for fans and teammates to see just what kind of player, and person, Ashbee was.

"I have always said that he taught the younger players on our team about what it took to win," Allen said in *Walking Together Forever*. "He was the toughest, and as it turned out, bravest man I ever have seen."

Things nearly didn't work out between Ashbee and the Flyers. When the old-school defenseman showed up for training camp in 1972, he didn't like the laissez-faire attitude he saw from some teammates. He believed his fellow players should have a burning ache from the last-day loss that cost the team a spot in the previous spring's playoffs. Instead, what he saw when the 1972–73 season started were teammates who didn't work hard enough in the offseason, didn't work hard enough in training camp, and who were staying out late and partying until all hours of the night.

To Ashbee, the personification of that lack of work ethic came in the form of promising young defenseman Rick Foley. Foley had what Ashbee didn't—great size, skating ability and a high offensive skill level. But to Ashbee, Foley had no heart and no

ASHBEE BULLIES THE REF

The Broad Street Bullies' brawling wasn't always limited to player-on-player violence.

During a game in Pittsburgh on January 25, 1973, defenseman Barry Ashbee protested a tripping call against him by punching referee Bryan Lewis in the face.

Ashbee was handed an eight-game suspension for his outburst.

The gritty Barry Ashbee led by example on the ice, and during his losing battle with leukemia off the ice.

desire, and when he reported to camp at 243 pounds—28 pounds more than the team expected—Ashbee exploded, telling Allen he wanted out, that he was getting too old to waste his time with players who had more interest in partying than working and winning. Allen talked Ashbee out of quitting, saying he would excise the malingerers, and as proof exiled Foley to the minors, never to be seen again in a Flyers sweater.

The players who remained shared Ashbee's work ethic and followed his lead when it came to grit, determination and toughness. Young players like Bobby Clarke, Bill Barber and Tom Bladon watched what Ashbee put himself through just to play, and it inspired them.

"He was the strongest guy mentally that I've ever seen," Clarke said in *Walking Together Forever.*

Ashbee played through torn knee ligaments in the 1972–73 season, ligaments that needed to be surgically repaired but weren't fixed until season's end. The following season, a chipped vertebra in his neck caused shooting pain from his shoulder to his hand, and forced him to wear a horsecollar-shaped brace on his neck. When the pain became too unbearable, Ashbee would tape his arm to his body and jam his stick into his glove.

"I sat next to him in the [locker] room," Bladon said in *Walking Together Forever.* "I would pat him on the back as we got ready for a game or a period, forgetting about his cracked vertebra, and he would collapse to the floor on his knees in pain. The next period, he would be out there knocking people around into the boards. He was something."

He had 17 points and was third in the league with a plus-52 rating in 69 games in 1973–74 and earned a second-team All-Star selection. That season, unfortunately, would be his last.

Game 4 of the Flyers' conference final series against the New York Rangers went to overtime tied 1–1. At 1:27 of the extra period, Rangers defenseman Dale Rolfe fired a shot from the point. Ashbee had moved into position to block the shot, but it rose faster than he expected, and the defenseman couldn't get his hands up in time to protect himself. The puck slammed into Ashbee's face, inches above his right eye.

"It was like a softball was stuck in my eye, and then there was just a big red ball of fire," Ashbee later told reporters.

He dropped to the ice in a pool of blood. He was rushed off the ice and taken directly to St. Clair Hospital, and then transferred to Wills Eye Institute in Philadelphia. Both eyes were patched as doctors waited for blood to drain out of the eye so the extent of the trauma could be assessed.

Tests showed damage to the retina, and while Ashbee's vision in general would be okay, he had lost almost all of his depth perception, meaning his playing career was over.

Publicly, Ashbee never showed any bitterness. In the press conference announcing his retirement, he said: "These things

BRUCE GAMBLE

Bruce Gamble was an overweight, 33-year-old chain-smoker, but he started in goal for the Flyers on February 6, 1972, in Vancouver.

Early in the first period, Gamble dropped to his knees to make a save. Barry Ashbee blocked the shot, but Gamble slumped over in pain. The referee blew the play dead, and Gamble got back to his feet as a trainer rushed onto the ice.

Gamble played the rest of the game, coming within 1:58 of a shutout in a 3–1 win, but felt lousy the whole time. He went to the hospital the next morning, and a doctor diagnosed the problem—the goalie had suffered a heart attack during the game.

happen and you just have to accept them. The one good thing I've found out from this is that this old world isn't such a bad place after all. I can't begin to count the number of letters I've had from people offering to give me one of their eyes.

"I'm just happy that I was able to get my name on the Stanley Cup once. I look at it this way: I'm only 35. I've got a long time to live."

Unfortunately, that wasn't true.

After he retired, Ashbee was asked to stay on as an assistant to coach Fred Shero. Donna Ashbee said coaching wasn't something Barry particularly was interested in, and saw the offer as a pity gesture by the Flyers.

"I'm not sure if he had even given any thought to what he was going to do after he was done playing," she said in *Walking Together Forever*. "Once he took the position, he grew to really enjoy it. He came to like the teaching aspect of the job, being able to answer questions the guys had, and working with them."

He got to like the job so much that he told Donna that maybe there was a future for him as a head coach.

Before he could explore those options, though, he had something much worse to deal with.

On April 11, 1977, Ashbee told team doctor Edward Viner about odd bruises on his arms and legs. Viner scheduled Ashbee for a follow-up visit, but the physician already was certain what the grim diagnosis was. Tests the next day proved him tragically correct—Ashbee had acute leukemia.

On April 13 Ashbee called Clarke and told him, and said he would inform the team before practice. But when Ashbee hadn't arrived by the time the players were ready to take the ice, Clarke bolted the locker room door and told his teammates about Ashbee's illness.

"It was like getting hit with a brick," Paul Holmgren said.

Ashbee talked to the team after practice, and then checked himself into Hahnemann Hospital for treatment led by Dr. Isadore Brodsky, one of the country's leading oncologists.

A shaken Flyers bunch lost their playoff game to the Toronto Maple Leafs that night; the next day, Ashbee called a press conference in his hospital room. He told reporters: "I don't want everybody in town to think I'm lying up here dying. Heck, I'm lucky. The doctors are optimistic. They think they caught it in time.

"I don't want this to be written up as a 'Win One for the Gipper' story. The players know I'm sick, and I'm going to get better, that's all."

Despite two rounds of chemotherapy, Ashbee never got better. His kidneys became infected and his body, overloaded with white blood cells, was incapable of fighting back. Players would visit, but Ashbee would drift in and out of consciousness.

"I saw him every day," Don Saleski recalled in *Full Spectrum*. "And to see a strong-willed guy like that wasting away was so hard."

Thirty days after he was diagnosed, on May 11, 1975, Barry Ashbee died.

The team flew to Toronto for the funeral, where Clarke gave the eulogy:

"It took an incurable blood disorder to quell a spirit that the loss of sight in one eye, a spinal fusion, torn ligaments in his knee and a pinched nerve in his neck could not dampen. Barry never gave in to the luxury of exhaustion or pain. He always played the hand the way it was dealt.

"He may be gone from us physically, but he will never be forgotten because he left a little bit of himself with all of us."

Ashbee's place in Flyers history is indelible. His retired No. 4 hangs in the rafters of the Wells Fargo Center. The annual award given to the Flyers' best defenseman is named the Barry Ashbee Trophy, and the biggest beneficiary of the annual Flyers' Wives Fight for Lives Carnival is the Barry Ashbee Research Laboratory at Hahnemann.

The best summation of Barry Ashbee's Flyers legacy was written by Bill Meltzer in a story on the Flyers' website:

"Barry Ashbee's retired number hangs in the rafters because he was the epitome of the type of hockey player that every team needs to win. He wasn't the most talented guy around, but no one was more dedicated to winning or persevered more tenaciously."

BERNIE PARENT: BEATEN UP, BEATEN DOWN

Bernie Parent was on top of the world after winning the 1975 Stanley Cup. He had won back-to-back championships, back-to-back Conn Smythe Trophies as playoff MVP, and had been on the cover of *Time* magazine. As Bernie himself likes to say, it was a beautiful thing.

But the beauty faded fast.

A week before the start of the 1975–76 season, Parent reported pain in his neck and elbow that nothing—not muscle relaxants, massage therapy or a few days in traction—could cure.

While the Flyers started 3–0 with Wayne Stephenson in goal, Parent learned what had been causing him so much pain—a herniated cervical disc. On October 14, 1975, Parent had major surgery performed—a cervical laminectomy.

The original diagnosis was for Parent to miss 3–4 weeks. But when the goalie tried practicing on November 27, he ended up back in the hospital, in traction.

On February 5, 1976, Parent put lingering pain in his arm aside and returned to practice. Three weeks later, on February 24 in Washington, he suited up for his first game, surrendering five goals on 19 shots in a 5–5 tie with the Capitals.

He would go on to play just 11 games that season, going 6–2–3 with a 2.34 goals-against average.

When the playoffs opened, coach Fred Shero wanted to start Stephenson, but assistant coaches Mike Nykoluk and Barry Ashbee convinced Shero to go with Parent. And while he helped backstop a seven-game series win against the Toronto Maple Leafs, Parent just wasn't the same.

After an uneven performance in Game 1 of the second-round series against the Boston Bruins, Parent saved Shero the embarrassment by taking himself out of the lineup.

"I'm tired," Parent told reporters. "I'm not in playoff shape. I don't want to cost the team a game. Let's make the move before it happens."

Parent's neck felt better when the 1976–77 season started, but he wasn't clear of injuries. A broken toe suffered during the preseason left him hobbled, but a special pad in his skate allowed him to play. He also missed time with a sprained knee, but in 61 games, he went 35–13–12 with a 2.71 GAA. He allowed three goals in a 4:42 span early in the first period of the playoff opener against the Toronto Maple Leafs, but settled down as the Flyers rallied, but fell short 3–2. After allowing four goals on 15 shots in the first two periods of Game 2, he was replaced by Stephenson and spent the rest of the series on the bench.

He came back in Game 1 against Boston in the next round, replacing Stephenson after the Flyers fell behind 3–0. The Flyers rallied to force overtime, but while trying to reach back and glove Rick Middleton's shot 2:57 into overtime, Parent knocked the puck into the net.

Parent didn't play again in the series, and the Flyers were swept out of the postseason for the second straight year.

In 1977 the Flyers brought Parent's idol, Jacques Plante, to training camp in an attempt to rebuild the netminder's confidence. Parent and Plante had been teammates during Parent's short stay with the Maple Leafs, and Parent credited Plante for turning him into the goalie he became.

"I went to the Leafs a pretty good goalie with a lot of talent but still very raw," Parent said in *Walking Together Forever*. "Plante

HOLMGREN'S NEAR-DEATH EXPERIENCE

Today Paul Holmgren is the Flyers' general manager, but he nearly never made it through his rookie season.

On March 26, 1976, the day after his first NHL game, Holmgren reported to a team meeting in Boston with a swollen right eye. Barry Ashbee and Bobby Clarke took the youngster to the Massachusetts Eye and Ear Infirmary, where doctors found a puncture wound caused by a skate blade when Holmgren had been at the bottom of a pile during an AHL brawl several days earlier.

An emergency operation was performed to stop a fluid leak that was endangering Holmgren's eyesight, but he had a severe reaction to the anesthetic and nearly died on the operating table.

He survived, but didn't play again until the following season.

worked with me on understanding the game, playing the angles, practicing properly, and all of those little things that I had been missing. Working with him really turned my career around."

It seemed to help as Parent won 14 of his first 20 games, and finished the season 29–6–13 with a 2.22 GAA and seven shutouts. Despite the strong stats, Parent remained inconsistent, and Shero was splitting the goaltending chores nearly 50/50 between Parent and Stephenson.

When the playoffs started, though, Parent looked like the Bernie of old. He shut down the Colorado Rockies in a two-game preliminary-round sweep, allowing just three goals in two games. In the quarterfinals against the Buffalo Sabres—a team that had gone 3–0–1 against the Flyers in the regular season—Parent held them to two or fewer goals in four of five games as the Flyers advanced with ease. Chants of "Bernie! Bernie!" again rained down from the Spectrum.

The dream, however, ended in the semifinals against Boston. The Bruins won Game 1 in overtime when Middleton knocked in a loose puck in front, and in Game 2 they scored seven times on Parent on just 33 shots in a 7–5 Bruins victory. Parent rallied to hold Boston to just one goal in a 3–1 Flyers win in Game 3, but the Bruins closed the series and the Flyers' season in five games.

At 33, Parent's best days clearly were behind him entering the 1978–79 season. When the Flyers took to the Spectrum ice against the New York Rangers on February 17, 1979, Bernie was 16–12–7 with four shutouts, but hadn't won a game in nearly five weeks.

Midway through the first period, Jimmy Watson and Don Maloney were jostling in front of the net when Watson yanked on Maloney's arm and the Rangers player's stick blade penetrated the tiny eye slit in Parent's mask. The goalie immediately yanked off his mask, clutched at his face and skated off the ice.

Dr. David Pollock, the Flyers' team optometrist, found blood in the interior chamber of Parent's right eye, and he was taken to Wills Eye Institute. There, Dr. James Tasman found Parent had suffered two conjunctival tears and admitted him to Pennsylvania Hospital. Both eyes were patched, and bed rest was ordered for at least a week.

"This is what happens to old goalies, I guess," Parent told the *Philadelphia Bulletin*'s Ray Didinger from his hospital room. "You forget to duck."

Three leading Philadelphia eye specialists all determined Parent should retire. The lens in his right eye had been

BAD VACATION

To keep some of his veterans fresh for the 1984 playoffs, coach Bob McCammon forced mini-vacations on some of his older players.

The players weren't in favor of them, especially Bill Barber, whose creaky knee was just starting to feel better when his time-out was ordered.

During four days in the Poconos, Barber was given a workout plan, which included modified squat thrusts—generally a bad idea for someone with chronic knee issues.

One morning while working out, Barber heard a crack in his leg like a gunshot, which was his femur snapping where it entered the knee joint. He never played again.

permanently subluxed, or pushed back, resulting in a build-up of pressure in the eye. Medication could control the condition, but his ability to focus and his depth perception never would be the same.

"He can't catch a ball his kids throw to him, let alone stop a puck," Flyers team doctor Edward Viner said.

"It was just one of those freak things," Parent said. "The good Lord was saying to me that it was enough and it was time to move on with my life."

Parent played 486 games with the Flyers over 10 seasons (1967–68 to 1970–71, and 1973–74 to 1978–79), and remains the standard by which every Flyers goalie is compared.

He won 232 games as a Flyer (a mark since passed by Ron Hextall) and posted a 2.42 goals-against average, a .917 save percentage, and a remarkable 50 shutouts. He's also the only goalie to win the Vezina Trophy, Conn Smythe Trophy and the Stanley Cup in the same season twice. He was elected to the Hockey Hall of Fame in 1984, and was a charter member of the Flyers Hall of Fame in 1988.

Were it not for the injuries Parent suffered after the second Cup season, said team chairman Ed Snider, "I think Bernie would have gone down without question as the best goalie of all time."

PELLE LINDBERGH

Sunday, November 10, 1985, is a date that still brings shudders and tears to Flyers fans. It was early that morning, on a sharp curve on Somerdale Road in the Gloucester County town of Somerdale that Pelle Lindbergh's souped-up Porsche 930 Turbo slammed into a three-and-a-half-foot-high concrete wall in front of Somerdale Elementary School.

According to the Lindbergh biography, *Behind the White Mask*, a heavily impaired Lindbergh, driving upwards of 80 mph, didn't hit the brakes until he was about 10 feet away from the wall. The goalie's car was pulverized, with the driver's side bearing the brunt of the impact. The entire front end was pushed into the passenger cabin, which was shorn away from the rest of what was left of the vehicle. The windshield was found 40 feet away.

Two passengers in the car with Lindbergh survived, but the goalie was left with a broken body and a dead brain.

It was a shocking turn for a player who seemed just to be reaching the prime of his life and career. He was coming off a season with 40 wins and a 3.02 goals-against average, and won the first of what was expected to be many Vezina trophies. He was mere months removed from backstopping the Flyers to the 1985 Stanley Cup Final, and at age 26, there seemed to be nothing but more winning on the horizon.

And then it all ended.

The night before, the Flyers had earned a 5–3 win against the Boston Bruins, ending a stretch of five games in eight nights. With five days off before a Cup Final rematch with the Edmonton Oilers, coach Mike Keenan gave the players Sunday and Monday off.

"He said, 'I don't want anybody at the rink the next two days. Everybody take the time off; you've earned it. Go and enjoy it, and we'll see you in a couple days,'" Mark Howe said.

Lindbergh didn't play that night against Boston, and with his mother and brother-in-law visiting from Sweden, Pelle and his fiancée, Kerstin, figured they all would just head home after the game. But with the extra time off, and in the midst of a 10-game win streak, the players wanted to celebrate, including a nice, long party at the Coliseum in Voorhees, which had an after-hours bar.

Lindbergh had no intention of going out that night, but later told Kerstin he would make a quick visit. She said she would stay home with his mom, and Pelle first met up with friends at the Bennigan's on Route 73.

The quick visit turned into an all-night drinking session, and at about 2:30 AM, Pelle and a friend, Ed Parvin, drove to the Coliseum to continue the party, where they drank and enjoyed themselves until 5:00 AM.

Lindbergh told teammates Rick Tocchet and Murray Craven that he was going to drive Parvin home to Mount Ephraim, then return so they could get some breakfast. Kathy McNeal, a friend of Tocchet's, jumped into the Porsche with Lindbergh, and the three took off.

Tocchet and Craven, who shared a house within walking distance of the Coliseum, barely were inside when there was a knock on their door. Two fans who had been partying with the players at the Coliseum said Lindbergh's car had crashed. Lindbergh and Al Morganti, then the Flyers' beat writer for the *Philadelphia Inquirer*, were the same age and had grown close.

"He was my best friend on the team and in Philly," Morganti said. "I would go out with my then-girlfriend, and we would go out with him and his girlfriend a lot."

Morganti called Lindbergh a "whack job," but meant it in the nicest, most respectful way. Lindbergh always was aggressive, living on the edge. He didn't just drive fast. He loved physical hockey, loved to fight. Morganti said he and Pelle would watch hockey fight tapes for fun.

"I loved hanging out with him," Morganti said. "He had a condo on the water at the Moorings [a section of the Kings Grant development in Marlton]. "He had a big raft we'd go out in, we'd bring crossbows and shoot. It was cool."

Kerstin brought Morganti into Pelle's hospital room, where the goaltender had been hooked to a respirator. It was Morganti who was given the awful assignment of explaining to Pelle's mother, Anna-Lisa, her son's condition.

"I remember I was the second one at the hospital. She [Kerstin] brought me in because his mom was over from Sweden, and [Kerstin] spoke English a little, but she asked me to help translate. The [doctor] went through the broken bones, and then she kind of asked, what about, can he play again. The guy just looked at her—'I'm the ortho [orthopedic] guy, and you had better talk to the neurologist.'"

The neurologist explained just how terrible Pelle's condition was. A CAT scan had shown that trauma to Pelle's brain stem had cut off the oxygen supply to the player's brain, making recovery impossible. He was brain dead, and the only thing keeping him alive was the respirator.

"He explains brain dead," Morganti said. "I'm in shock, and she's waiting for the translation. I had to tell her what it meant. It was awful."

Doctors said the only thing the family could do was say good-bye, and their only remaining decision was whether surgeons would be allowed to harvest Lindbergh's organs for donation.

Two days later, after Sigge Lindbergh, Pelle's father, made the sad flight over from Sweden, he and Anna-Lisa made the decision to remove Pelle from life support. His heart, kidneys and corneas were donated to needy patients.

"Pelle's organs are going to save other lives," Keenan said. "It's appropriate. He died making one more save."

Players, some still hung over in the early Sunday morning hours, couldn't believe the phone calls they were getting. That grim task fell to team captain Dave Poulin, who had gotten the call from Craven.

"I was supposed to go down to Egg Harbor," Howe said of that day. "I was anticipating buying a new boat, so I was going down to look at boats, and I got a call about 7:30 in the morning from Dave Poulin, and I couldn't believe what I heard."

"I was heading to the [Jersey] Shore," Brian Propp said. "I had a home I was going to do some work on."

One by one, they all received the call.

"You became numb to it," Poulin said. "You were just contacting them and trying to make it clear to them that they had to come down to the hospital.

"You had to explain. Some said 'We'll come down in a little while,' but I said, 'No, you have to come down now.'"

Team chairman Ed Snider got his own early phone call from John Brogan, who was an assistant to team president Jay Snider.

"It was just awful," Snider recalled. "Poor kid. I felt a little guilty because everybody knew he loved his Porsche, loved to speed. I felt like I could have done more before it happened. Whether it would have worked or not I don't know. He had that souped-up Porsche, and he loved to open it up."

Lindbergh had bought the 1983 Porsche 930 Turbo in Germany new for $52,000 and immediately sent it to the Stuttgart factory for another $41,000 of modifications. The speedometer went to 190 mph, and Lindbergh told friends he got it up to 150 on the Autobahn.

GRETZKY DONATION

Wayne Gretzky isn't called the Great One just for what he did on the ice.

In November 1985, Gretzky's Oilers were the first opponents for the Flyers following the death of star goalie Pelle Lindbergh. The Flyers asked that in lieu of flowers, and out of respect for Pelle's sister, Ann-Christine, who was fighting cancer, donations be made to a cancer research fund established in Pelle's name.

The only opposing player to make a donation was Gretzky.

"He scared me," Clarke said in *Full Spectrum*. "We told Pelle he had to slow down."

"I had stopped driving with him about a month before [the accident]," Morganti said "I'd go to Atlantic City with him, and I'd be there before we left. We all told him to slow down."

Players met that Sunday morning at the hospital. Some saw Pelle, while others cried or sat like zombies. After a while, they went to Poulin's house to watch football, but mostly they sat and stared at the television for a few hours and then went home.

"It's something you can't believe is happening," Dave Brown said. "We were poised to go to the Final again that year and he was the guy that was going to lead us there. There's no plan on how to get through things like that. Something like that happens, you lose your number-one goalie, and most of all a friend. It sends the whole team into turmoil. What do you do? He was dead. You just try to cope with it after that."

The next day, on what was supposed to be their day off, Keenan got the players on the ice at the Coliseum.

"There was nothing else to do," Tim Kerr said. "Getting back out there on the ice was somewhat of a distraction at the time. It was the only place we could go where it wasn't an issue for a while."

Snider and GM Bob Clarke had chosen to leave all decisions related to the team to Keenan, the 36-year-old second-year coach.

"He was magnificent," Poulin said of Keenan. "He was stellar. His feel of the pulse of the team, and his decision-making process through that was just remarkable. He was at his best."

"Mike did an excellent job," Howe said. "He got the guys together at his house a couple times. If anybody watched Mike in practice, if the team made a bad pass or two bad passes, the whistle blew and you paid, because you weren't focused. We were practicing a few days later and we were as bad as a team can be, and Mike was patient with everybody. He kept everybody together."

On November 13, Lindbergh's funeral was held at the Gloria Dei (Old Swedes) Church on Delaware Avenue in Philadelphia.

Poulin delivered the eulogy: "We'll always carry him with us and draw from his energy.

"Pelle, we love you. We all love you."

Clarke and Jay Snider had discussed playing the Edmonton game as they would any other, to help foster a sense of normalcy and closure. But it was decided the proper thing to do for the fans, who had no other chance to bid farewell to Lindberg, was conduct a pregame memorial service.

The boards were stripped of advertising, and fans were given wallet-sized pictures of Lindbergh with a message written on the back: "In loving memory of Pelle Lindbergh. Our friend. Our goalie."

By sheer coincidence, Lindbergh's picture had been pre-printed on the tickets for that night's game. Rather than tear them, ushers put a black *X* on the back and returned them to fans.

Behind a wreath of flowers in the shape of Lindbergh's No. 31, Gene Hart led the service, saying the evening should be about "not the mourning of a death, but the celebration of a life."

After the service, the players were given a 15-minute chance to collect themselves. Then they returned to the ice for the game.

The Oilers had volunteered to postpone the game, but the Flyers players said the show must go on. In fact, it had to; it needed to. The ice was their safe haven from the horrors of reality.

"Once you step on the ice, everything else fades away," Howe said. "Just getting on the ice, your mind is on [the game], and your focus and your thoughts are there."

"The only thing Pelle would want us to do is go out and play great hockey," Propp added. "It was tough the first little while, then it was like someone got traded. You have to realize they're not going to be there anymore."

The game started tentatively, but once the skating, shooting and hitting began, the sole focus became the next play, the next shift.

The Flyers took a 1–0 lead late in the first when Poulin beat Mike Krushelnyski on an offensive-zone faceoff. The puck went back to Howe, who shot a wrister that went off the glove of goalie Andy Moog and into the net.

"I came back to the bench and remember sitting down and almost crying," Howe said. "The emotions of losing a teammate like that."

Ilkka Sinisalo and Propp scored early in the third to break a 1–1 tie, and Rich Sutter and Brad McCrimmon added goals to cap an emotional 5–3 win, a victory that pushed their forgotten win streak to 11.

But no win streak, no matter how long, could soothe the pain of their tremendous loss.

"We lost a little invincibility there," Poulin, who back then was the grizzled leader at the not-so-grizzled age of 26, said. "We had 19- and 20-year-olds, we had Tocchet, [Peter] Zezel, [Derrick] Smith, Craven—they were all so young. How could they not think they were invincible?"

"One thing that helped our team was the closeness of the team and leadership we had," Propp said. "We made sure we talked it out. We knew we had a job to do professionally. It was difficult. I still have a picture of Pelle in my office that I keep all the time. It's a shame."

CHELIOS LAYS OUT PROPP

Those who know Ron Hextall say there is a thick line that separates the man from the player.

The Flyers assistant general manager is a devoted husband and father to four children. That's far removed from the player who hacked and whacked his way to more than 500 penalty minutes, including an NHL record for goalies of 113 in the 1988–89 season.

"The only thing I think I can say was when I was on the ice I had a job to do, and I took my job very seriously," he said. "I'm opposite that off the ice, but on the ice I had a job to do, and I tried to do it to the best of my abilities. Sometimes my emotions got the best of me."

One of the most memorable of those moments occurred May 11, 1989, at the end of Game 6 of the Flyers' Wales Conference Finals loss to the Montreal Canadiens.

The bad blood had started in Game 1 of the series with spilled blood. Midway through the second period, Brian Propp skated into the left corner to clear the puck out of the Flyers' end. Montreal defenseman Chris Chelios skated toward Propp and left his feet to deliver a crushing elbow to Propp's jaw. The blow drove Propp's head into a metal glass support, knocking him unconscious. Propp dropped like a rock, with the back of his head bouncing off the ice like a basketball.

When teammates and medical personnel reached Propp and took off his helmet, blood began pouring from the back of the forward's head.

Referee Kerry Fraser made no call on the play, and Chelios told reporters after the game that Propp "was coming around the net and had just got rid of the puck when I hit him—I don't know how."

Propp was taken to Montreal General Hospital, where he was diagnosed with a concussion and a cut lip.

Two days later, Propp returned to the rink as the team skated. "These things happen in hockey," he said to reporters. "It's too important just to go out looking for revenge. We're looking for a win. That's the best way to get revenge."

While Chelios said he wasn't out to hurt anyone, Propp is sure it was a deliberate cheap shot. His anger hasn't dulled one iota in more than two decades since the play.

"I know it was [a cheap shot]," he said. "If you want to take a look at it, it's on YouTube.

COOPERALLS

The Flyers' uniform generally hasn't changed much in 45 years, but there was one notable exception.

For two seasons, starting in 1981–82, the Flyers wore Cooperalls, full-length pants that were supposed to be a more streamlined wardrobe. Instead, they looked like tuxedo pants and thankfully were banned by the league in 1983.

"At the time, I was the leading playoff scorer. There was no remorse, nothing. ... I have no respect for him."

Propp returned for Game 3 at the Spectrum, but that didn't stop the Canadiens from routing the Flyers and taking a 2–1 series lead. Game 4 also went to the Canadiens, with goalie Patrick Roy earning a 3–0 shutout that featured irate Flyers fans pelting the Canadiens bench with all manner of debris.

The Flyers won Game 5 when Dave Poulin knocked in the rebound of Gord Murphy's point shot at 5:02 of overtime, setting up Game 6 back at the Spectrum.

Scott Mellanby gave the Flyers a 1–0 first-period lead, but Jeff Chycrun accidentally put the puck behind Hextall on a Montreal power play, tying the game.

In the second, Bobby Smith scored with Ron Sutter in the penalty box to give Montreal the lead, and then Chelios took a drop pass from Bob Gainey and fired through a screened Hextall to make it 3–1.

Ryan Walter capped it for Montreal in the third when he finished a two-on-one break.

Propp scored with 6:05 left to make it 4–2, but any Flyers momentum was stopped when Sutter took a head-high run at Chelios with 3:42 left. Chelios got his stick up in time to block Sutter's stick from crashing into his skull, and the Flyer was sent off for high-sticking.

"It wasn't planned," Sutter said in *Full Spectrum*. "I just saw who it was, remembered what he had gotten away with on Proppie, and did it."

179

THE HOLMGREN GATES

The Spectrum always had the feel of a zoo. And to separate the animals, there were two steel gates between the locker rooms, which were separated by about 90 feet down a narrow hallway.

But the gates weren't always there. They were installed to prevent another riot like the one between the Flyers and Bruins in a 1977 preseason game.

Paul Holmgren fought Boston's Wayne Cashman, and the brawl spilled into the hallway. Holmgren, who thought Cashman had tried to gouge his eyes, charged after Cashman, who grabbed a stick out of the locker room to defend himself.

The next day, two steel gates, bolted to the floor and ceiling, were installed between the rooms. According to Pat Croce's book *I Feel Great*, they became known as the Holmgren Gates.

Also remembering was Hextall. He had watched Game 1 from the stands due to an injury.

"It was just a dirty hit," he said. "I respect the hell out of Chris Chelios, but that was a dirty hit. And obviously it could have been a lot worst for Proppie than it was, but it was bad. I have an attack mentality, and someone did something to one of my foot soldiers. I felt like there had to be retribution."

Hextall delivered that retribution in the final two minutes of the game. When Chelios brought the puck in offside, Hextall attacked. The goalie charged out of the net, waffled Chelios in the head with his blocker and began whaling away at him in the corner. The referees tackled the two combatants to the ice, and Hextall emerged from the pile missing his sweater and still screaming at Chelios.

As the pair was separated, Hextall threw his blocker at Chelios. That's when Roy skated into the fray, and he and Hextall began jawing at each other. Were it not for a linesman dragging Hextall to the Flyers' bench, the pair might have gone at it.

As Chelios was taken out through the Zamboni tunnel, fans pelted the ice with trash and chanted, "We want Chelios!"

Chelios, though, stayed in the locker room during the post-game handshake line for fear of further antagonizing the situation.

"You never know what to expect with Hextall," Chelios said after the game. "But I saw him and was ready. I was fortunate I didn't get a skate in the head or anything."

Hextall was unrepentant for his action. "Did you see what he did to Brian Propp?" he said after the game. "Come on, I think we owed him something. God almighty, he just about took [Propp's] head off. I think that's good enough reason."

Flyers general manager Bob Clarke backed his goalie, saying, "I don't think you like to see a series end on that type of incident, but we like the fact that a player will stand up for one of his teammates."

For his outburst, Hextall was hit with a 12-game suspension, at the time the fourth-longest ban in NHL history, a decision which still rankles Propp.

"Chelios never got anything for [the hit]. Hextall threw his blocker and he gets suspended for 12 games at the beginning of the next year, which really hurt our club," he said. "That was the most ridiculous thing I've ever seen the league do."

Years later, a far more mature Hextall admitted that perhaps he went a bit too far.

"I look back and think, 'How could I be so into it to do that?'... The guy almost killed my teammate. Did I overreact? I don't know. Would I like to take it back? I don't know."

ROGER NEILSON'S PAINFUL ADMISSION

During his tenure as Flyers coach, Roger Neilson had pulled off the amazing goal of achieving détente at the height of the Cold War between Bob Clarke and Eric Lindros. Clarke considered Neilson a good friend, while Lindros viewed Neilson as his biggest supporter in the organization.

"As a person, you always know you've got someone to trust," Lindros told reporters. "Roger means a lot to me—coming to the rink every day and knowing someone is there who is honest with you. He knows when to kick you in the butt to get you going and when to pat you on the back when you need it. Never too high, never too low. And he always keeps things humorous."

Neilson even made cancer a joke.

The coach had fought a persistent sinus infection through the early part of the 1999–2000 season; he eventually beat that bug, but never felt right. Further tests diagnosed multiple myeloma, a form of bone cancer; the announcement was made December 10, 1999.

Neilson, known for his goofy ties and even goofier personality, told his players in a manner consistent with his persona—he showed them a video which featured Chris Therien's embarrassing attempt to fight from the previous game, which included the defenseman flopping and flailing, and at one point having his back to the player he was trying to slug it out with. Interspersed were scenes of the Black Knight losing his arms and legs from the film *Monty Python and the Holy Grail*. Laughter could be heard echoing throughout the Flyers' practice facility.

When it was over, Neilson told his players about his cancer.

"Everyone is laughing, and then all of a sudden Roger tells us," Craig Berube told reporters that day.

While doctors believed Neilson could be cured, the entire organization was devastated. "I couldn't believe how positive and upbeat he was," Lindros said then.

A visibly shaken Clarke added, "He's such a good man, a good person."

Neilson was put on a regimen of chemotherapy and decided to coach through the pain. The plan was for the treatments to go on for three months; if after that time they weren't working, Neilson then would need a bone-marrow transplant. That plan, though, was shelved, and it was determined that Neilson would have to leave the team in late February to have the transplant procedure.

"He should be able to make it back for the playoffs," Dr. Isadore Brodsky, chief of oncology hematology at Hahnemann University Hospital in Philadelphia, told reporters.

It also was decided that assistant coach Craig Ramsay would stand in for Neilson during the coach's absence.

Neilson's last game was February 19, 2000, a 4–2 defeat of the Washington Capitals. He told his players that morning that it would be his last regular-season game.

"I think it was Mark Recchi who said in the locker room before we went out, to win this one for Roger," goalie Brian Boucher told reporters. "It'll be his last game for a long time. I think we were really inspired by that."

The Flyers didn't miss a beat when Ramsay took over, winning 16 of their final 25 regular-season games.

Unfortunately, this is where the real ugliness comes into play.

On April 10, the day after the end of the regular season, Neilson told Clarke he felt healthy enough to resume his coaching duties. However, Clarke and the doctors weren't so sure. Neilson spent Game 1 of the first-round series against the Buffalo Sabres advising Ramsay and fellow assistant Wayne Cashman via headset from the press box. But after Game 1, Neilson left for his home in Dallas, saying he didn't want to be a distraction to the team.

The Flyers walked through the Sabres in five games, setting up a semifinal match with the Pittsburgh Penguins.

Neilson again said he felt strong enough to return, but Clarke didn't want to make a big change during what had potential to be a long playoff run, so he made the decision to keep things status quo for the remainder of the postseason. In other words, Ramsay

LAUREN HART'S CANCER

On January 5, 2000, six months after watching her father succumb to cancer, Lauren Hart was diagnosed with non-Hodgkin's lymphoma.

Lauren, who has sung the national anthem before Flyers home games since 1997, vowed to stay on, and on January 15, 2000, she received a louder ovation than normal when she sang before a game against the Devils.

As she walked off the ice, there to greet her was coach Roger Neilson, who just a month earlier had been diagnosed with cancer.

was the head coach for the rest of the playoffs, and Neilson would continue to advise from the above.

"You can't make a change when the team is going good," Clarke told reporters. "Roger knows that."

It wasn't a scenario Neilson had foreseen, or one he was pleased with. He had intimated to reporters that during a meeting with Clarke after the regular season that a new two-year contract had been verbally agreed to. Neilson's original deal, signed when he was hired in March 1998, was set to end after the 2000 playoffs. Clarke, though, said no deal had been made, and that nothing would be discussed until the season was over.

The next day, April 25, 2000, Neilson was asked about his job status during an interview with a Toronto radio station. He replied, "I don't think they want a cancer patient who's a friend of Eric Lindros behind the bench right now."

All through Neilson's illness, the battles had restarted between Lindros and his family and Clarke and the Flyers. Lindros was suffering through another concussion, and in early March had started a firestorm when he criticized the club's training and medical staff. Neilson's past loyalty to the player apparently pushed him onto the Lindros side in the war, and the coach viewed his diminished status with the organization as punishment.

Clarke said Neilson's relationship with Lindros and his coaching status were completely unrelated. Neilson himself said the statement was meant as a joke that just didn't go over well. Clarke and team CEO Ron Ryan accepted Neilson's response, but the peace wouldn't last long.

Neilson watched from the press box as the Flyers advanced past Pittsburgh but then fell apart after taking a 3–1 series lead against the New Jersey Devils in the Eastern Conference Finals.

After the series ended, Neilson said he either wanted his old job back with the Flyers or an early release from his contract so he could seek work elsewhere.

"I still want to be a head coach," Neilson told reporters. "If not here, then somewhere else."

The Flyers made Ramsay the full-time coach, and Neilson signed on as an assistant coach with the Ottawa Senators. He substituted for Jacques Martin for two games in the 2001–02 season to reach the milestone of 1,000 career games coached.

Not long after, however, Neilson's cancer returned, this time as skin cancer, and the great coach, a pioneer in his field, died June 21, 2003.

THE BARBER REVOLT

Bill Barber was the epitome of a team-first person. As a player, coach or front-office executive, Barber always saw the crest on the front of his sweater as far more important than the name on the back.

Barber's Hall of Fame career ended after a serious knee injury in 1984, but that only started his second life as a Flyer.

"I said to Clarkie [GM Bob Clarke], put me where you need me. It doesn't matter," he said. Clarke first utilized Barber's hockey mind as coach of the team's AHL affiliate, the Hershey Bears, than as an NHL assistant coach and director of pro scouting. When the Philadelphia Phantoms were born in 1996, Barber was named the team's first coach. In Barber's four seasons, the Phantoms won at least 44 games, and won the Calder Cup in 1998.

When the Flyers started slowly in the 2000–01 season, coach Craig Ramsay was let go, and Barber stepped into the breach. He inspired the team to a 31–13–7–3 finish (after a 12–12–4–0 start under Ramsay), a 100-point season, and a second-place finish in the Atlantic Division. Barber won the Jack Adams Award as the NHL's best coach.

The playoffs, though, were a different story. The Flyers couldn't solve Dominik Hasek and the Buffalo Sabres, losing twice in overtime and suffering an embarrassing 8–0 loss in Game 6 in Buffalo.

As bad as things were on the ice, it was nothing compared to what was going on at the Barber home. Barber's wife, Jenny, had been diagnosed with lung cancer in April 2001. Bill told few people—and almost none of his players—because he didn't want to cause a distraction. Instead, he came to work every day.

Bill and Jenny Barber had met when both were teenagers and Bill was playing for Jenny's hometown Kitchener Rangers of the

Ontario Hockey League. They were married when Bill was 21 and Jenny was 20. They bought a house in Cherry Hill shortly after Bill began playing for the Flyers in 1972.

"It was a high school–type romance," Orest Kindrachuk, who roomed with Barber when they were in the minors, told the *Courier Post*. "Nowadays those romances don't last. This one did."

"We knew his wife was not doing well," Chuck Gormley, the longtime Flyers reporter for the *Courier Post*, said, "but we didn't know how bad she was doing. He let us in a couple times. He let us in on how she was feeling, [but] not very often. He wanted to keep it business."

Jenny's condition worsened early in the fall of 2001, but Bill stayed with the team, never missing a game and rarely skipping a practice. He always said that's what Jenny wanted.

At 12:05 PM, on Saturday, December 8, 2001, Jenny Barber, Bill Barber's wife of 28 years and mother of the couple's two children, lost her battle with cancer. She was just 48 years old.

The Flyers had a game that afternoon against the Minnesota Wild. For Bill Barber, the only place he could have been, should have been, was behind the bench. And when the puck dropped at 3:00 PM, there he was, coaching his team.

"We heard that morning in the press box before the game that she had passed away," Gormley said. "When I saw him on the bench, I couldn't believe it. How you coach in those circumstances is beyond me. Especially when you know he's a good husband and father."

After the game, Barber allowed people to see into his emotionally ravaged soul.

"She was a champion," he said. "I'll miss her more than anyone knows."

Few players knew Jenny had died that morning, but Barber's late arrival that afternoon clued them in.

"He was a little late to the game, and we knew what the situation was, but we didn't know the finality of it," forward Paul Ranheim told reporters. "After the game, Keith [Primeau] gave him the team puck. Billy said a couple words. It was very emotional."

"We can't even imagine or fathom the intense stress this caused him," Primeau said that afternoon. As team captain, he was one of a handful of players who knew of Jenny's passing before the game. "His only release was to come to the rink. Bill Barber has two passions, his family and the Philadelphia Flyers."

"After that game I walked down to the coaches' room, and it's the only time I've ever walked down to the coaches' room, to offer my condolences," Gormley said. "He [Barber] showed me a ring that his wife had given him, and he had it around his neck on a chain, and he said something like, I'm never going to take this off. It was something that you could see how much he was impacted by this."

Barber was encouraged to take time off from the stress of his job, but instead did what he always did. He showed up for work.

"It's not like this was a sudden thing," he said. "This was going on for a long, long time. As a family we stood tall for what we believed and we prepared ourselves right to the very end. We were all mentally stable and understood what really happened here. It's not like it was happening that day. This was going on for around seven months. The family prepared, I was prepared. I didn't let anything family-wise intrude on the team.

"Time off? Where would it lead? My honest opinion is it would have went worse."

At the time, Gormley was one of the people who believed time away was the right thing. Years later, he can understand why Barber chose to stay.

"When we asked him why you would coach, he said, 'My wife understands how much this team means to me, and this is my way of dealing with stress.' ... She gave him her blessing to do whatever he wanted to and whatever he needed to do. How can you take that away from somebody? It's easy to criticize somebody for that, but until you've been through that situation, you can't. He did what he felt was right."

Barber did his best to keep his personal issues out of the locker room. The team finished the 2001–02 season 42–27–10–3 (30–19–5–2 after Jenny's death), and captured the Atlantic Division title and the second seed in the playoffs. The seventh-seeded Ottawa

Senators were their first-round playoff opponent, but that's where things fell apart.

After scoring 234 goals, fifth-most in the conference, the Flyers started handling the puck like it was a concrete block. They scored just once on the underwhelming Patrick Lalime through the first four games of the series—an overtime marker by Ruslan Fedotenko in Game 1.

The Flyers scored just one other goal in the five-game series, and were shut out for a remarkable 243:53 in regulation. Dan McGillis' goal at 3:53 of the first period of Game 5 was the only time the Flyers scored in regulation.

The Flyers lost Games 2, 3, and 4 by identical 3–0 scores, with Game 4 marred by goalie Roman Cechmanek skating to center ice and screaming at his teammates on the bench.

Brian Boucher started Game 5, and after McGillis gave the Flyers the 1–0 lead, Daniel Alfredsson scored late in the first, and Martin Havlat netted the overtime winner.

The series was over, but the Flyers still were firing shots.

A group of disgruntled players first complained about Barber to Clarke and team chairman Ed Snider, then took their issues public.

"There were a lot of problems," Boucher told reporters. "Not only in the playoffs, but in the last two, two and a half months. There were meetings about meetings ... and it seemed like nothing ever got solved.

"Everybody made suggestions, what we felt we needed, and I think for the most part we felt we didn't get it. I know that people are saying that the players are crybabies, but we're players and we needed to be led in the direction that the players suggested. It was frustrating because it wasn't just something that popped up at the end."

The players said the problems went back as far as October, and that in the final two months of the season, Primeau said he and Rick Tocchet, rather than the coaching staff, began making in-game adjustments between periods.

"You can't have 20 guys coaching," Mark Recchi said. "You have to have one guy take charge. It was very tough. ... It's been

COACHING CAROUSEL

When Fred Shero was hired as Flyers coach in 1971, *Philadelphia Inquirer* columnist Frank Dolson called Ed Snider the "Charlie Finley of the Atlantic Seaboard," for changing coaches so often.

Shero was the third coach in the first five seasons of the franchise.

That's nothing compared to what Bob Clarke accomplished between 1997 and 2002, when he went through five head coaches.

After 61 games in 1997–98, Wayne Cashman was replaced by Roger Neilson. Neilson's illness ended his Flyers tenure in favor of Craig Ramsay 57 games into the 1999–2000 season. Ramsay was fired 28 games into the 2000–01 campaign, replaced by Bill Barber. Barber was fired at the end of the 2001–02 season, replaced by Ken Hitchcock.

a very tough year for him [Barber]. I know that; we all know that. And that's probably why we left it as long as we did. You have to respect the man for what he went through and how he handled it, but ultimately, things didn't get done at the end."

Primeau had a number of meetings with Barber about what the players felt needed to be done.

"[The power play] was one issue," Primeau told reporters. "We had the worst power play in the league; why are we not practicing it?

"Then there were the systems, and the tirades on the bench. All season long we said we know when we make mistakes out there and we're getting yelled at. We say when we come to the bench make the adjustment, and he wants the players to make the adjustments. Well, our job is to play."

According to Primeau, any time he brought ideas from the locker room to the coaching staff, Barber's response was, "Don't make suggestions. Work harder."

"All season long we tried to be on the same page and get the situation addressed," Primeau said. "So that's why everyone is so discouraged, because our thoughts weren't accepted.

"We go in there and say, 'Look, we'll do whatever is asked, we just want to be led, just lead us in the right direction. Do the things that will make us successful.' Then we hope that occurs, and we felt we were spinning our wheels."

When asked why he went public with his complaints, Primeau said, "I'm sticking up on behalf of my teammates because I want to walk out of here with my pride intact."

"The fact that the captain did that showed everyone there was a real problem," Gormley said. "That would not ordinarily be addressed like that. That he addressed it like that spoke volumes that Barber wouldn't be back if everyone felt that way."

Barber refused to comment on his players' biting barbs, and days later was fired. The loyal soldier, the player who took below-market contracts to stay with the team, the man who said put me anywhere, let me help, I just want this organization to win, was dumped after 30 years of faithful service.

Barber landed on his feet, spending the next six years as director of player personnel with the Tampa Bay Lightning, and got his name inscribed on the Stanley Cup for a third time when the Lightning won it in 2004. He returned to the Flyers in 2008 as a scouting consultant, a job he continues to hold. He also remains a regular presence at Flyers home games.

"I had a year and a half here [as coach] from the NHL standpoint, but it was good. I enjoyed it," he said. "Times were tough, expectations were high, and we fell short. There's no secret to it. As a coach you have to take responsibility for that, and as a coach I had no problem understanding the direction they were going. I was on a different page at the time, to be honest. I know what it takes to win, and I'll stand my ground on that. It was unfortunate that I had to go, but it was time to move on."

For his part, Primeau said he'd like to have a mulligan on his public tirade against Barber.

"I grew up in Toronto and I was a huge Darryl Sittler fan," Primeau said. "He was captain of the Maple Leafs and a Hall of Famer and all those things that I loved about the Toronto Maple Leafs. [My dad] said to picture somebody coming out and saying something about Darryl Sittler, and that really put it into perspective for me.

"My thought process when all of that was taking place, I was going to let people on the outside see exactly what was going on in our locker room, and that was probably the wrong thing to do. As a player you don't want to be called out on the carpet by your coach, and that's basically what happened, and it was now public knowledge. And whether I was defending teammates or speaking the truth because I was the leader in the locker room, it could have been handled differently."

Boucher, 25 at the time, also believed he should have handled the situation differently.

"I answered the questions honestly," he said. "But as an athlete you should know better how to handle questions and whether you want to answer questions honestly or be politically correct.

"I have regrets about how I answered those questions. Looking back on it now, being an older guy, it was unprofessional how I handled it."

For Barber, there are no hard feelings. He said he still speaks to Clarke and holds Ed Snider in the highest regard.

"There's no peace factor involved," Barber said. "It was time for me to move on. ... I have no complaints."

TERTYSHNY AND HART—TRAGEDY TIMES TWO

In more than 45 years of Flyers hockey, no single time period could have been worse than the month of July 1999.

In a nine-day double-barrel shotgun blast of tragedy, the club lost a giant piece of its past and a potential piece of its future.

Gene Hart, 68, the team's broadcaster from the club's inception until his retirement in 1995, passed away from liver cancer and kidney failure on July 14, 1999.

Nine days later, on July 23, defenseman Dmitri Tertyshny was killed in a boating accident at the far-too-young age of 22.

Hart was a hockey minstrel, spreading the gospel of the sport throughout the Delaware Valley. His voice was the one coming through the transistor radio as children huddled in their beds, staying up far too late to listen to games. His voice was the one that filled smoky bars and living rooms from Allentown to Cape May, from Cherry Hill to Conshohocken. His voice provides the soundtrack to fans' personal highlight reels.

"I would fall asleep with Flyers games," said the one-named Eklund, the anonymous proprietor of the popular hockey Web site Hockeybuzz.com. Eklund was a hockey fanatic growing up in Cherry Hill in the early 1970s. "I would put the [radio] underneath my pillow. The old AM dials would give off heat, and my parents would worry that I would start a fire."

Joe Watson remembered a Flyers fan who told him that when he went to college in South Carolina during the heyday of the Broad Street Bullies, the student would try to find the highest point in the area to pick up the games on WCAU radio. That was the length people would go to hear Gene Hart's voice.

"We used to turn the television down and put the radio on," Al Piazza, a life-long South Philadelphia resident and 45-year Flyers fan, said of the days when Hart was shifted from TV to radio. "You didn't want to hear anybody else."

Hart was hired in 1967 only because the team didn't have enough money to employ a better-known Canadian broadcaster.

"And," Hart said in a 1992 interview, "they needed someone who wasn't too concerned with how much money he made or didn't make."

He got the job for $50 a game that first season, and went on to call every Flyers game, either on TV or radio, between 1967 and 1995. Along the way his calls became synonymous with Flyers hockey, whether it was joyously counting down the seconds to the Flyers' first Stanley Cup in 1974, or his signature sign-off, "Good night, and good hockey."

"When they went to the Final against Edmonton [in 1987], I remember saying to my parents, we have to listen to Gene tonight," Eklund said. "Because if the Flyers win the Stanley Cup tonight, I have to hear Gene Hart call it. It's got to be Gene Hart calling it."

Hart's most memorable call came May 19, 1974, when he proclaimed over and over: "The Flyers win the Stanley Cup! The Flyers win the Stanley Cup!"

"His voice kept getting stronger and louder," Flyers chairman Ed Snider said in a story accompanying Hart's death, "And to this day, I think it remains one of the greatest calls in sports I've ever heard."

As the voice of the Flyers, everyone became Gene Hart's friend. He was their link to the Flyers family, making him a kind of wizened old uncle to the masses.

"We didn't know hockey. It was a foreign sport," Eklund said. "The fact that he had this passion for it and made you love it, that's what Gene Hart did for the city. He taught us to love hockey, and that taught us to learn everything about it. I think Hart should be up there with [Bob] Clarke and [Bernie] Parent and Snider. If there were four pillars that made hockey work in Philadelphia, he should be there."

And when he died, a part of them died with him.

"There's not a single game where someone doesn't come up to me and say I loved your father," Lauren Hart, a Wells Fargo Center staple since she began singing the national anthem before every game during the 1997–98 season, said. "He became a friend to people in a way that sportscasters don't do anymore. People always come to me and say, 'I hope you don't mind but ...' It's my fear when people stop and forget him. It's especially exciting when a younger fan comes up and is informed and knows because their parents or brother or sister has passed it on.

"It's really moving. When I'm in the building ... they're playing the clips, to hear him, his great voice. Inevitably someone will come up to me and say, 'When I was a little boy, my dad and I would watch together.' It was a coming of age, a passing of time. The birth of the Flyers, having a championship so early in their history, really cemented [the relationship] in a way that is so unusual. It doesn't happen with lots of teams. Because it happened during the time my father was teaching everybody the game, people feel such an amazing connection."

Players also were fond of Hart.

"He would bring up games that you played in that you wouldn't even remember," Eric Lindros told reporters at the time of Hart's death. "He remembered every little detail."

Lindros was so fond of Hart that he drove two hours from his lakeside cottage in Ontario to Toronto to fly back to Philadelphia for the funeral.

And Hart was as devoted to the club as any player who ever wore the sweater.

"What convinced me to hire him was that Gene had a tremendous amount of enthusiasm, even though he didn't have a major background in the sport," Snider told reporters. "We knew he'd do a fabulous job for us. A lot of people don't realize that for about 10 years, he would do games on the road and then take a red-eye back to New Jersey to teach school the next day."

For years the Flyers simulcast Hart's radio call on television, but in 1988 they added a separate TV broadcast, pushing Hart and partner Bob Taylor to radio. In response to a survey the club sent to season-ticket holders, fans said the one thing they would change is for Gene Hart to be on television; their wish was granted when he worked on the telecasts from 1993 to 1995.

Hart called more than 2,000 Flyers games, including six Stanley Cup Finals; he was inducted into the Flyers Hall of Fame in 1992 and the Hockey Hall of Fame in 1997. And the press box at Wells Fargo Center is named in his honor.

He retired from the broadcast booth after the 1994–95 season, but worked in various capacities for the team, including as the man at the microphone when the Philadelphia Phantoms won the Calder Cup in 1998.

That would be the last call he would make; fittingly, the champion broadcaster went out with a championship call.

A memorial service was held days after his death, attended by more than 2,000 fans, not to mention present and former Flyers, the club's front office, media members and friends from Gene's other loves—members of the Opera Company of Philadelphia and the Philadelphia Orchestra performed throughout the service.

"When you think of Gene Hart," Snider told the audience, "you think Flyers."

The team chairman then used Hart's own words from years earlier, when Hart had led Pelle Lindbergh's memorial service, as a reminder of the true purpose of the ceremonies.

"Rather than mourn," Snider said, quoting Hart, "we are here to celebrate the life that enriched all of us."

While Gene Hart was a legend in Philadelphia and beyond, Dmitri Tertyshny was a little-known Russian-born defenseman hoping to make an impact in North America.

Tertysnhy was taken in the sixth round of the 1995 draft by the Flyers, but stayed in Russia for three more seasons, playing for his hometown team, Chelyabinsk. He came to the Flyers for the 1998–99 season, and in 62 games had two goals, 10 points and 30 penalty minutes. At 6'2" and 180 pounds, the only thing that stood out about Tertyshny was his stringy, collar-length black hair. His teammates called him Tree, more as a play on his name, but apt enough to describe his frame.

While not considered one of their prime prospects, the Flyers were interested enough in Tertyshny to send him on a retreat to Kelowna, British Columbia, with other players and prospects for a two-week skating and conditioning camp run by strength coach Jim McCrossin and skating coach David Roy.

On the final day of the camp, Tertyshny and two team-mates, Francis Belanger and Mikhail Chernov, rented a 17-foot boat for a ride around Okanagan Lake. Belanger was driving the boat when it hit a wake. Tertyshny was thrown over the front of the boat, which then went right over top of him. Tertyshny was mangled by the motor's propeller; he made it back to the boat, but the blades had, among other gruesome damage, sliced both his carotid artery and jugular vein. He bled to death on the boat.

Many of Tertyshny's teammates were at John LeClair's golf tournament in Vermont when they got the news. The grim task of informing them fell to Eric Lindros and Rod Brind'Amour. As team captain, it also was Lindros' unenviable job of expressing the players' condolences, with the help of a Russian interpreter, to Tertyshny's family, including his wife Polina, now a far-too-young widow who at the time was pregnant with the couple's first child.

Lindros described Tertyshny as, "a real gamer. Consistent. A terrific person. Kind of quiet with a great sense of humor. He was outgoing; his wife was just wonderful. He'll certainly be missed.

... He always put the team first, always worked extra hard. He was going to be an All-Star one day."

CHRIS PRONGER

Lots of players have pulled on orange and black Flyers jerseys since the Broad Street Bullies last dominated the NHL, but none would have fit in with that memorable crew like Chris Pronger.

"I think he was born to wear orange," former NHL GM Brian Burke, who played for the Flyers' AHL team at the tail end of the Broad Street Bullies era, told NHL.com. "He's got the whole package—size and skill, as well as being a leader. But the fans in Philadelphia will love that mean streak he brings to every game."

Pronger didn't just have a mean streak—his whole persona was mean. A five-time All-Star who won the Norris and Hart trophies in 2000—he's only the seventh blueliner to win League MVP honors—he had helped the Edmonton Oilers reach the Stanley Cup Final in 2006, his first season there, and helped the Anaheim Ducks win the Cup the following season, his first with that team.

The hope was Pronger's snarl, skill and experience was the missing element the Flyers needed, so the team dealt forward Joffrey Lupul, defenseman Luca Sbisa, first-round picks in 2009 and 2010, and future considerations to the Anaheim Ducks for Pronger on June 26, 2009.

"I think Chris Pronger is still one of the top defensemen in the league," Flyers GM Paul Holmgren said after making the deal. "I think he makes everyone around him better. He's a winner, he's won a championship. He's a tremendous character player, he works hard. I wanted a guy who would make life miserable for the other team. Chris is one of those guys."

Holmgren showed just how much he thought of Pronger 10 days after acquiring him by signing the 34-year-old to a seven-year, $34.55 million contract.

"I am very excited to be able to retire a Philadelphia Flyer and I am looking forward to many years with the Flyers logo on my chest," Pronger said that day.

Pronger arrived with a reputation for being, as teammate Braydon Coburn put it, "the alpha dog."

"I knew he was a great guy," Coburn said. "I knew that from talking with other guys, that he was a great leader. Seemed liked everywhere he went, he won. He was a great leader. Prongs doesn't take shit from anybody. He's his own man."

Teammates weren't the only ones Pronger wasn't taking any guff from. His sparring sessions with reporters were a constant source of amusement. Tim Panaccio of CSNPhilly.com even wrote a column on the daily interactions between Pronger and the media during the 2010 Stanley Cup Final, writing how "the banter with Pronger is exactly what [the media] want. We live for it. So does Pronger. ... Only a handful—usually the Canadian writers—seemed to 'get it' with Pronger. That his daily routine with the Philly media ... was an act. Designed to entertain at the Cup Final."

Pronger's sometimes-abrasive personality first made a few of his own teammates fairly miserable. An up-and-down 2009–10 season reportedly was marred by clashes between Pronger and team captain Mike Richards. Whether those issues were real or not, that became as much of a story as anything the team accomplished on the ice.

Pronger finished with a team-best plus-22 rating and was third with 55 points while playing all 82 games. However, the team suffered through coaching and goaltending changes and only made the playoffs after a final-day shootout win against the New York Rangers.

In the playoffs Pronger stole the headlines on and off the ice. He led all defensemen with 18 points, and led the League by playing an average of 29:03 per game, including eight games of over 30 minutes of ice time. Just as memorable were his off-ice antics. After the Blackhawks won Game 1 of the Stanley Cup Final—the team's first win in the Final since 1973—Pronger snagged the puck at the final buzzer. He did it again after the Blackhawks won Game 2, nearly starting a melee as in response to the Hawks' Ben Eager yapping at him, Pronger flipped a towel at Eager as he skated off the ice.

When asked what he did with the puck after Game 2, Pronger replied, "It's in the garbage—where it belongs." When asked about enraging Eager, he added, "Apparently it got him upset. ... It's too bad. I guess little things amuse little minds."

"I don't have a problem with it," Richards said of Pronger's thievery. "If he wants to grab the puck, let him have the puck. It's kind of funny. You can tell him not to take it if you want, but I'm not going to."

The move clearly was calculated to put the focus of the media on Pronger, rather than his struggling teammates, who were down 2–0 in the series.

"I'm sure there's a method," Danny Briere said. "He seems to be disturbing a lot of people. We're a team that disturbs a lot of people. I guess he fits right in."

Whether the ploy worked or not, the Flyers responded by winning Games 3 and 4 in Philadelphia to even the series. Game 5, however, was a different story. Pronger was a career-worst minus-5—he was on the ice for six goals and in the penalty box for a seventh as the Blackhawks won 7–4.

If Pronger was upset, disappointed or angry, he showed none of it after the game, telling reporters, "I'm day-to-day with hurt feelings."

The next day provided a little more salt in the wounds, as the Chicago Tribune ran a full-page poster of Pronger wearing a black practice jersey and a figure-skating skirt, with the tagline, "Looks like Tarzan, skates like Jane."

Pronger was nonplussed, saying, "I don't read what you guys write, good or bad. ... I really couldn't care to be honest with you. I'm worried about playing the game."

Despite his best efforts, the Flyers lost the series in Game 6, bringing an end to a memorable first season for Pronger in Philadelphia.

"I wasn't sure what this group of fine young soldiers was going to be like," Pronger said. "It was a lot of fun. Obviously a bit of a tough start to my first year, but good things in life are never easy."

Sadly, that first season was as good as it would get for Pronger. The next 10 months would see Pronger undergo four surgeries and play just 50 regular-season games, the fewest since knee and wrist injuries limited him to just five games in 2002–03.

He had knee surgery in July, which sidelined him for all of training camp and the first two regular-season games. He missed a month after breaking his right foot in December, and in March had surgery on a broken hand that sidelined him the last month of the regular season and the first five games of the playoffs. He came back for the final two games in the first round to help the Flyers get past the Buffalo Sabres in the first round, then left the lineup after the first game of the second round against the Boston Bruins with a back injury that led to surgery to repair a herniated disc, which had been impinging on a nerve root and causing pain and weakness in his leg.

"[Rehabilitation] was an option, but in order for me to try and play hockey again it was pretty cut and dry," Pronger said. "I could have went through the whole summer rehab and get another steroid injection and see if that calms the nerve down, but it was a pretty bad herniated disc. The odds of it becoming an issue again were very high."

Pronger said spending as much time rehabilitating as playing was a drag, but he was determined to return healthy for the 2011–12 season.

"I felt good when I played this year," he said after the back surgery. "That's the funny thing—every time I started to feel better and started to get my feet underneath me and get back into the groove, I had another injury. ... Mentally I feel like I can play. When I was healthy, my play speaks for itself. It's a matter of staying healthy. This year was very tough. Every time I turned around I had another injury. It wasn't like it was a bump and a bruise, it was something broken that needed surgery to fix. That can be a little disappointing and frustrating, when you know you can still play at a high level and your play speaks to that and you're not able to go out and play. That's tough, especially when you feel like you can add another element to the team when you're out there. Mentally I've got a lot left; it's how my back feels. Basically, if the surgery works and I am able to train properly and get healthy, I don't see why I can't continue to play as long as I want, as long as everything else holds up."

Pronger was named team captain in the preseason, and his health was where he wanted it to be at the start of the 2011–12 season. Entering the eighth game of the season, against the Toronto Maple Leafs on October 24 in Philadelphia, he had a goal and six assists.

With 8:02 left in the first period, Pronger was pursuing a puck in the Philadelphia end along with Toronto's Mikhail Grabovski. Grabovski got to the puck first and took a shot, but on the follow-through the blade of Grabovski's stick hit Pronger in the right eye.

Pronger immediately sprinted off the ice, with one person working between the Flyers' bench and the locker room reporting hearing "terrifying" screams as Pronger went past them.

"It's scary," Scott Hartnell said, "You get a high stick, especially around the eye, it's a dangerous thing. ... Hopefully he is all right."

"Unfortunately I've been around to see when guys get pucks or sticks or whatever in the eye, you always kind of hold your breath because it's always scary and such a sensitive part of the body," Braydon Coburn said. "You can tell that something was wrong right away, the reaction he had. You don't see that reaction very often."

Once the initial shock wore off, Pronger's vision returned to normal, and he missed just over two weeks, returning for a game November 9 in Tampa Bay. More problems struck, though, in his fourth game back, November 17 against the Phoenix Coyotes. With 2:09 left in the third period, Pronger chased a puck in the defensive zone with Coyotes' Martin Hanzal in pursuit. Pronger got to the puck first, but Hanzal arrived with a big check that sent Pronger head-first into wall, where his face appeared to strike the metal stanchion between the planes of Plexiglas.

The hit left Pronger on his hands and knees, but after a second he was back to his feet, finished his shift and played his usual complement of minutes in the third period. However,

Pronger played just one more game, two days later in Winnipeg. When the team returned home he was scratched from the lineup, with the cause being a virus. His recovery from that was delayed by surgery to fix a bothersome left knee issue, sidelining him until after Christmas.

Despite yet another injury absence, Holmgren said in announcing the knee surgery that he wasn't worried about Pronger's long-term health.

"I think Chris is a player who takes good care of himself, looks after himself, does the proper rehabilitation and conditioning to stay in top shape," Holmgren said. "Long-term, I still think Chris has a lot of miles left on his body. Based on his attitude about this and the way he takes care of himself, I believe he'll be fine."

Days later, it was revealed that Pronger was far from fine.

On December 15, Holmgren announced Pronger would miss the remainder of the 2011–12 season due to "severe post-concussion syndrome."

Pronger almost immediately disappeared from the public eye—as he said, "I kind of went dark there for a while." He moved back to St. Louis with his wife and children to be closer to his wife's family, and refused to speak publicly about his health for 16 months. In March 2013 he finally opened up about his condition.

"I don't think the eyesight part will [come back]," he said. "The peripheral vision has not come back. My eye is not functioning. ... And that makes me dizzy when I do a lot of different things. I get lightheaded. That's probably the biggest thing posing a lot of problems for me right now.

"I've made improvements. I still have [concussion] symptoms. I still get symptoms with loud noises and a lot of moving parts, bright lights, things like that. Not to the level it was, but I still do get them. There's a lot of things that have gotten better. My eye is still troubling. It's not working properly. I don't have peripheral vision. I don't have a lot of the things that have worked well for me in the past."

Pronger said the worst part of his recovery was the first six months, when depression was a major issue.

"You get headaches, you start not wanting to do anything, you get a little depressed," he said. "You're not able to work out; you're not able to do anything you want to do. You try to work out and you get nauseous and a headache and you want to go lay down. It's an awkward feeling and something ... when you have an experience you don't fully understand what [the doctors are] talking about, it can be debilitating. I think the biggest part is the depression and how you feel about yourself and how you feel about the injury and how dark you go down."

During that time period, Pronger admitted to not being the father and husband he should have been.

"You get agitated very quickly," he said. "When the symptoms start piling up, you start getting a headache and it gets loud in the house, there's bright lights, kids running around screaming [Pronger and his wife have two sons, ages 10 and 8, and a 4-year-old daughter], all that stuff, you are on edge as it is. You're pissed off that you are not playing the game you love, you're pissed off that you can't go do what you want to do every day. Then you are even more pissed off because you've got a headache and it's getting worse and worse and your eyes are bothering you and you're light-headed and dizzy and your kid comes over and you snap. You're not being the father that you want to be. It changes your personality a little bit. I've gotten a little better with it. But I still get a *grrr* on from time to time and got to catch myself, kind of take myself out of the room and make sure I'm a little better."

But Pronger said as his condition has improved, his home life has gotten better. And while he can't do much physical activity—anything strenuous that gets his heart rate up still brings on the concussion symptoms—he said he was beginning to push himself just a bit more in order to keep healing.

"I'm at the stage now where they want me to push the envelope to see where symptoms occur," he said. "I get up, I have breakfast, go work out, go to my eye appointment, come home, relax for a couple hours, and then go get my kids from school and start carpooling them around to their different activities and things they do. Really it's just about pushing the envelope a little bit, doing a little bit more, and then when I have symptoms back off a little bit and keep trying to move the threshold."

However, it's near certain that the one threshold he'll never cross is the one that allows him to play again.

"I've got no regrets," he said. "I played to the best of my ability. Played to win and was fortunate enough to have won a Stanley Cup and a couple gold medals and played on some really good teams. ... I'm not going to look back and say I wish I could have done this or that. I can say I left the game, if that is it, with nothing to prove.

"I have to continue to work at trying to get healthy and that's my main focus and goal. We'll see what happens."

If what happens is retirement, it comes after just 171 games in three seasons with the Flyers; however, his impact on the players around him will be felt for a long time.

"When I was growing up Prongs was one of the guys that I looked up to and he was one of the guys that you always wanted to be like," Coburn said.

"His name still sits on my board down on the lower end under the injured part of it," added coach Peter Laviolette. "I'd certainly rather have him up in the top-six part of it somewhere, contributing, but that's just not the case right now."

ERIC LINDROS

WELCOME TO PHILADELPHIA

No one personifies the title of this book—the good, the bad, and the ugly of the Philadelphia Flyers—quite like Eric Lindros.

At 6'4" and 240 pounds, Lindros had attributes that left scouts drooling—Wayne Gretzky's skills packed into Mario Lemieux's body, with Mark Messier's temperament and physicality. He was the next great hockey player, the future face of the game, the player destined to lead whatever team was lucky enough to land him to championships well into the 21st century.

Heading into the 1991 NHL Draft, that team looked to be the Quebec Nordiques, who finished the 1990–91 season last in the league.

There was just one problem: Lindros and his parents, Bonnie and Carl, had made it clear that Eric never would play in Quebec. The Lindroses believed going to Quebec would stifle Eric's earning potential. They also believed Nordiques owner Marcel Aubut wouldn't have enough money to pay Lindros what he was worth and build a winning team around him.

The Nordiques still took Lindros with the first pick, but soon realized Lindros would stick to his threat to sit out two seasons and re-enter the draft in 1993. Heading into the 1992 NHL Draft, Aubut and general manager Pierre Page let it be known that Lindros was available for the best offer.

FLYERS SHOW SOME INTEREST

A year before it happened, the seeds were planted for Eric Lindros to bloom in Philadelphia.

The Flyers held the sixth overall choice in the 1991 NHL Draft, giving them no shot of landing Lindros. Still curious, *Courier Post* writer Chuck Gormley asked GM Russ Farwell about him.

"I asked the question, what about this kid Lindros, what will he bring to any team?" Gormley said. "He [Farwell] was so excited about Lindros. He said he was the type of player who is going to make kids want to play hockey. Kids in the playground are going to say they want to be Eric Lindros.

"I thought to myself, Russ really likes this guy. I wonder if he'll try to create something for him?"

"Marcel Aubut was trying to run not a trade but an auction," Russ Farwell, who was the Flyers' general manager at the time, said.

According to Farwell, the Nordiques were looking for certain players, but Aubut demanded a minimum of $15 million in any deal.

"They would always talk whatever the cash was going to be in addition [to the players]," Farwell said. "We had a number of meetings, and we met with Jay [Snider, team president] and his dad [owner Ed Snider] one time, and we kind of worked it out, and there were very few teams that could meet what Quebec was looking for. We were down, we were motivated, and yet we had a little more depth than other teams in the market. And teams that had players couldn't satisfy them from a cash standpoint. We thought at the end of the day we would be one of the only one or two available contenders."

The day before the 1992 draft in Montreal. Aubut and the Nordiques bunkered down in a Montreal hotel suite, where they would host their own version of *Let's Make a Deal*. According to Tim Wharnsby in the (Toronto) Globe and Mail, the list of possible trade partners had been whittled from 14 to four: the Flyers, New York Rangers, Toronto Maple Leafs and Chicago Blackhawks.

Negotiations dragged on as the Nordiques attempted to get the best deal possible for their asset.

"They [the Nordiques] had a suite and were holding meetings in their suite so they were shuttling teams in and out of there," Jay Snider said. "I don't remember how many times we were up there negotiating a package, but it was a lot of times. This went on pretty much day and deep into the night for several days. I can't remember if it was two or three days."

Rumors ran everywhere. The Toronto Maple Leafs reportedly offered the Nordiques a package of center Doug Gilmour, goaltending prospect Felix Potvin, forwards Wendel Clark and Craig Berube, defenseman Dave Ellett, multiple draft picks, and $15 million. Another story had the Chicago Blackhawks ready to surrender goalie Ed Belfour, forward Steve Larmer, and defenseman Steve Smith as part of a five-player, seven-pick trade that reportedly was nixed when Blackhawks owner Bill Wirtz balked at sending the Nordiques $5 million to complete the deal.

"I put together the hockey part of the trade," Farwell said. "And Jay came up with … I don't know if Marcel just set that financial number or if there was any bargaining at all, but I wasn't involved with spending the $15 million. He didn't push back. At one point I remember they wanted [Rod] Brind'Amour in that trade and we just didn't feel we could do that. We set what we wouldn't do from a hockey standpoint. That's where I was involved."

Farwell stated early in the process that Brind'Amour and fellow forward Mark Recchi were off the board, but everyone else the Flyers had was available. The wild card was a 19-year-old Swedish center the Flyers had drafted five spots after Lindros in 1991—Peter Forsberg.

The Flyers had tried to convince Forsberg to come to Philadelphia immediately after drafting him, but Forsberg believed he needed another season of development in Sweden. The Flyers again wanted him to come over for the 1992–93 season, but Forsberg felt he still wasn't NHL ready.

"We wanted him to come," Farwell said of Forsberg. "They thought it over and decided he wasn't ready, he wasn't prepared to come that year. We were looking at another year with not putting anything meaningful into our lineup."

When the Flyers let the Nordiques know Forsberg was available, it turned out to be a big turning point in the process.

After an all-night negotiating session, Snider returned to his hotel room, only to be awakened around 9:00 AM by a phone call from Aubut. Aubut said the Nordiques wanted Forsberg, forward Mike Ricci, defensemen Kerry Huffman and Steve Duchesne, goalie Ron Hextall, the Flyers' 1993 first-round draft pick and $15 million. Snider agreed, and the deal was made, with one condition—a very important one, as it turned out.

"One of the things we had asked for was before we completed the deal was we wanted to speak to them [the Lindros family] and make sure that he would play in Philadelphia, and that was a final condition of ours, knowing that family was keen on making their own decision on where he played," Snider said. "Marcel continued to insist you can't talk to him until we have a deal. I said once we have one then we have to talk to him before it's finalized. He called and said we have a deal and gave us the number—that meant we finally had him."

Even with a deal in hand, however, Aubut wasn't done. Unbeknownst to the Flyers, he took their deal to Rangers GM Neil Smith and Stanley Jaffe, president of Paramount Corp., which owned the Rangers. New York offered forwards Doug Weight, Tony Amonte and Alexei Kovalev, defenseman James Patrick, goalie John Vanbiesbrouck, three first-round picks and $12 million. At 11:50 AM, 10 minutes before the start of the draft, the Nordiques and Rangers agreed on a deal for Lindros.

And that's when the circus started.

"I left to go to the draft floor, and Jay comes in and says here's what happened," Farwell said. "[Aubut] came into our room, changed his mind, and said they're going in a different direction."

A fuming Snider went to NHL President John Ziegler, who immediately convened a meeting in a back room with Aubut, Smith, Snider and NHL general counsel Gil Stein. A decision was

MUSICAL LAWYERS

If the Lindros arbitration case had been a hockey game, the Flyers would have been skating shorthanded.

Club attorney Phil Weinberg arrived Saturday night, hours after the Flyers and Rangers were sent to arbitration to settle their difference over the Lindros trade. However, Weinberg's wife, nine months pregnant, went into labor later that evening, and Weinberg flew home on the first available flight Sunday morning.

The arbitration case also started that morning, forcing the Flyers to scramble for representation.

"We borrowed an attorney from the Blackhawks to start the proceedings," Russ Farwell said.

The Weinbergs welcomed their daughter into the world at 1 p.m. Monday, and Weinberg was back in Montreal later that afternoon.

made to take the matter to arbitration, with Toronto lawyer Larry Bertuzzi appointed to the job.

Bertuzzi flew to Montreal to begin meeting with all parties on Sunday, June 21, 1992. Nine days later, he rendered his decision.

"It was the natural thought that the NHL is going to take care of the Rangers because they're New York," prominent Philadelphia media personality Howard Eskin said. "[Philadelphia fans] always have that defeatist attitude that thinks New York gets everything. [Fans] were waiting, but the only thought they had was, it's New York and there was no way the Flyers would get him."

But the Flyers did get him.

"One of the key things was they [the Flyers] related the conversations they had with Marcel," Bertuzzi said. "But they also portrayed that Marcel had said nobody gets to talk to Eric until I get a deal. And Marcel gave them Eric's phone number at a certain point to talk to the kid at his family's cottage and find out about his preparedness to come to Philly. On its face that was a pretty good piece of evidence. If they were right that Marcel had set the threshold that you don't get his number until we've got a deal and he gave them the number, at one blush they must have made a deal."

Bertuzzi ruled that if the Rangers' deal with the Nordiques at 11:50 AM was valid by league standards in place at the time, then by the same standard, the Flyers' deal with the Nordiques at 10:00 AM was valid.

Eskin, who at the time hosted the top-rated afternoon sports-talk radio show in the Philadelphia area, said the fan response over the ensuing days was overwhelmingly positive.

"They had already put him up on that pedestal," he said of Lindros. "The fans thought the Flyers had the next Wayne Gretzky. It wasn't just they were going to win one Cup, it was they were going to win multiple Cups. They had put the Flyers in the same realm as the Edmonton Oilers when Gretzky was there and they won all those Cups."

OFF-ICE ISSUES

Eric Lindros' troubles weren't limited to on-ice injuries and bad losses. At 6'4" and 240 pounds, with Hollywood-star looks and a load of money, he was easy to find and made a ready target.

In November 1992 Lindros strained ligaments in his left knee. During his rehab, he flew home to Toronto—with the team's permission—to see his own doctor and work himself back to health.

During his time at home, Lindros and friends visited a night-club in Whitby, Ontario, called Koo Koo Bananas. While partying with friends, he was accused of spitting on a woman and pouring beer on her. The woman further alleged that when she confronted Lindros in the club's parking lot to ask for an apology, he said, "I make $3.5 million a year. What are you going to do?"

Lindros was cleared of all charges in February after three independent defense witnesses all said no one saw the player pour beer on anyone.

Things got uglier in May 1996. In a report in *The Fan* magazine, a short-lived Delaware Valley sports publication, a story was published linking Lindros to Philadelphia mob boss Joseph "Skinny Joey" Merlino. The story also was broadcast on WIP 610

When Eric Lindros arrived in Philadelphia in 1992, the eyes of the hockey world were upon him. *Photo courtesy AP Images.*

AM, the Philadelphia-based sports-talk radio station that also was the team's radio broadcast rightsholder.

The publisher of the magazine and the radio host who broke the story was Mike Missanelli, at the time one of WIP's most popular hosts.

The genesis of the report was a *Philadelphia Daily News* story that had reported Merlino had sat in Lindros' seats during a game at the Spectrum.

Lindros downplayed any "relationship" with the local mafia boss, saying he had been introduced to Merlino a handful of times during his first four seasons with the Flyers. And while the seats in question were Lindros', he claimed he had returned them to the team for resale, a common practice among players. That Merlino got them was a coincidence.

"That was such [expletive]," Lindros told the *Philadelphia Daily News* in August 1996. "That was just one person [Missanelli], coming up with ... they were nothing comments, wanting to publicize his radio show."

One of the ways Lindros and Merlino met could have been through a relationship Lindros was having with one of Merlino's sisters. In a story in late February 2006 in *City Paper*, a free Philadelphia daily, a former girlfriend of Joey Merlino said Lindros went on a number of dates with one of Merlino's sisters.

Merlino himself said he never used any relationship with Lindros as part of any illegal activity. Merlino said he was a fan of the team and of Lindros. He also admitted to losing a significant amount of money betting on the Flyers, something he said never would have happened if he had inside information.

THE LINDROS CASE INTRIGUE

The Lindros arbitration case had all the machinations of an episode of *Law and Order*.

In making their case, Flyers CEO Ron Ryan wanted to obtain a copy of the phone bill from the Flyers' hotel suite from the day before the draft, which would include Jay Snider's call to the Lindros cottage in Ontario.

But when he got the bill, the phone call mysteriously was missing. When Ryan pressed the issue with hotel management, he learned that someone had gotten into the closet where the telephone computer was and deleted the record of the call.

Ryan subsequently got phone records from Bell Canada to prove that the Flyers had spoken to Lindros the day before the draft.

The NHL investigated and apparently agreed. Carl Lindros said he and Eric discussed suing Missanelli, the magazine and the radio station, but decided it wasn't worth pursuing.

In 1997 WIP became the source of more frustration for Lindros and the Flyers.

There's a bit of irony that the local all-sports talk station could cause so much agita for the club. When WIP shifted into an all-sports format in 1987, the station was owned by Ed Snider (he sold it to Infinity Broadcasting in 1994).

On February 28, 1997, WIP host Craig Carton reported Lindros had missed a game against the Pittsburgh Penguins on February 15 of that year because he had been suspended by the team for being drunk the night before and hung over the day of the game.

The story immediately became front-page news across the Delaware Valley.

"There is only so much I can take," an emotional Lindros said on March 4 of that year. "I haven't done anything at all. I'm innocent."

That same day, club president and GM Bob Clarke told reporters: "You know where Lindros was the night before that Pittsburgh game? He was sitting in a hyperbaric oxygen chamber with our trainer [John Worley]."

Carl Lindros, still smarting from the embarrassing publicity surrounding the Merlino report less than a year earlier, said from his suburban Toronto home: "Eric is very upset about this. This is unbelievable to us. It's sad. It's sick. ... These things wear you down."

The Flyers said Lindros missed two games—February 15 and 16—due to a lower back strain. Newspaper reports said Lindros was injured in a game against the Ottawa Senators on February 13 when he leaped to avoid a check and landed hard on his back.

Carton, who cited four unnamed sources for his information, including two within the Flyers' organization, stood by his story, and WIP stood by Carton.

In response, Snider and the Flyers filed a libel suit against Carton, WIP and Infinity Broadcasting in Philadelphia Common Pleas Court.

"We're seeking damages for libeling of this organization and to Eric Lindros," Snider said March 5 in announcing the suit.

Asked why he took these actions now and not during the Merlino brouhaha, Snider said: "Because this is one step too many. They finally went over the ledge. We were willing to give them the benefit of the doubt last time, but we're not willing to do it any longer. We're not going to sit back and take it. We understand that they have the power of the airwaves, but we have the power of our integrity and our pride, and we're not going to sit back and take this garbage."

Clarke said the organization had to sue to show its support for the shoddy treatment Lindros was receiving.

"If management and ownership won't support their players, then you don't really have a team, you have a bunch of people playing hockey," Clarke said. "It happens to be Eric this time, but if it was any other player, we'd do the same."

Carl Lindros also threatened a lawsuit on behalf of his son, saying he had evidence to document Eric's whereabouts on February 14 and 15, including a video rental receipt and phone bills that showed Eric making long-distance calls from his South Jersey home.

After first backing Carton, WIP changed course and didn't renew his contract in July of that year. About a year after the suit was filed, WIP settled with the Flyers and Lindros, giving the player an on-air and written apology and making a donation to a charity of Lindros' choosing. Also, hosts and callers were barred from discussing the settlement.

THE LEGION OF DOOM

When Bob Clarke returned to the Flyers in 1994, he took one look at his team and realized there was a certain element missing.

"[Eric] Lindros was going against the biggest players from the other teams and he needed help," he said in a June 1995 interview

LINDROS CHANGES HOW DEALS ARE DONE

In the aftermath of the Eric Lindros trade debacle, many things changed about the NHL.

Most importantly, it altered the way trades were made. Previously, deals were worked out over cocktails and written down on restaurant napkins until they officially could be called into NHL Central Registry during normal business hours.

"Trades were still done just on your word and you talk about it, you'd agree and the deal was made," Farwell said. "We just agreed it was done and we announced it the next morning. That's how trades happened before. But it was on that Lindros deal that things were more standardized and that was the start of the system they have today. No deal is final until they [the league] has gone through it."

with the *Philadelphia Inquirer*. "His line had to have more size. And we knew we had to have a veteran defenseman."

With one transaction, he managed to fill both holes.

Clarke had a chip in Mark Recchi, who entered the 1994–95 season coming off his second straight 40-goal, 100-point season. Knowing the Montreal Canadiens needed scoring help, he first tried to peddle Recchi to them for 25-year-old defenseman Mathieu Schneider, but was rebuffed. Clarke then turned his attention to another 25-year-old Montreal blueliner, Eric Desjardins.

He also inquired about a giant forward who had taken up residence in the team's doghouse. John LeClair had scored a pair of overtime goals in the Canadiens' 1993 Stanley Cup run, but had been flip-flopping between center and left wing, with no success at either spot.

"We thought we could try him with Lindros," Clarke said in *Full Spectrum*.

On February 9, 1995, Clarke sent Recchi and a draft pick to the Canadiens for Desjardins, LeClair and forward Gilbert Dionne.

"That trade changed the whole atmosphere and confidence level of our entire organization," Clarke said in a 2005 interview on the Flyers' website. "Desjardins was an All-Star and LeClair was about to turn into one. We had no idea that LeClair was going to be that good. But that deal turned out pretty good."

That's certainly an understatement.

With Mikael Renberg completing the threesome, a new day had dawned in Flyers history.

In the first period of their second game together, against the New Jersey Devils, Lindros chased the rebound of a Desjardins shot into the corner, looked up and found LeClair all but blotting out Devils goalie Chris Terreri, an immovable object the Devils' defense couldn't handle. Lindros fed a pass in front that LeClair stuffed into the net, which started the Flyers on their way to a 3–1 win.

"That was the game where things started to go with Renny [Renberg] and Eric," LeClair said. "We had a game with lots of chances. I scored my first goal as a Flyer, and you could tell there was some good chemistry there."

Watching Lindros(6'4", 240), LeClair (6'3", 233), and Renberg (6'2", 235) run over, around and through their Devils counterparts, Flyers fourth-line center Jim Montgomery said, "They look like the Legion of Doom out there."

"Nobody could get the puck off them," Chuck Gormley, the Flyers beat writer for the *Courier Post* at the time, said. "Once they dumped the puck into the corner, regardless of which corner it was, no defenseman was strong enough to stop that line. Nobody in the league. Even if you had a big, tough defenseman, there was only one of them out there, and there were three of these guys."

The threesome rained down doom on teams throughout the league. Lindros had 25 goals and 34 assists in 36 games after the trade, while LeClair had 25 goals in 37 games with the Flyers. Renberg scored 25 times in the final 37 games of the season.

The Flyers, 3–6–1 the day of the trade, went 25–10–3 after the deal, including separate eight- and nine-game win streaks.

The Flyers marauded their way into the playoffs, making it to the 1995 Eastern Conference Finals. Two years later, it would

THE FIRST CONTRACT

Future problems were foreshadowed by the first meeting between the Flyers and Carl Lindros.

That first sit-down was held at a hotel in Syracuse, New York, about halfway between Philadelphia and the Lindros home in Toronto.

"Prior to meeting with Eric, we [Farwell and team president Jay Snider] met with [agent] Rick Curran and Eric's dad [Carl]," Russ Farwell said. "It didn't go well."

An angry Carl Lindros left the meeting, presumably to get some air and cool off. Instead, he got in his car and drove home.

"It was Jay's first dealings with the family, and he reported back to me," Ed Snider said. "It was, 'Oh my god, what did we get into?'"

be more Doom for the East as the Flyers topped the Rangers to take the conference title and were the heavy favorite against the Detroit Red Wings in the Stanley Cup Final.

In the first three rounds of the playoffs, Lindros racked up 11 goals and 12 assists, LeClair had seven goals and 11 assists, and Renberg had four goals and five assists.

It was thought the Red Wings didn't have the size to handle the Flyers, especially down low in the Detroit zone, and over time the Flyers would push the Wings right off the ice.

Rather than go power on power, the Wings used a combination of skill, finesse and grit to exasperate the Flyers' big line.

"It was incredibly frustrating," LeClair said. "Both those guys [Detroit defensemen Nicklas Lidstrom and Larry Murphy] are very skilled, especially with their sticks. Those guys are also very talented defensemen; they just used a different tactic. They definitely stayed away from our strength, trying to outmuscle guys in the corner and stuff."

The result was a Red Wings four-game sweep. Lindros finished with a pair of assists in Game 1 and scored the final Flyers goal of the series, which came with 15 seconds left in regulation in Game 4, with the Flyers down 2–0. He finished a minus-5 in the series, as did LeClair, who had two goals and an assist in the four-game series. Renberg had one assist and was a minus-2.

"They confused the Flyers with the left-wing lock," Gormley said. "The Flyers had never seen that and I think that they were baffled by it. They [the Red Wings] were more ready. They had veteran guys who were willing to pay the price and understood the glare of the spotlight. The Flyers, they looked like deer in headlights."

Two months after the Final, Renberg was traded to Tampa Bay to recoup the four first-round picks the team lost as compensation for the signing of free agent Chris Gratton. The Legion of Doom was no more, but in three seasons together, they had accomplished a lot.

Renberg had three straight 20-goal seasons. LeClair had the first two of his three straight 50-goal seasons and wrote the definition for what an NHL power forward was. Lindros won the Hart Trophy as league MVP in 1995, and in 1995–96 had the best season of his career, finishing with professional-bests of 47 goals, 68 assists and 115 points.

"I turned into a different player," LeClair said of his time with Lindros. "Being able to play with them [Lindros and Renberg], confidence is a big thing. You play with them, you have some success and your confidence grows.

"When I came to the Flyers, I got the confidence in me as a player. Playing with Eric and Mikael, I had some success and built that confidence."

That confidence made the Legion of Doom one of the most dominant in NHL history.

"In my opinion, they changed the game," Gormley said.

THE COLLAPSED LUNG

When the Flyers took the ice against the Nashville Predators on April 1, 1999, Eric Lindros was in the midst of his best season as a Flyer.

It was Lindros' 71st game of the season, and he had 40 goals, 53 assists and 93 points, the third-highest total in the league. The

"MORE SASKATCHEWAN THAN SASKATCHEWAN GUYS"

In 1991, the year of the heralded Eric Lindros draft, the Flyers held the sixth overall choice. Atop their list were two players, Richard Matvichuk, a defenseman with the Saskatoon Blades of the Western Hockey League, and a center who played like he was from the rough-and-tumble WHL. But actually he was from a small village in eastern Sweden—Peter Forsberg.

At the time, Swedes were considered soft players, not worthy of a top–10 draft pick, least of all for a team like the fearsome Philadelphia Flyers.

"We just felt he may have been born in Sweden, but he's more Saskatchewan than Saskatchewan guys," Russ Farwell said. "They can hardly handle him in his hockey league because he plays so hard and so tough. We felt he was the ideal guy."

A year after passing on Jaromir Jagr with the No. 4 pick because they didn't want the stigma of spending such a high draft choice on a European player, the Flyers couldn't pass on Forsberg.

Farwell spent two years trying to lure Forsberg to the NHL, but each time he said no. Which is why when the opportunity arose to acquire Lindros, Farwell reluctantly put Forsberg in the deal.

71 games already was a personal best, and he was evolving into the captain and leader the Flyers had hoped for.

The Flyers slogged their way to a 2–1 win as the Predators, like most teams, targeted Lindros physically and held him to zero shots in 21:16 of ice time. The big center looked slow, which was chalked up to it being his first night back after a two-game suspension for high-sticking the New York Rangers' Petr Nedved.

During the game, Lindros complained to teammates and trainers of soreness in his side and chest, but he never missed a shift. He received ice and electrical stimulation on his upper body after the game, and left the arena for a late dinner and drinks with teammates. Still not feeling right, he made it an early night and returned to his hotel room.

When Keith Jones returned to the room he shared with Lindros, he found Lindros awake, watching a movie, and still complaining of soreness in his chest. Jones wrote in his autobiography *Jonesy: Put Your Head Down and Skate*, that he got Lindros some Advil and went to sleep.

A few times during the night Jones wrote that he heard the bathtub running, but that didn't concern him.

"I don't think much of it, because when you play hockey sometimes guys will hop in the tub and try to give the body some relief, so I just assumed that's what Eric is doing," Jones wrote.

Early the next morning, Jones wrote that Lindros still was in pain, and looked pale. He called trainer John Worley, but Worley had taken Mark Recchi to the hospital the previous evening with concussion-like symptoms.

Jones wrote that at about 7:30 a.m. he finally reached Worley, who was just returning from a night at the hospital with Recchi. Jones explained Lindros' situation, and Worley said he would come to their room after he cleaned himself up.

Jones then went for breakfast, but when he returned, Lindros' condition had worsened. "I come back up and Eric is back in the tub, pale and in even worse shape than he had been," Jones wrote. "I say to him, 'Something is wrong here. Maybe it's something internal. I'll go get John right now. I think we got to get you to the hospital.'"

THE HOUSE THAT ERIC BUILT

The Wells Fargo Center is a lot of things to Ed Snider, but it's absolutely not The House That Eric Lindros Built.

"That's bullshit. That's pure, unadulterated bullshit," Snider said. "There's no role he had in building this building. I can tell you that unequivocally. The lender couldn't care less who was on the team at a given time. ... That's an old wives' tale by sportswriters who don't understand finance. Eric Lindros had nothing to do with this building being built. It's absolutely untrue. I don't think our lenders even knew who Eric Lindros was."

As Jones approached the elevator, Worley stepped out and the two went back to see Lindros. With Worley handling things, Jones gathered his bag and Lindros' to catch the team's flight to Boston for their game against the Bruins the next night.

Worley considered having Lindros fly back to Philadelphia so Flyers doctors could examine him, but changed his mind and called Rick Garman, the Predators' team physician, and an ambulance. Paramedics rushed Lindros to Baptist Hospital in Nashville, where Garman met them. Lindros was admitted at 9:44 AM on April 2.

When he arrived at the hospital, Lindros said he was having more pain in his chest and shortness of breath. X-rays showed a collapsed lung due to the loss of three liters of blood—half of Lindros' total blood volume. The blood had filled his chest cavity, collapsing the lung.

Doctors performed emergency surgery in the intensive care unit out of fear Lindros wouldn't survive long enough to get to an operating room. A chest tube was inserted between two ribs, and as blood began draining out, Lindros' breathing returned to normal.

Teammates had no idea of the drama unfolding back in Tennessee. About the time doctors were cracking open Lindros' chest, they were skating in Boston.

"It's incredible," teammate Sandy McCarthy told reporters. "No one knows what happened."

Not even Lindros. Jones said Lindros told him during the game that he had been cross-checked in the upper body in the third period, while Rod Brind'Amour said he heard Lindros complain of sore ribs during the first period. Garman said Lindros told him he had been cross-checked hard during the Rangers game and felt back pain for a day or two after that.

Regardless of what caused it, Lindros' life had been in serious jeopardy. Garman said that Worley's decision to not send Lindros back to Philadelphia kept a severe injury from turning into a fatality.

The Flyers immediately ruled Lindros out for the remainder of the regular season, but wouldn't close the door on a playoff return.

THE 1998 OLYMPICS

When Bob Clarke named Eric Lindros the captain of the 1998 Canadian Olympic hockey team, the first to include NHL players, the criticism was unyielding.

Hall of Fame Edmonton Journal columnist Jim Matheson wrote, "He's wearing the 'C' and that's a heavy letter of the alphabet. ... Most wonder why he was given the 'C' over more established players."

Jack Todd of the *Montreal Gazette* was even blunter, writing that Lindros would be "the worst captain since Ahab."

Carl Lindros, though, thought otherwise.

"It's premature right now to be even contemplating this," he told the *Philadelphia Daily News*. "It's going to take a couple of doctors to convince me that common sense shouldn't apply. I'm not a doctor, but as a parent and as an agent, we've got to see the rationale that it makes sense for him to be back this spring. I'm not saying that there won't be a good argument. But probably it will take more than a couple of doctors to convince me."

Carl also told the *Philadelphia Inquirer* he had trouble getting in touch with Flyers doctors, and had yet to speak to general manager Bob Clarke. He added that when Eric returned home, he would be placed in the care of Larry Kaiser, the director of thoracic surgery at the Hospital of the University of Pennsylvania—and a doctor unaffiliated with the Flyers.

A day later, Ed Snider responded and agreed with Carl Lindros.

"We are operating on the assumption that we are not going to have Eric for the rest of the season or the playoffs," he told the *Philadelphia Inquirer*. "We have to figure out a way to win without him."

Lindros returned home April 12, and within a few days was able to visit with teammates, ride an exercise bike, even jump on the ice for a few minutes at a time. His blood count and stamina seemingly rising each day, he practiced in pads and remained steadfast that he would return for the second round of the playoffs if the Flyers made it that far.

Doctors and Carl Lindros said otherwise, and were worried that members of the organization were pressuring Eric to return sooner than safety should allow. *Toronto Star* columnist Damien Cox wrote as much in a May 1, 1999 column: "Within the Philly organization ... there exists the ludicrous sentiment that Lindros should ... courageously shake off the lingering effects of the collapsed lung he suffered exactly 30 days ago and leap back into the fray like a comic-book hero."

Cox wrote that in the days following Lindros' ordeal, Eric was pressed into considering having a blood transfusion to help speed his recovery. He also wrote that Lindros met with Clarke, during which time he asked Clarke why he was being "overtly challenged to rush back."

Clarke, Snider and Lindros all denied any undue pressure ever was placed on Eric.

It all became a moot point when the Flyers' season ended with a six-game first-round playoff loss to the Toronto Maple Leafs.

MOMMA AND POPPA LINDROS

Carl and Bonnie Lindros will be remembered as polarizing figures in hockey circles. Some see them as fine people who doggedly defended the health and welfare of their oldest son and refused to allow him to be exploited for the financial gain of others.

"Carl's an extremely meticulous, extremely thorough person," said Rick Curran, Eric's first agent, who added that he found his work with the family to be "a worthwhile experience."

There are others, though, who saw them as paranoid, overprotective pains in the butt who did more to hurt their son's career than help it.

"The big interference came from his mom and dad," Terry Murray, who coached Eric from 1994 to 1997, said. "When they came into town and were staying with him for several days at a time, you could always see a different Eric coming to the rink every day. He had different questions, he had a lot of concerns on his mind, he was a little more distracted. When everybody was away and he was there and just playing hockey, he was a real good player."

In Lindros' early days in Philadelphia, Al Morganti was covering the NHL for ESPN, putting him on the receiving end of frequent phone calls from Carl Lindros.

"Carl could be oppressive," he said. "Because I was with ESPN, I was one of the key media people and Carl would call. ... They had this agenda—they wanted [GM Bob] Clarke gone. I remember I went into the Coliseum to see Clarke with [assistant GM Paul] Holmgren and said you've got a big problem here. They're trying to engineer stories and I'm just telling you this, what's going on with this guy.

"They said, 'We already know.'"

Chuck Gormley, who covered the Flyers for the *Courier Post*, also got his fair share of phone calls from Carl Lindros.

"[Carl] would call me and say, 'Chuck, I was on vacation last week, and I'm going through all my stacks of newspapers, and I saw here you wrote on Wednesday such and such, that's not true," Gormley said. "And I want to make it a point that that's not true.' He would try to let you know what was fact and what was not fact. And the real challenge in covering Lindros was that he would not give you a lot of information. And so a lot of things were left to speculation, and as soon as you speculated they would call and say that's not what happened. So you would ask what happened and they would say, 'I'm not going to get into that.' They would profess to take the high road and we would be left to guess. And so often you would lose their respect and they would lose yours, because no one was telling you the truth. Lies were getting in the paper, in their opinion. It became an untenable situation because you couldn't distinguish between who was telling the truth and who wasn't. And that became an every-day issue. The Flyers would say one thing, his agent would say another."

Morganti said he tried to prod Lindros into finding a new agent.

"I liked Eric," he said. "I told Eric to get another agent, and he'd listen to you and then he'd hear from Toronto."

Morganti wasn't the only person to suggest Lindros needed new representation. In a July 31, 1998, story in the *Philadelphia*

CURRAN DISMISSED

To the Lindros family, loyalty is an honor above all else. And if you go against the family, you get whacked—figuratively, of course. They're the Lindroses, not the Sopranos.

Rick Curran, Lindros' agent since he was about 14, learned that after negotiating Eric's first Flyers contract.

"The day that I completed the negotiation for his first contract, there was a press conference," Curran said. "We all went out and had lunch together, the family and myself, [attorney] Gord Kirke. And we've never spoken since."

Curran's offense? Moving his office from Canada to Devon, Pennsylvania, near his wife's family.

Inquirer, Clarke said upcoming negotiations for a new contract might go smoother if it wasn't Carl Lindros he was dealing with.

"I don't know if it would make it easier, but it probably would," Clarke said. "But that's the way it is. I get along with Carl. I like Carl. I have no problems with Carl. But certainly, having a father as an agent ..." Clarke never finished the thought, but the story served as a public glimpse into the growing chasm between the team and its star player.

The gulf only would grow over the ensuing years. What had been limited to private spats became public brawls played out daily in the newspapers. Lindros accepted a one-year contract for the 1999–2000 season rather than a long-term deal, and rumors swirled that Carl Lindros wouldn't let Eric sign a multi-year deal as long as Clarke was general manager. The Lindros family believed signing one-year deals was their only assurance Eric would not get traded.

As the situation continued to devolve, the best solution looked like a complete divorce, and trade rumors started to run rampant.

"There is no basis for trust anymore in the relationship between Flyers management and the Lindros [family]," an anonymous source told the *Philadelphia Inquirer.* "And because there is no ability to have honesty in that relationship, neither side believes each other's intentions are sincere. That's the reality."

The story went on to describe unnamed teammates who were pushing for Lindros to find a new agent, believing the acrimony between Carl Lindros and the Flyers' front office was affecting Eric's play.

"My agent does what I say, whether it is my father or anyone else," Eric replied. "It shouldn't matter who the agent is."

The 1999–2000 season was Eric Lindros' last with the Flyers, and it certainly was a memorable one.

He suffered four concussions, none bigger than the violent shoulder to the head thrown by the New Jersey Devils' Scott Stevens in the first period of Game 7 of the 2000 Eastern Conference Finals.

In the aftermath of the end of the Flyers' season, and with yet another contract negotiation on the horizon, Snider received a letter from the Lindros camp outlining where they felt they had been the aggrieved party in the relationship.

The jump-off-the-page line came from the events surrounding Eric's treatment in Nashville following his near-fatal collapsed lung in April 1999. It was an accusation worthy of a daytime soap opera.

"We did everything right," Snider said years later, "and the mother said that Bob Clarke tried to kill her son."

A frustrated Clarke lashed back, torching whatever remained of the bridge between him and the Lindros family. In an interview with the team's beat writers and columnists, he said: "It's pretty hard to believe that [trainer] John Worley wouldn't treat Eric properly [or that] I would put him on a plane and try to kill him.

"This is the kind of stuff that just never ends, and it's hard on a hockey club. It's disruptive. And as hard as it's been on all of us on this team, it's been a lot harder on Eric.

"You can't tell me how a 27-year-old man can have his dad speaking for him, taking him to the doctor, showing up in the darn locker room. ... You do that to a 14-year-old kid, he'd be embarrassed."

Clarke said that after years of meddling from Carl Lindros, he was done with it, and said Eric, who was going to be a restricted free agent in the summer of 2000, could return to the Flyers, but only Eric—not his family.

"We want to retain his rights," Clarke said. "We want him back. If he comes back, it's going to be his own self. We don't want his mom and dad back. We've had enough of them."

Carl Lindros' reply came a few days later, when he said, "It's somewhere between humor and tragedy, sort of like a play from Shakespeare."

Things only would get more tragic for both player and club. Lindros sat out the 2000–01 season to recover from his injuries, and then declared he never would play for the Flyers again.

Clarke replied that he was done letting the Lindros family dictate where Eric might play, and that his responsibility was to make the best trade possible for the Philadelphia Flyers. That finally happened August 20, 2001, when Eric was dealt to the New York Rangers for forwards Jan Hlavac and Pavel Brendl, defenseman Kim Johnsson and a draft pick.

According to team chairman Ed Snider, the move was a long time coming.

"He and his parents are the most difficult people I've ever dealt with in any field, in any business," he said. "In my entire life I've never met people like this. We always thought he would grow up and speak for himself, but whatever gene that family has, it's everywhere. Everyone is guilty until proven innocent, and Eric is never guilty. They would take facts that we had and say they aren't the facts."

THE END

When Eric Lindros took the ice on the last day of May 1997, the day of Game 1 of the Stanley Cup Final, it was high point of his career with the Flyers.

And from a peak, there's only one way to go—down.

It started March 7, 1998, in Pittsburgh. Lindros had played in 59 of the Flyers' 60 games to that point in the season, and scored his 28th goal 7:59 into the second period.

Forty-nine seconds of game time later, Lindros' life, and the course of Flyers history, would be changed forever.

Pittsburgh's Jiri Slegr scored moments after Lindros. On the ensuing faceoff, Lindros grabbed a loose puck at center ice and cut toward the right-wing boards. As he moved around one Penguin, he lost the puck and kicked it ahead toward the Pittsburgh blue line. Lindros looked down to find the puck, which was within inches of his stick as he skated through the neutral zone.

Lindros had developed an awful habit, going to back to his youth hockey days, of skating with his head down. He always was so much bigger and stronger than other kids, so anyone who dared venture into his path would bounce off him like tennis balls off a concrete wall.

NHL foes don't bounce as well.

And it wasn't a tennis ball that night in Pittsburgh—it was a wrecking ball named Darius Kasparaitis, who drove his right shoulder into Lindros' jaw.

The hit separated Lindros from the puck and his senses. The force of the blow snapped his head back and dislodged his helmet. Lindros landed on his back and immediately put his hands up to his head. He rolled onto his knees and twice tried to get up with help from the Flyers' medical staff, but twice fell down. On his third try he found his feet and was helped off the ice by teammates.

"He wasn't himself as I was helping him off the ice," John LeClair recalled. "For me, that was the disturbing part, to see him like that."

Lindros walked to an ambulance under his own power and was diagnosed at a Pittsburgh hospital with the first concussion of his career.

According to a story in *ESPN The Magazine*, during the ride to the hospital Lindros got a call on his cell phone from his mother, Bonnie. The story, as related to writer Tom Friend, said GM Bob Clarke, riding with Lindros, rolled his eyes and said, "Isn't that nice—Mommy called."

Lindros missed the last five weeks of the regular season but was able to return for the playoffs. It didn't help, though, as the Flyers were eliminated in five games by the Buffalo Sabres.

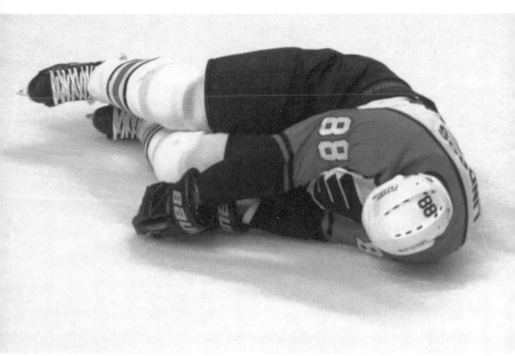

Eric Lindros lies on the ice after getting hit in the first period of Game 7 of the Eastern Conference Finals against the New Jersey Devils in Philadelphia, Friday, May 26, 2000. Lindros was skating up the ice with the puck when the Devils' Scott Stevens blindsided him with an elbow. Lindros left the game. No penalty was called. *Photo courtesy AP Images.*

The summer featured Lindros passing on a five-year contract that would have paid him between $45 and $50 million, instead agreeing to a one-year, $8.5 million deal, and he reported to training camp in 1998 free of any distractions, on or off the ice.

"He's looked dominant the whole preseason," goalie John Vanbiesbrouck said during camp. "He's using his body, playing strong at both ends of the ice. We feed off his intensity and it's fun to watch."

Lindros played the first 35 games of the season injury-free, but that's where the streak would end. On December 29, 1998, Calgary's Jason Wiemer waylaid Lindros, giving him the second concussion of his career. He sat out two games, and when he

TEAMMATES

Those who played with Eric Lindros hold him in high regard, but temper it with a bit of wistfulness—a what-if sense pervading their opinions.

"I always got along great with Eric," Rod Brind'Amour said. "I thought he cared, I thought he played hard and I always supported him."

"[Eric] is one of the guys that [my son] Brett thinks back on that I played with that was the nicest guys to him," added Ron Hextall.

Keith Primeau said when he came to the Flyers in 2000, Lindros invited he and his wife to stay at his home.

"Eric was a very nice person, a really nice guy," Primeau said. "I think he's another one of those guys that because of his stature and because of his ability was always front and center, and I don't know if he necessarily wanted to be front and center."

came back went on an 18-game scoring streak, tying Clarke's team record.

That season ended after his near-fatal lung injury in April, and after signing another one-year contract, he started the 1999–2000 season healthy, but it wouldn't last.

On January 14, 2000, Atlanta's Darryl Shannon elbowed Lindros in the head, and he was diagnosed with a "mild" concussion—number three, if you're counting—but Lindros said he felt worse after concussion number three than he did after number two.

The forth concussion came March 4, 2000, when 6'7", 240-pound Bruins defenseman Hal Gill elbowed Lindros in the head. Despite feeling less than 100 percent, Lindros played the next four games before getting pulled from the lineup prior to a game in Phoenix.

"This is not a concussion injury," team doctor Jeff Hartzell told the press. "We don't believe it has anything to do with that." He said the headaches could be the result of a sinus problem, muscle contractions or Lindros grinding his teeth while asleep or chewing gum.

Days later, though, Hartzell said the Gill hit had given Lindros a Grade I concussion—the most mild on the scale, and less severe than the Grade II injury Lindros had suffered in Atlanta.

But in a report in the *Philadelphia Inquirer*, an unnamed member of the organization said Lindros actually had a Grade II concussion from the Gill shot. The source added the team knew about Lindros' headaches and treated him with over-the-counter headache medication and massages, despite Lindros having suffered his second concussion of the season and fourth in three years.

Clarke defended his medical and training staff and said Lindros never let on to the extent of his injuries.

"We're very confident that our trainers did the right thing, that our doctors are the best doctors you can get, that our trainers are the best trainers you can get," he said. "The speculation against our doctors and trainers is very offensive. ... If Eric has a problem, he can bring it up."

The Flyers sent Lindros to visit Dr. Stephen Silberstein, a headache specialist at Thomas Jefferson University Hospital, who agreed with Hartzell and said Lindros had a Grade I concussion.

The Lindros family felt differently, though, and sent Eric to see concussion expert Dr. Larry Kelly in Chicago, who diagnosed a Grade II concussion, which would sideline Lindros through the first round of the playoffs.

The difference in the diagnoses could be chalked up to two reasons. One is the difference in expertise, while the other is slightly more sinister—Silberstein was recommended by the Flyers, while Kelly wasn't. Days after returning from Chicago, the tenuous strings binding the Flyers and Lindros were irreparably torn.

During a press conference, Lindros described the culture around the organization as "wacky," ripped the team for its handling of his latest concussion issues, and said Clarke had insulted his father/agent. He added that Clarke nor team chairman Ed Snider had called him since his latest injury, saying the only Comcast-Spectacor representative he had heard from was Pat Croce, the 76ers president and a minority partner in the Flyers.

FEELINGS TODAY

Years removed from day-to-day dealings with the Lindros family, Bob Clarke said he holds no grudges.

"I liked Eric," Clarke said. "I liked Eric, and through most of all the messes that went on, I liked Eric. I liked his dad. I wish it had worked differently."

Clarke is unsure where the breakdown first started, but said, "It got a life of its own, and I'm not quite sure how to describe it all.

"I don't know or understand so much that went on. Everybody had the right intent, but the results were different."

A sampling of Lindros' statements, taken from the March 24, 2000, edition of the *Philadelphia Inquirer*:

"I tried to explain my symptoms and that things were not real good, but I was not going to pull myself out of the game. ... John Worley knew what I had. I was clear in what I told him. I was not concealing it. I might not have been up front with the doctor in Boston [after suffering the injury there]. ... I knew what would happen [if I had requested to sit out]. ... It's a wacky situation around here.

"I was hoping the team would take me out—knowing what went on and expressing to them for days about my headaches. Another reason I kept playing is this environment here. The last time I had a concussion, I didn't talk to Clarke for three weeks. What he would say off the record was that my agent was a fool and disruptive for insisting the team follow the [league's] return-to-play guidelines [for concussions]."

The team issued a bland statement later that day, but a different statement was made days later. Clarke convened a meeting with coach Craig Ramsay and alternate captains Eric Desjardins, Mark Recchi and John LeClair, during which Clarke said he was stripping Lindros of the captaincy and handing the role to Desjardins.

"He criticizes our trainers, criticizes our doctors, criticizes our organization," Clarke told reporters. "If he's that unhappy with us all, he shouldn't be the captain of our team."

Years later, Clarke said Lindros left him with no choice. "When our organization, our team, our other players were being hurt by what was going on," he said, "I guess it just had to change. I didn't want this organization to be hurt by things that Eric and his family were trying to accuse us of, so we started to fight back. I only saw Eric as a hockey player who was responsible to his teammates, like any other hockey player.

"Our doctors never tried to do anything to hurt Eric, or our trainers, the team didn't, but we were accused of it."

On May 4, 2000, while his teammates were in Pittsburgh, about to engage in the longest playoff game in modern NHL history, Lindros suffered concussion number five when he collided with Phantoms forward Francis Lessard during a four-on-four scrimmage at home.

The hope was Lindros could return for the Eastern Conference Finals, but his father said, "We're shutting everything down. We're all the way back to where we were before," meaning when the early March hit first took place.

Despite Carl's proclamation, Eric received medical clearance to play on the day between Games 5 and 6 of the conference finals against the New Jersey Devils. With one day to practice, Lindros was a surprise addition to the lineup for Game 6.

"I still think it was a foolish decision," Chuck Gormley, who chronicled the Lindros saga for the *Courier Post*, said. "I remember standing in the parking lot at the Coliseum, and I remember saying to myself, you can't [let him play]. You can't do that because of all the animosity."

It was animosity, Gormley said, that had developed because Lindros had set himself apart from the team one time too many.

"I remember Rick Tocchet saying all hands on deck," Gormley said. "Whether we have Lindros or not, we don't care. We don't have time for individuals. That's what I sensed from that team. Eric became an individual and they would not allow that. As an organization, they had to take a stand. I don't think it had as much to do with criticizing John Worley as it did, we have an individual on this team, and we're not going to stand for it."

Keith Jones said Lindros' return, "changed the entire dynamic, because we had played as a team. Then your superstar comes back and everyone settles in and says, 'Okay, take over.' And it wasn't about the team as much as it was about him coming back into the lineup and everyone taking a breath of fresh air and saying, 'Okay, now he's going to take it.'"

For one night, though, he did take it. In his first game in two and a half months, he was the Flyers' best player. He played 14:47 at center and right wing, and scored their lone goal, even though it came with 30.1 seconds left in the third period and with the Flyers trailing 2–0. He also had a goal disallowed because it came after the buzzer to end the second period.

And the few cheers coming Lindros' way in a raucous Continental Airlines Arena came from a surprising source—Clarke.

"I sat there in the press box for Game 6 right next to Clarke," Gormley said. "I never saw Clarke root harder for somebody than for Lindros that night. He was just, 'Come on Eric, come on Eric.'"

Despite the loss that night, there was hope that if Lindros could play Game 7 the way he played Game 6, the Flyers could survive what was shaping up as a monumental collapse from a 3–1 series lead. Those hopes were dashed quickly and painfully. The video proof is readily available online.

On May 26, 2000, on his fourth shift of the game, with 12:10 left in the first period, Lindros skates across the Devils' blue line, his head down. He never sees defenseman Scott Stevens skating in from his right. Two Brahma bulls moving at top speed collide; Stevens drives his left shoulder and upper arm into the side of Lindros' head and jaw. The force of the blow spins Lindros 180 degrees, his stick pinwheeling out of his hands. Lindros lands hard on his back, the back of his helmeted head snapping violently off the ice, and he bounce-rolls onto his left shoulder. His legs wrap around him, nearly curling him into the fetal position.

"When that hit occurred, when they say the air went out of the building, the air went out of that building," Gormley said. "It was very frightening."

Lindros was taken by ambulance to Pennsylvania Hospital, where he was kept overnight for observation. He was diagnosed with concussion number six, and his fourth in four months.

"Once that [Stevens hit] happened," Gormley said, "everyone knew his career was over. I thought his career as a Flyer was over the second that hit happened."

Gormley was right, as Lindros remained silent while home in Toronto recovering from his injuries, and then on November 16, 2000, he declared he was done playing for the Flyers.

"I made it clear when I turned down $8.5 million [qualifying offer] that I would not play there again. It's time to move on," he told reporters. "Moving on with a trade is the best thing for that organization, and the best thing for me."

He added, "I'm open to meeting with [Clarke] with regard to trade possibilities, but not for any other reason."

A fuming Clarke fired back: "I don't give a crap whether he ever plays again or if I ever see him again. All he ever did was cause aggravation to our team. If he wants to play, he might have to come back [to the Flyers] if no one else wants him in the NHL."

Lindros said the only team he would play for is the Toronto Maple Leafs, but Clarke wasn't about to be dictated to. "My responsibility is to the Philadelphia Flyers, not to Eric Lindros, and we're going to do what's right for the Flyers," Clarke told reporters. "Eric may want to play in Toronto, but that may not happen. ... We want the best compensation we can get for this player."

The story dragged on throughout the 2000–01 season, with the Flyers unable to work out a deal with the Leafs, while Lindros killed any trade possibilities with other clubs by threatening not to report.

The stalemate continued into the summer of 2001, but a bit of daylight came through the dark skies on July 4 —Independence Day—when Lindros family attorney Gord Kirke told Clarke that Eric would consider a trade to the New York Rangers. On August 20, 2001, Eric Lindros finally received his independence from the Flyers when he was dealt to the Rangers. In return, the Flyers received forward Jan Hlavac, defenseman Kim Johnsson, forward prospect Pavel Brendl, and a 2003 draft pick.

Clarke initially took the high road, telling reporters, "No point in rehashing old stuff." But later he couldn't help himself, saying of Lindros: "He hurt this organization. I couldn't care less about him."

Snider said if he had to do it all over again, he would have cut the cord much sooner than 2001: "I really regret my own role in all this because I put up with it for too long. We put up with a lot of crap that we shouldn't have put up with, hoping. It was always the hope that Eric would step up to the plate and be accountable."

While Clarke is content to let the past stay in the past—"That was a long time ago, and it turned out okay for everybody in the end," he said—Snider isn't as delicate.

The chairman's loyalty to former players is well-known throughout the league, and when he had a more active daily role, he made it a point to thank players traded away for their service to the club.

"I have a special affection for most players," he said. "The only player that we ever traded up until the last couple years ... that I didn't call was Eric Lindros. The only guy."

REBIRTH

SOLD!

In 1996, after 30 years of majority ownership of the Flyers, Ed Snider no longer was the rambunctious young executive who was as willing to drop the gloves as his players.

Times had changed, and the Ed Snider of 1996 was a sports mogul, one of the longest-tenured owners in the NHL, the owner of one arena with another, his hockey pleasure palace, going up across the parking lot. Spectacor, the arena management company he had started to run the Spectrum, had become incredibly successful.

"I'm one of the few guys who made his money in sports," he said.

Heading a major corporation as well as a major sports team had taken its toll on Snider. His contentious dealings with 76ers owner Harold Katz and the city of Philadelphia over the construction of what would become the Wells Fargo Center had worn him out.

But as Snider was slowing down, one of his former employees had made the jump from a 33 RPM record to a 78.

Pat Croce had been the strength and conditioning coach for the Flyers and 76ers in the 1980s, and then turned a physical fitness and therapy center in Broomall, Pennsylvania, into a 40-franchise chain before selling out in 1993.

Looking for a new challenge, Croce took Katz to lunch in November 1995. Croce knew Katz had grown weary of the

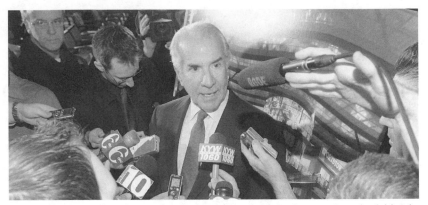

Despite the ownership shakeup in the 1990s that brought Comcast into the fold, Ed Snider remains at the center of the Flyers organization as shown here in a January 2008 press conference.

negative press surrounding his ownership of the NBA team and asked if he could become Katz's partner. Katz rejected the overtures, saying the team wasn't for sale; if he would sell, he told Croce, he would get out completely.

Croce kept pressing Katz, and with Philadelphia real estate magnate Ron Rubin in tow—Rubin had developed the Bellevue Hotel complex and the Suburban Station building, among others—Croce finally wore Katz down. On February 5, 1996, the 76ers owner gave Croce and Rubin 30 days to make a formal offer.

Rubin told Snider, an old friend, that he planned on speaking with Comcast Corp., the Philadelphia-based cable television behemoth, about financing their deal to buy the 76ers. Rubin had watched media companies like ITT/Cablevision buy the New York Knicks and Rangers, as well as Madison Square Garden and the MSG television network, and thought that was the way of the future. To Rubin, that future needed to involve Comcast. At the time, Comcast was the nation's third-largest cable television provider, with more than 9 million subscribers.

Comcast chairman Ralph Roberts and his son Brian, the company's president, shared Rubin's belief that media companies owning sports teams—which would provide relatively inexpensive, easy programming—was a good direction in which to head.

"Ron Rubin was in the shower one day and came up with the idea that it would be fantastic if Comcast got involved in buying the Sixers and buying me and all the other stuff [the two buildings]," Snider said.

"I was starting to think about having some exit strategy sometime in the future," he added.

Snider and Rubin met the Robertses on February 24 at the Comcast offices in Philadelphia. When the meeting started, Snider was unsure of where it would go. But by the end, he said, he was on board, and on March 19, 1996 the deal was finalized.

"I wouldn't have made the deal if I had had doubts," Snider said. "It made sense for everybody. I really like the Robertses."

It helped that Snider had an extra ace in his pocket. The Flyers' boss had agreements in place with the 76ers and Phillies to start a new all-sports television network.

"It was the most important part to Comcast," he said.

In 1976 Snider had created PRISM, a pay-cable channel built around Flyers, 76ers and Phillies games, plus first-run movies. He sold the channel in 1989 to a company owned by Cablevision founder Charles Dolan.

"I was very unhappy with the job Dolan was doing, so I worked the job with the Phillies, and when all of our contracts would end, I would start a new channel. I was in the process of starting the channel when I made the deal with Comcast. They have never really wanted to own teams, per se, but they felt the ownership would be an advantage if they were going to come into partners with the channel."

The deal saw the Robertses and Snider merge to form Comcast-Spectacor. The newly created company purchased the Flyers, 76ers, the TV network (later named Comcast SportsNet), the Spectrum, and the under-construction CoreStates Center. Comcast owned 66 percent of the new venture, with Snider retaining the other 34 percent. He was named chairman of the new company and was given full control of the Flyers and 76ers, as well as the management of the two buildings. Croce held a minority interest in the company and was named president of the 76ers.

"They [Comcast] wouldn't do the deal if I didn't stay in," Snider told the *Philadelphia Daily News*. "The management contract gives us complete control."

Snider relished the fact that he maintained control of the Flyers while being relieved of the financial burdens that came with majority ownership.

"I didn't need a partner in what I'm doing now," he told the media the day the deal was announced. "There are no financial problems. But I felt what Comcast brings into the fold will be very important to our future.

"I have no financial worries at all. There's been an awful lot written in the press that's erroneous. ... I just feel that this was an incredible opportunity for a synergy with people who don't really want to get involved in the operations. It gives us control of the whole operation, including the Sixers, and we'll be in control of our own destiny. We have a tremendous partner that has far-reaching tentacles, particularly in the media, and we hope to grow in those areas and make a whole lot more money."

That partnership has gone even better than Snider could have foreseen.

"I have to almost beg them to give input," he said. "They're just wonderful people in the sense that when they have a partner or an executive, they let them run with it. In sports, everybody knows better than the owner or the GM. When you think of a two-thirds partner, you'd think you'd have problems because things aren't always done the right way all the time. I've never heard a bad thing from Brian and Ralph Roberts. They're great partners."

And the success of that partnership is the only reason Snider continues to come to work every day.

"I didn't think I'd be here [17] years later," he said. "The relationship with Comcast and Brian and Ralph has been positive for me, not just from a partnership point of view, but it's really fun being around a company like Comcast. ... It's been fun to be on that end, too, to watch what they've done and be in the inner circle. It's expanded my view. It's expanded my horizon."

REBUILDING

On Sunday, October 22, 2006—the Flyers' version of Black Sunday—the team was 1–6–1, the worst start in franchise history. That morning, team chairman Ed Snider replaced Bob Clarke as general manager on an interim basis with assistant GM Paul Holmgren; Holmgren's first move was firing coach Ken Hitchcock and replacing him with assistant coach John Stevens.

The change was an attempt to spark a struggling team that, at least on paper, looked like a playoff squad. Instead, it was a band-aid on a sliced artery.

The Flyers continued to hemorrhage losses while Holmgren, along with team president Peter Luukko, formulated a plan.

"As we got into the season, we saw the team wasn't heading in the right direction," Luukko said. "And we said, 'What are we going to do to make this team better long-term?'"

Ahead of the Flyers were two paths.

"There were two courses we could take," Luukko said. "One was trade away some of our youth to get some older veterans and maybe just make the playoffs, but probably knowing that you don't know how much better you'd be the next year. That could have been Plan A, but Plan B was the better one. In sports, if you build short-term, you're in trouble. We said, don't give up on young players. Maybe they're in situations that you wouldn't really want them in at that time, but they're gaining in experience.

The plan was to build the core of the team around their rich crop of youngsters—Jeff Carter, Mike Richards, R.J. Umberger, Joni Pitkanen, Antero Niittymaki—and complement them with high-character veterans.

Snider gave his blessing, but as Luukko said, "It's one thing to have a plan; it's another to execute it."

Holmgren's first moves, though, looked like he was reverting back to Plan A. Out went young defenseman Freddy Meyer, traded to the New York Islanders for veteran blueliner Alexei Zhitnik. Not long after, forward Randy Robitaille went to the Islanders for center Mike York.

ONE FINAL LOSS

Even after the disastrous 2006–07 season ended in April, the Flyers still suffered one more loss.

Finishing with the worst record in the league, the club had a better than 50-percent chance of winning the draft lottery. But when the Ping-Pong balls were pulled, the Flyers slid to the No. 2 spot, one position after the Chicago Blackhawks. They selected James van Riemsdyk with the second pick, one spot after the Blackhawks drafted Patrick Kane.

Years later that lottery loss cost them dearly—Kane scored the series-clinching overtime goal in Game 6 of the 2010 Stanley Cup Final.

While on the surface those moves looked like a desperate grab for a postseason berth that seemed farther away by the day, Luukko said there was more to it.

"He [Holmgren] said to me, 'Peter, I'm going to do this, but this is what I'm thinking. These guys will make our team better if we start going, but if we don't, they're also assets that teams are going to want at the trade deadline. I can move these guys at the trade deadline.'"

Holmgren's biggest decision, though, was what to do with Peter Forsberg. The sublimely talented Swede had spent more time in doctor's waiting rooms than the locker room. Besides his chronically sore feet, there was his impending unrestricted free agency.

It became a daily soap opera. What would Peter do? Re-sign? Retire? Accept a trade to a contending club? It all added another drag to a team plummeting to new depths by the day.

"We all took turns trying to convince Peter to re-sign," Holmgren said. "The players, myself, even Mr. Snider. To Peter's credit, he couldn't commit due to his own personal health issues. Once we were able to begrudgingly make that trade, we were able to move forward."

"That trade" came February 15, 2007, as Forsberg waived his no-trade clause and was dealt to the Nashville Predators, in exchange for forward Scottie Upshall, defense prospect Ryan Parent, and first- and third-round picks in the 2007 NHL Draft.

"Peter helped us because he wouldn't commit because of his health issues," Holmgren said. "That really got the ball rolling to retooling. He was a strong asset we were able to parlay into different assets along the way."

While Parent was the major defense prospect the Flyers needed, Upshall had an immediate impact. He had six goals and 13 points in 18 games, and his speed, energy and exuberance almost single-handedly fueled some strong, late-season play.

Holmgren continued to retool his team at the trade deadline. Zhitnik was sent to the Atlanta Thrashers for defense prospect Braydon Coburn, a 6'5", 220-pounder who could skate like a greyhound. Out went disappointing forward Kyle Calder to Detroit as part of a three-way trade which landed the Flyers young shot-blocking defenseman Lasse Kukkonen from Chicago.

"When we acquired Alexei, we had no intention of moving him on at any point," Holmgren said. "We liked the player, we liked the fact that he had two years more remaining on his contract at a fairly reasonable [salary cap] number for a player of that caliber. When Braydon Coburn's name came into the equation, it was something we felt we couldn't pass up."

Holmgren liked Kukkonen after seeing him play against the Phantoms with the Blackhawks' AHL team, and thought he was stuck behind fellow young Chicago blueliners Duncan Keith, Brent Seabrook, and Cam Barker.

"I think they have a lot of young players," Holmgren said, "but at the end of the day, you can't play them all. He just became available."

Also coming available was goaltender Martin Biron.

Biron had spent most of the last decade on the Sabres' bench, first as a backup to Dominik Hasek and then Ryan Miller. He had opportunities at the starter's spot, but injuries usually seemed to sidetrack him.

"The Marty Biron thing came about over a month of conversations back and forth trying to work that out," Holmgren said. "I think Marty was a sought-after guy by a couple other teams."

Biron was set to become an unrestricted free agent in the summer of 2007, but the Flyers took a chance, sending a 2007 second-round pick to the Sabres. "Giving up a high pick to get him, it's a little bit of a gamble," Holmgren said. "You know he's going to be an unrestricted free agent, you have no idea whether you can sign him. You have no idea whether he's going to like Philadelphia. We all liked the goalie, had a lot of good knowledge because of Donnie Luce [the Flyers' director of player development had served a similar role for years in Buffalo]. His character, what type of guy he was. You're giving up the 31st pick in the draft, and you have to talk him into staying."

The Flyers, though, gave Biron the chance he always had wanted—to be the unquestioned starter. He played well enough—and liked his time in black and orange enough—that he signed a two-year contract extension just before the season ended.

"Personally, this is very big for me," Biron said the day he signed the new deal. "It was big that they came in and got me at the trade deadline, to be able to know more about me and introduce me to this organization and move forward. I want to move forward, too. That was a big part of my decision."

The decisions made by Holmgren at the trade deadline put an end to any lingering doubts that he was the right man for the job. Holmgren had been installed as the full-time GM months earlier, but it came after the embarrassing news broke in early November that Snider had offered the post to NHL senior vice president and director of hockey operations Colin Campbell. Shortly after Campbell rejected the deal, Snider removed Holmgren's interim tag.

"I thought he was very steady and calm during the process," Luukko said of Holmgren. "Also, he acted like that job was definitely going to be his. He didn't panic, make this move or that move and they'll give me the job. He was very comfortable in doing what was right for the team long-term, which I thought was very impressive."

"Once the initial thing with Colin Campbell was put to rest, I just went about doing what I was going to do anyway," Holmgren said.

But he couldn't rest on his successful trade-deadline moves. Part of the plan he had put into place was clearing cap room to make a big splash in free agency.

"We knew we were going to have some money to spend in the summertime, and we knew there would be free agents," Holmgren said. "It would be a pretty good market, and there would be players that could plug holes in the areas we needed."

Those needs included scoring depth on the wings, a top-line center and a stronger leadership core. In a two-week span that summer, he completed his to-do list.

His first step on the road back to success was for the GM at the southern point of the standings to turn his gaze south on the map. In June 2007, Nashville Predators owner Craig Leipold, claiming he was tired of losing money, put the team up for sale. To make the team more buyer-friendly, GM David Poile was told to cut payroll. That meant impending unrestricted free agents like forwards Forsberg, Paul Kariya, and Scott Hartnell, along with defenseman Kimmo Timonen, likely would not be re-signed.

"I called David a little bit after they had lost out in the play-offs, and we talked for quite a while that first time," Holmgren said. "There was a lot going on about Nashville, with their team's status, and he had the pending free agents—Kariya, Timonen, Hartnell and Forsberg—and I asked him the question, are you going to try to get any of your guys signed. He said, 'We're going to try, but I don't know how successful we'll be.' I raised the idea of, 'Maybe there's something we can do where you don't just lose the players for nothing.'"

Holmgren was focused on Timonen and Hartnell. Timonen, a two-time NHL All-Star, was considered one of the best all-round players at his position. Hartnell brought size at 6'2" and 210 pounds, and skill, shown by consecutive 20-goal seasons.

Holmgren and Poile spoke a few more times, and in late June, Poile gave Holmgren a 48-hour window to negotiate deals with Timonen and Hartnell.

"We agreed to a timeframe where I could talk to the players themselves, and if we came to an agreement with those players, there would be a return for Nashville," Holmgren said. "If we could only sign Timonen, it was a certain price; if we could only sign Hartnell, it was a certain price; and if we could sign both, it was the first-round pick." That first-round pick would be the one the Predators had given the Flyers in the Forsberg deal months earlier.

Hartnell agreed to a six-year, $24 million deal before the deadline. Getting Timonen signed proved a bit harder.

"As the time was ticking down, I had to call [Poile] for a half-hour extra," Holmgren said. "We just had to finalize a few things with Timonen."

The blueliner eventually agreed to a six-year, $37.5 million pact. Drawing assists on the signing were Kimmo's brother Jussi, a defenseman playing for the Phantoms, and Sami Kapanen, a long-time friend from Finland.

"I talked to my brother and I talked to Sami right away," Kimmo said after the deal was done. "There were so many positive things about this city of Philadelphia and the Flyers.

"They had a bad year last year, but I believe that we can turn it around and have a really good team next year. The one big thing was maybe getting a couple more players before the start of the season, and talking to Holmgren, he said he was going to do everything he can to get a couple more guys."

Holmgren lived up to his words. On July 1, the first day of free agency, he went fishing for the biggest catches. He put hooks in the water for centers Danny Briere, Chris Drury and Scott Gomez, as well as power forward Ryan Smyth.

All the offers went out about noon. Then, like any other fishing trip, it became all about patience.

"To me, that was more nerve-wracking than the trade deadline," Holmgren said. "It was the first time I ever went through that as a manger. You're just waiting. There's nothing you can do but wait."

Holmgren's patience paid off when Briere took the Flyers' bait.

"We talked again, it was 3:30, and we were able to get it done by 4:15," Holmgren said. "There was a lot of excitement in my office that day."

There was a lot of excitement in the Briere household, as well. The league's 10th-leading scorer with 95 points in 2006–07, Briere inked an eight-year, $52 million contract that was front-loaded to pay him $10 million in the 2007–08 season.

Danny Briere (third from left) is shown with coach John Stevens (left), team general manager Paul Holmgren, and Peter Luukko, president and C.O.O. of Comcast-Spectacor (right) after a news conference at the Philadelphia Flyers offices in Voorhees, New Jersey, July 12, 2007. *Photo courtesy AP Images.*

While Holmgren was celebrating reeling in Briere, another fish jumped in his boat.

The Flyers' GM had been talking to his Edmonton counterpart, Kevin Lowe, for months regarding forward Joffrey Lupul. The 24-year-old had dropped from 28 goals to 16 in his first season in Edmonton and was in desperate need of a fresh start after a disappointing season in his hometown. In return, Lowe demanded Pitkanen.

Holmgren long had hoped Pitkanen would live up to his vast potential, but the enigmatic Finn, taken by the Flyers with the fourth pick of the 2002 draft, would flash one moment of brilliance for three moments of mind-boggling ineptitude.

"I had a hard time even talking about moving Joni," Holmgren said. "But when Jason Smith's name came up that morning, I think something just said I better think about that one."

The defenseman had served as Edmonton's captain longer than either Wayne Gretzky or Mark Messier, and his toughness and dependability were unquestioned. Once Smith's name was added to the equation along with Lupul, Holmgren added winger Geoff Sanderson to complete the transaction.

Timonen and Hartnell also officially signed their deals, making July 1, 2007, one of the most productive days in Flyers history.

"That was the first time in our 40 years that we ended with the worst record in the league, and not only was it embarrassing, it was unacceptable, and I certainly hope that the moves that we've made will fix that problem," Snider told reporters that day.

Briere was the big catch, turning down more money from other teams to come to Philadelphia.

"They were the best fit, the best organization, and the team that committed to winning the most," he said days after he signed. "I don't think money was an issue at all."

But it certainly helped, as did having a few familiar faces in the locker room. Biron was Briere's best friend and road roommate in Buffalo, and defenseman Denis Gauthier was a teammate in junior hockey.

"Having some friends on the team, playing with Marty, being his roommate in Buffalo [helped]," he said. "I played with Denis Gauthier in junior. [Defenseman] Alex Picard is from my home-town. And Simon [Gagne], knowing him from here and there. There were a lot of guys I knew in the dressing room that I felt very comfortable with."

And while he signed on the first day possible, Briere didn't just jump at the first big-money contract thrown his way.

"I'd been watching [the Flyers] since the trade deadline," he said. "What they did at the trade deadline, what they did before July 1, it was something that was very interesting. They're com-mitted to winning. And they showed everybody they were serious about turning things around. A lot of teams will say that, but here we had a team that was doing it—acting it, as well."

"I never want to go through this again as long as I live," Luukko said. "But there is something to be said that things need to get worse before they get better. We had a chance to take a core of guys we believe in and really build for the future."

CHANGING COURSE

When the Flyers drafted Jeff Carter and Mike Richards in the first round of the 2003 NHL Draft, the thought was the team had found building blocks that would carry the club to success well into the next decade.

The pair debuted in the 2005–06 season and quickly grew into the kind of cornerstone players the team had hoped for. The organization showed how much it believed in them by signing Richards to a 12-year, $69 million contract extension in December 2007, and naming him team captain in September 2008. And in November 2010 they locked Carter in with an 11-year, $58 million deal.

However, there were issues on and off the ice with both players. Rumors of excessive partying dogged the team during the 2008–09 season, with Carter and Richards seen as part of a cabal

"DRY ISLAND"

When Peter Laviolette was hired in December 2009, one of his first acts was to institute a "Dry Island," with players pledging to abstain from alcohol for a month by writing their uniform number on a board. According to a source, the *Philadelphia Inquirer* reported Mike Richards and Jeff Carter chose to take themselves off the island.

The *Inquirer* report stated that in five other instances where Laviolette brought back the Dry Island concept, Richards and Carter refused to sign on.

GM Paul Holmgren confirmed the report that Carter and Richards stayed off Dry Island, but added other players did as well, saying, "We carry 23 players and there weren't 23 numbers up there."

of young players spending too much time in the bars in the Old City section of Philadelphia. GM Paul Holmgren told the Bucks County Courier Times that he spoke to his players about being more disciplined in their personal lives.

"It's off-ice discipline," Holmgren said. "It's night before a game taking better care of ourselves. That's a natural maturation process that a lot of our younger players are still going through. We've addressed that. So am I concerned about it? We'll see how it goes this year. All our players have been talked to about it. Is it an issue? The fact that we've talked about it, I guess it is an issue."

Holmgren attempted to solve the issue by bringing in a new voice for the locker room—in June 2009 he traded for brash defenseman Chris Pronger. It looked to be a caustic mix early in the season. Coach John Stevens, who had formed a special bond with Carter and Richards dating to their AHL championship in 2005, was fired that December and replaced by Peter Laviolette. There also appeared to be a divided locker room, with younger players—among them Richards and Carter—on one side and veterans—Pronger, Ian Laperriere, Kimmo Timonen and Danny Briere among them—on the other.

A détente appeared to be reached during the 2010 Olympic break, when Pronger and Richards were teammates in Vancouver and helped Canada win the gold medal, and the peace allowed the Flyers to go on their remarkable run to the 2010 Stanley Cup Final.

After the Flyers went out in four games in the second round of the 2011 playoffs, however, Holmgren knew something needed to change with the makeup of his roster. At the top of his list was solving the team's goaltending issues, which he addressed June 7, 2011, by acquiring the rights to goaltender Ilya Bryzgalov from the Phoenix Coyotes.

That only solved part of the problem, though. Holmgren had decided the Flyers as led by Richards and Carter had gone as far as they could and wanted to make a change before the no-trade clauses in both players' contracts kicked in.

So on June 23, 2011, Holmgren made a pair of trades that rocked the franchise and stunned the rest of the league. First,

Carter was dealt to the Columbus Blue Jackets in exchange for forward Jakub Voracek, the eighth pick of the 2011 draft and a 2011 third-round pick. Next, he sent Richards to the Los Angeles Kings for forwards Wayne Simmonds and Brayden Schenn, plus a 2012 second-round draft pick.

"What we've done today is change the direction of our organization with these two moves," Holmgren said.

That change didn't come without some pain. It was Holmgren who led the scouting department when the Flyers selected Richards and Carter; it was Holmgren who signed off on Richards receiving the captaincy; and it was Holmgren who negotiated the long-term deals for Richards and Carter.

"Those are two hard phone calls to make," an emotional Holmgren said the day of the trades. "I think the world of both of them. That's difficult. That's the hard part of the job. That was tough, obviously."

Luukko also was scarred by the moves, mostly because of a special relationship he and his family had developed with the Carters.

"I've known Jeff and his mom and dad since he was about 12 years old," Luukko said. "We [Comcast-Spectacor] built an arena

CHAMPIONSHIP TRADES

Mike Richards and Jeff Carter never wanted to leave the Flyers. But in the end, it worked out okay for them.

Richards had 44 points in 74 games as the Kings' second line center, but Carter struggled in Columbus with a foot injury, and while he had 25 points in 39 games, never was happy as the Blue Jackets plummeted to the bottom of the league standings.

He earned a reprieve when he was dealt to the Kings in February 2012, and reunited with Richards, helped Los Angeles win the franchise's first Stanley Cup. Richards was fourth on the team with 15 points in 20 games, while Carter had a team-high eight goals, including the game-winning goal in the Kings' Cup-clinching victory.

in London, Ontario, and Jeff's mom worked for the construction company. My family is very friendly with the Carter family, so it was very, very difficult."

Carter and Richards also were shocked by the trades.

"Mike and Jeff were extremely upset," Holmgren said. "It's a call that they ... not only was it tough for me to make, it was tough for them to receive. When you're around this business long enough, you get to know that it is a business. Hopefully everyone will move on. They're both good players in our league and they'll go on to be productive players on their new teams."

The Flyers also moved on. While announcing the trades, the Flyers also revealed they had signed Bryzgalov to a nine-year,

CUTTING THEIR LOSSES

The Philadelphia Flyers had high hopes for Ilya Bryzgalov when they traded two franchise cornerstones to free up cap space to sign the goaltender to a nine-year, $51.5 million contract.

But just two seasons later, the Flyers used one of the two compliance buyouts granted each franchise in the 2013 collective bargaining agreement to terminate the final seven seasons of Bryzgalov's deal.

The Flyers will pay Bryzgalov more than $1.6 million per season through the end of the 2026–27 season not to play for the team.

Despite widely reported issues with Bryzgalov in the locker room, general manager Paul Holmgren said the decision to cut ties with Bryzgalov was a financial issue more than anything.

"It's a costly mistake that we made," he said. "You know Ilya, it's hard to fault him. I still believe he played pretty good, but in a salary-cap world you need to make decisions from time to time that put you in a better light moving forward and this is one of those."

Including bonuses, the Flyers paid Bryzgalov $16.5 million for a two-season record of 52–33–7 with a 2.60 goals-against average, .905 save percentage and seven shutouts in 99 games. He also had a 5–5 record with a 3.46 GAA and .887 save percentage in 11 Stanley Cup playoff games—all in his first season.

JAGR HOCKEY SCHOOL

Jaromir Jagr asked for one perk when he signed with the Flyers—a key to the Skate Zone, the Flyers' practice facility, for 24-hour access.

Jagr enjoyed going to the rink late at night to work out, sometimes skating wearing a weighted vest or shooting and stickhandling with a weighted stick. Teammates sometimes would join him. It became known as the Jagr Hockey School.

"I went a couple times," Jakub Voracek said. "It was interesting to see what he was doing on the ice at night. He's working on little things. It's not like he's here working out for two, two and a half hours, or he's skating for two and a half hours. He just goes every night for 30, 35, 40 minutes. But if you do that every night, eventually you're going to get better, or you're going to end up as the best at it."

$51.5 million contract. A day later, they used the eighth pick of the draft on center Sean Couturier.

The salary-cap savings also allowed the Flyers to make even more shocking moves in free agency. On July 1, they signed future Hall of Famer Jaromir Jagr to a one-year contract.

Jagr had spent the three previous seasons playing in Russia, but had expressed interest in returning to the NHL. Despite being 39 years old, teams were clamoring for his services, and it appeared he was destined to return to the Pittsburgh Penguins, the team he started his career with. Instead, it was Holmgren swooping in thanks to a text message and some persuasive words.

"It sort of just started innocently," Holmgren said the day after the signing. "I just sent a text to Petr Svoboda, his agent, who also represents Jake Voracek, and I didn't know who was involved. I read over the last few days it was just Detroit and Pittsburgh were the teams, so I just sent him a text about if Jaromir would have interest in playing for Philadelphia and it just kind of went from there, and culminated today with our signing of him."

SKATING WITH HIS IDOL

Growing up in the Czech Republic town of Kladno, Jakub Voracek idolized the city's most famous hockey player, Jaromir Jagr. He even had a picture taken of himself at age five with Jagr when Jagr played in Kladno during 1994–95 lockout. Little did the 5-year-old Voracek know that eventually he would be sharing a locker room with his hockey hero.

"I got traded [to the Flyers] on June 22 and he signed July 1 and I signed [that day] as well," Voracek said. "Signed at the same time, so that was pretty cool."

Voracek and Jagr share the same agent, and Voracek said he was present during the Flyers' negotiations to bring Jagr to Philadelphia.

"I was in the same house with [agent] Petr Svoboda, so I knew what was going on with everything," Voracek said. "As soon as he put the phone down and I realized I was going to play with Jagr on the same team, I said it's going to be a pretty cool year."

Jagr was an immediate hit, with his legendary work ethic turning him into a role model.

"He's been a terrific influence on our younger players ... having them after practice or getting them extra work or coming back to the rink for some extra work," coach Peter Laviolette said. "Just having his experience in the locker room, you wouldn't know that he's closing in [on age 40]."

"To see Jags ... and the work he put in and the time he put in just to make sure he was ready and improving his game," Braydon Coburn added. "Even at 40 he still felt like there were many things he could improve on. That was really good for a lot of guys in our dressing room to see."

Some of that work came at late-night skating sessions—sometimes solo, sometimes with teammates. It became known as "Jagr Hockey School."

Teammate Jody Shelley told Yahoo Sports! that the Jagr Hockey School, "is just one example of how much he likes to be here and what he expects from himself. That's something that rubs off on you, when you have a guy that expects so much of himself. ... He loves hockey more than any guy maybe in the room. I've never seen guys do it before, let alone Jaromir Jagr."

Jagr spent the season on the Flyers' top line, alongside Claude Giroux and Scott Hartnell, and the trio became one of the league's most dynamic lines. Both Giroux and Hartnell were All-Stars and posted career-best offensive numbers. Giroux was third in the NHL with 93 points, the most by a Flyer since Eric Lindros had 93 in the 1998–99 season. Hartnell had a career-best 37 goals, tied for sixth in the league, and his 16 power-play goals were second.

Jagr, who turned 40 in February 2011, finished with 19 goals and 54 points in 73 games, and helped the Flyers reach the second round of the playoffs. He left in the summer of 2012 to sign with the Dallas Stars, but his one season in Philadelphia provided a lifetime of memories for those lucky enough to play with him.

"He just has input on anyone's game if they're open for any ideas," Shelly told Yahoo! Sports. "He's just got a lot of things to tell me and talk about. It would have been nice to meet him 20 years ago."

STADIUMS

THE SPECTRUM

In 1965 Ed Snider was putting together his bid for a professional hockey team. At the top of his to-do list was finding a home for his club.

Owning a pro hockey team was a second job for Snider, who also was treasurer and part owner of the Philadelphia Eagles. One of his major roles with the football team at the time was developing a new multi-purpose stadium on the south end of Broad Street, near the Philadelphia Navy Yard, which would be the new home of the Eagles and the Philadelphia Phillies.

While struggling to move the project through the Philadelphia city machinery, Snider was approached by Ike Richman, who owned the Philadelphia 76ers. Richman wanted to move his team out of the Philadelphia Convention Center and wanted to know if Snider thought Eagles majority owner Jerry Wolman, a real estate developer, could help him build a new arena.

"I said we're not in the business of building arenas," Snider said, "but let me think about it."

Snider still was thinking about it as he was contemplating his bid for an expansion NHL team. In the plan for what would become Veterans Stadium, he saw room for two buildings.

"I thought to have it in South Philly because I always thought this was the best location because of the roads all converging here, from New Jersey, from Northeast Philadelphia, the

Schuylkill, from Delaware," he said. "I thought this was the [perfect] location."

Snider met with Philadelphia City Councilman Paul D'Ortona, with whom he had been working on the Veterans Stadium project. Snider proposed that since the city owned the land where the new stadium was being constructed, as well as the surrounding parking lots, an arena could be built in one of the lots between the new building and JFK Stadium. Snider said his group would lease the land and parking lots from the city, but the arena would be privately built and owned. The building would house the Flyers and the 76ers, as well as concerts and other events.

"You have to understand, I was talking to a guy who had been involved with a stadium project that had been delayed 10 years in haggling over the use of city funds," Snider said in *Full Spectrum*. "It had become a huge political football. And I'm talking about putting down an arena at no cost to the city that would generate all kinds of revenues to help pay off the [stadium] debt."

D'Ortona loved the idea, and he and Snider took their plan to Philadelphia Mayor James Tate, who didn't need much convincing. According to Snider, "They all agreed to it, and we made a deal in 15 minutes."

Snider, in *Full Spectrum*, said, "Tate turned to the city solicitor and said, 'I want you to do everything humanly possible to cut through all the garbage so that they can get this thing done.'"

On February 9, 1966, the NHL announced Philadelphia would receive one of six new expansion franchises. That afternoon, Snider and Tate announced plans for the new 15,000-seat South Philadelphia indoor arena.

On April 4, 1966, team president Bill Putnam announced the architectural firm Skidmore, Owings and Merrill had been hired to develop the new arena, and ground was broken June 1, 1966. A two-tier design was planned, which would seat 15,000 for hockey and 16,500 for basketball. The tiers were tapered sharply to provide the best sight lines, and there would be no obstructed views.

"The guidelines the architects used was that if you were sitting in the last row, you could see the goalies," Hal Freeman, first president of the new arena, said in *Full Spectrum*.

BROKEN WINDOW

The large windows that ringed the Spectrum concourse weren't supposed to open. But they did March 13, 1993.

During the first period of a game against the Los Angeles Kings, a vicious wind and snow storm—which dropped two feet of snow on some parts of the Delaware Valley—blew out one of the windows, sending shards of glass through the concourse and down to the ice. Thankfully only one person suffered a minor injury.

The teams finished the first period tied 1–1, and the game was canceled, much to the chagrin of the 2,000 or so hearty souls who braved the elements to see it.

Finding a name for the new building fell to team vice-president Lou Scheinfeld, who Snider had hired away from the *Philadelphia Daily News'* city hall beat.

Scheinfeld didn't know what name to use, but he knew what he didn't want—no use of the "A" word: Arena. Scheinfeld and Bill Becker, an executive for the company designing the Flyers' uniforms, donned hard hats and walked around the construction site, hoping an idea—and not a steel beam—would hit them.

"I'm thinking about how this building will host a number of different events," Becker recalled in *Full Spectrum*. "I thought of color and this being a stadium or auditorium, and 'Spectrum' popped into my head and out my mouth.

"I remember Lou saying, 'Doesn't that sound a little pharmaceutical?' I told Lou no, that it suggested blocks of colors which would be great for a billboard and a logo."

The pair came up with a proposal to take to Snider and Wolman. They turned Spectrum into an acronym—SP for sports, E for entertainment, C for concerts, T for theatrics, R for recreation, and UM for stadium.

Snider and Wolman thought it was a grand idea, and the new building would be named the Spectrum.

In making the announcement, Freeman said, "Spectrum is a series of images which form a display of colors. We have the only Spectrum in the whole world. It sounds like spectacle and spectacular."

Not everyone, though, was on board with the idea.

"It sounds like they've reached too far in groping for something unique," wrote *Philadelphia Daily News* columnist Stan Hochman.

Snider recalled other dissenting opinions.

"People were coming up to me and saying, 'It sounds like a doctor's instrument,'" he recalled in *Full Spectrum.*

The original plan was for the seats to play off the "display of colors" motif, with the chairs to come in four colors—blue, apple green, magenta and orange—and be arranged in concentric circles throughout the building. That plan was scrapped, though, when the fabric company couldn't get all the right shades in time for an August installation. Instead, a uniform dark red was chosen.

The Spectrum opened September 30, 1967, less than 16 months after ground was broken, and at a cost of just $6.5 million. The first event at the building was the two-night Quaker City Jazz Festival.

The Flyers took their first laps around the new ice October 15, 1967. The practice was open to the public, but only about 10 people took the team up on the offer. Those that stayed away missed little, as shooting was kept to a minimum due to the boards having not yet been delivered due to a manufacturers' strike. Snider allegedly had to bribe a union worker to open the gate so his trucks could come in and get the boards out.

The first official sporting event at the Spectrum was held October 17, 1967, a boxing card headlined by Philadelphia native Joe Frazier. The building's official dedication came the next day, prior to the Philadelphia 76ers' home opener.

The pundits weighed in on the arena, with one calling it the "Fish Can on the Delaware Flats," while another wondered why a building named for an array of colors would have such a bland, brown brick exterior.

The interior, though, was a different story, as the ushers wore blue suits and the usherettes were attired in burnt-orange blazers and hot pink miniskirts.

Finally, the first Flyers home game arrived, on October 19, 1967. A curious crowd of 7,812 paid between $2 and $5.50 for tickets. The high prices were blamed for the poor turnout, but NHL president Clarence Campbell, on hand to drop the ceremonial first puck, said the league had to "charge luxury prices for a luxury product."

SPECTRUM II—THE FIVE-YEAR, FIVE-DAY DEAL

In November 1989 the Spectrum was just 22 years old—not ancient by any means, but in the world of sports arenas, 22 is like 62. And with just 14 lucrative luxury suites to sell and player salaries ever on the rise, the Flyers had just about maxed out their building revenues.

76ers owner Harold Katz was in a similar boat, but his was a little leakier. He shared the Spectrum with the Flyers, but was just a tenant in Snider's hockey home. He paid about $1.5 million yearly in rent and shared in none of the money the building raised in suite sales or concessions.

In 1988 Katz opened talks with Robert Mulcahy, the chairman of the New Jersey Sports and Exposition Authority, about moving the team to an arena on the Camden waterfront.

At a Police Athletic League event in November 1989, Snider, seated next to Philadelphia Mayor Wilson Goode, mentioned Katz's talks with Mulcahy. Goode replied that a deal for a new arena in Philadelphia could be done in five days.

With Goode's assurances in hand, Snider told Katz that building a single-tenant arena was a bad idea. Katz agreed, and the pair formed a partnership to construct a new arena, ostensibly in Philadelphia. Spectacor, the company Snider had created to manage the Spectrum, would take the lead role in negotiations.

Katz signed a 30-year lease agreement with Spectacor to have the 76ers play in the new building. In return, Katz was given a $1 million reduction in yearly game-night costs, and he would receive a share of parking, concession, luxury box and advertising revenue generated by the new building.

Goode suggested JFK Stadium, which had fallen into disrepair and had been shut down in July 1989, as the best site. Spectacor agreed.

Despite promises from the state of New Jersey to pay for nearly two-thirds of the projected $100 million cost of an arena in Camden, Snider and Spectacor's first choice was to stay in Philadelphia. There was no way the city, nearly bankrupt at the time, could equal New Jersey's offer, but Snider was committed to staying where he was, even if it meant privately financing the building in a similar way to how the Spectrum was built.

That Spectrum deal—a trade of city land for a privately financed building that paid no property taxes—came under serious political scrutiny. Regardless, all Snider needed to do was look at a map.

"We were in the best location in the Delaware Valley," Snider recalled in *Full Spectrum*. "The subway and I–95 are right there. I was reluctant to go to another location that I thought was less desirable."

In late 1990 Spectacor and the city of Philadelphia reached an understanding on a 21,000-seat arena to be built to replace JFK Stadium. Nothing could be announced, though, until the state of Pennsylvania was able to provide a financial bail-out for the city. New Jersey, though, learned of the offer and countered with a proposal to pay for as much as 80 percent of a new arena.

PHANTOMS

When the Flyers moved across the parking lot from the Spectrum to the newly-built CoreStates Center, the club wanted a new tenant for the old building.

Enter the Philadelphia Phantoms, the Flyers' new American Hockey League affiliate.

The team was a hit right from its debut in the 1996–97 season, and excelled on the ice and at the box office during its 13-year run. The club won a pair of AHL championships and developed a number of players and coaches for the Flyers.

Following the 2008–09 season, with the closing of the Spectrum, the Phantoms were sold and moved to upstate New York.

SAME BUILDING, DIFFERENT NAMES

The Flyers' new home may have taken five years to go from conception to completion, but the building has changed names like the team changes coaches.

In September 1994 CoreStates Financial Corp. spent $40 million to buy the naming rights to the Flyers' new home, as well as the Spectrum. The contract with CoreStates was for 29 years, but the name lasted four. First Union merged with CoreStates, and on September 1, 1998, the buildings were renamed for First Union.

On July 28, 2003, Wachovia Security's purchase of First Union meant another new name for the buildings. That lasted until July 1, 2010, when Wells Fargo's purchase of Wachovia meant a fourth name for the building in 16 years.

With a solid deal in hand from New Jersey, a push was made by Katz and members of Spectacor to move across the Delaware. Snider, though, held firm and continued to negotiate with the city of Philadelphia.

Part of the preliminary deal would see the city give a $6.5 million gift to Spectacor, which would pay for half of a multi-level parking garage, from which the city would receive no money. Frank Rizzo, running for re-election as mayor, used that part of the deal as a bullet point in his campaign, forcing Spectacor and the city back to the bargaining table.

The sides agreed to make the payment a low-interest loan, repayable by Spectacor over a 24-year period, and make it the only money laid out by the city. On June 10, 1991, at the Hershey Hotel, schematics were unveiled for the new arena, tentatively titled Spectrum II. The design called for 19,000 seats for hockey and included 78 luxury boxes. Included in the original design was a store-lined concourse that would connect the new building with the original Spectrum. Total cost was approximated at $200 million.

The land for the building would be leased from the city at a cost of $100,000 per year, with the cost rising by $5,000 a year through 2057. In return, Spectacor received a five-year tax abatement; starting in the sixth year, the property tax would be $2 million per year until 2024, and from that point it would go up $100,000 per year, until it maxed out at $4 million per annum. The state of Pennsylvania also agreed to pay $5 million to demolish JFK.

City councilwoman Anna Verna, who represented the stadium district, wasn't pleased by the deal, but when the contract went up for approval, the vote was unanimous, and on July 7, 1991, the contract was ratified.

Meanwhile, there was another deal, nearly just as big, happening a few hundred miles away. At the 1991 NHL Draft the Quebec Nordiques used the first choice on 18-year-old phenom Eric Lindros, who was going to lead the NHL into the 21st century. The Flyers were floundering. Russ Farwell, Bob Clarke's replacement as general manager, had made a number of deft moves, including obtaining defenseman Steve Duchesne and forwards Kevin Dineen, Mark Recchi and Rod Brind'Amour. The work went for naught, though, as the Flyers were forced to watch the 1992 playoffs on television, making it an unprecedented three-year drought.

Even in the pre-Internet days, Lindros was a name on the lips of even casual hockey fans. The legend of the hockey prodigy with gargantuan size and Gretzky-like touch had spread throughout the U.S. Lindros had vowed never to play for Quebec, and in June 1992, the Flyers' trade for Lindros was upheld by an arbitrator. Five players, two draft picks, and $15 million went to the Nordiques for Lindros, who then signed a six-year, $20.5 million contract with the Flyers.

In the days following the trade, fans swamped the Flyers' ticket office with requests.

"I've never seen anything like it in my 10 years here," recalled Jack Betson, then the team's vice president of sales, in *Full Spectrum*. "Some people who had canceled their season tickets called to say they want them back." Larry Rubin, a Spectacor spokesman, said calls regarding luxury boxes were running 60-percent higher than normal.

Interior view of the Wachovia Spectrum in July 2008. The Spectrum closed in 2009 to make way for a new entertainment development. *Photo courtesy AP Images.*

Snider had his star to put on the marquee of his new home. What he didn't have, though, was progress. More than a year after the city council had approved the deal, ground had yet to be broken.

Still without financing on November 28, 1993, Snider ripped up his deal with Katz and started all over. Katz, freed from the constraints of the new stadium, nearly secured his own deal from New Jersey Governor Jim Florio for an arena on the Camden waterfront near the state aquarium. But when Florio lost his re-election bid to Christine Todd Whitman, the new governor flushed the deal.

Eventually, Snider received $140 million from Prudential Power Funding Associates, and he and Katz made a tenuous peace. On February 1, 1994, Spectrum II again was announced, and on June 23, the new contact was ratified by Philadelphia City Council. On September 13, 1994—five years after Wilson Goode told Ed Snider the city could approve a new arena in five days— ground was broken.

"From the time I had the idea to build the Spectrum to the time it was completed was 16 months," Snider said. "Construction was 11 months. On the same parking lot, that building cost $6.5 million to build. This one [Wells Fargo Center] cost $200 and something [actually $210 million]. The agreements with the city and everybody else for [the Spectrum] was about [3–4 inches] thick; the agreements for this building filled a whole conference room. Same city, same parking lot, same circumstances.

"Just the workmen's compensation for this building cost more than that building [the Spectrum] to build."

On August 31, 1996, the Flyers' new home, initially named the CoreStates Center, finally opened.

FAREWELL TO THE SPECTRUM

For 40 years, the Spectrum served as the center of the winter sports universe in the Philadelphia region.

The building hosted a number of major events, topped by the final game of the 1974 Stanley Cup Final, which saw the Flyers become the first expansion team to win the Cup. Cup Finals in 1975, 1976, 1980, 1985, and 1987 also were played there, as was the famed 1976 game that saw the Flyers beat the Soviet Red Army team. Two NHL All-Star Games were played there, in 1976 and 1992.

The AHL Philadelphia Phantoms also won their first Calder Cup title at the Spectrum, in 1998.

However, the building mostly is remembered for being the lion's den opposing hockey teams most wanted to avoid, and caused the "Philly flu" to become an illness afflicting various visiting players.

"There was some intimidation involved," Gary Dornhoefer said of the Spectrum. "Number one, you had the noise factor. You couldn't even hear yourself talk on the ice, that's how loud it was. And because we played a very physical game, the combination of both made it a very intimidating place to play."

However, with the Flyers departing for the Wells Fargo Center in 1996, and with new stadiums for the Philadelphia Eagles and Philadelphia Phillies opening in the years after, the Spectrum began to look like an out-of-touch relic.

The building still was being used, mostly for the Phantoms but also for other minor events, like the Philadelphia Wings lacrosse team, monster truck rallies, ice shows and concerts. But by 2008, executives at Comcast-Spectacor found it was costing more to keep the building open.

"We had kept it alive and kept it going," Comcast-Spectacor and Flyers president Peter Luukko said. "The American Hockey League attendance was beginning to dip a little bit and we had a lot of infrastructure we had to put into the facility.

"When we built the Wells Fargo Center there was Veterans Stadium. To see the Eagles build a state-of-the-art facility and then obviously Citizens Bank Park is one of the nicest [baseball stadiums] in the league. The allure of the Spectrum, and even the Phantoms at that point, was waning.

"It was time to go."

Alternate uses for the real estate occupied by the Spectrum started being discussed.

"Ed [Snider, team chairman] had always said for years that he wanted a sports bar on the corner of Pattison and 11th," Luukko said. "And then we were able to meet with the Cordish Company. I had had an earlier meeting with them and we really got along. We researched their concepts around the country and realized they would be our best partner."

Cordish, a real estate development company based in Maryland, is best known for its re-development of the Baltimore's inner harbor with Power Plant Live. They've also opened success-ful entertainment districts in Kansas City, Louisville, Ky., and Toronto, among other areas.

In July 2009, Comcast-Spectacor and Cordish unveiled a sprawling $100 million plan for the Spectrum site, a 400,000-square-foot complex that included entertainment, restaurant and retail venues, as well as a hotel, and would link the Wells Fargo Center and Citizens Bank Park.

All that was needed to make it happen was to demolish the Spectrum. While that may have been an easy decision from a financial standpoint, the reality behind it was far harder.

"It was obviously the hardest on Ed," Luukko said. "He gave birth to the Spectrum. He's so visibly known for the Flyers, but the Spectrum was a big part of his life and his baby, also."

The first step was the sale of the Phantoms, who were moved to upstate New York. As the building was closed for events and demolition day neared, fans were allowed to buy just about any part of the Spectrum they could remove, from seats to pieces of the hockey boards and glass, to even a piece of the arena's ice—the water from the final rink was drained into five-gallon drums and shipped to a company in Chicago, which re-froze the water in drink coasters.

With the building stripped to its studs, it was time to bring in the heavy machinery. On November 23, 2010, a crane with an aptly-hued orange wrecking ball was driven in for the beginning of the demolition of the Spectrum. A public farewell for the building was held, with about 1,000 fans filling the Wells Fargo Center parking lots at 8:00 AM, about 4½ hours before the wrecking ball was scheduled to swing.

Among those in attendance for the event were Flyers legends from throughout the years, as well as Philadelphia Mayor Michael Nutter and other dignitaries. While most of the talk was centered on progress for the sports complex, it was a bittersweet day.

"To me it's not a celebration," Snider said, "but in another way it is. I'm very emotional about it."

"All of the great accomplishments that the Flyers had and I had as an individual were in that building," Flyers Hall of Famer Bob Clarke said. "That's home for me."

"For me, this is my childhood," Flyers anthem singer Lauren Hart said. "I spent it growing up here and running around this building. It's the first time I sang in a really big place. It holds so many memories for me other than sports. It's so personal with my father [Flyers Hall of Fame broadcaster Gene Hart] and my family."

After a few eulogies for the old barn, Snider said some final words and the signal was given for the wrecking ball to swing. Showing how tough the building was, the large steel ball hit the brick façade and bounced off. Like the players who once skated there, the building would not go down easy.

It took a few more swings, but the ball finally put a dent in the building. Unlike Veterans Stadium, which was imploded and turned into a pile of ash in mere seconds, the Spectrum demolition took months, with the building dying a little more each day.

"Our offices face the Spectrum," Luukko said. "To watch that thing get torn down day by day, it seemed to go forever."

Eventually the final beams were removed and the ground was paved smooth. Meanwhile, work was completed on what has become Xfinity Live!

The original sprawling plan was reduced to one 60,000-square-foot building that opened in March 2012. The center is the NBC Sports Arena, a sports bar which features a 32-foot LED HD television as well as a number of other HD televisions. Six restaurants branch off from the sports bar, among them the Spectrum Grill steakhouse, the PBR Bar and Grill, and the Victory Beer Hall. There's also an outdoor plaza and walkway lined by the statues that had stood around the Spectrum, as well as a bar and stage for musical acts.

"It's more than met our expectations," Luukko said. "It's been incredible. ... It's been a destination not only on events but off-nights. It's done very well from people coming to see the teams when they're on the road, or to see bands and have a fun time. It's also turned into an entertainment center on its own."

Luukko said there is room to expand, with a team-store concept being discussed, as well as more restaurants and possibly a hotel. He said the option also exists to leave Xfinity Live! exactly as-is.

"If we never did anything more, we'd be fine," he said.

NUMBERS DON'T LIE

THE STREAK

The 1979–80 season started with Pat Quinn in his first full season as coach. Quinn had replaced Bob McCammon 50 games into the previous season, and worked hard to rebuild relationships with players that had soured during McCammon's tenure.

Quinn also installed an up-tempo style of play, encouraging defensemen to join the rush and allowing forwards to move freely through the offensive zone. Helping install the new plan was Quinn's new assistant, player/coach, Bobby Clarke.

GM Keith Allen also drafted well, tabbing Brian Propp with the 14th choice of the 1979 draft. The left wing had totaled a remarkable 94 goals and 100 assists in 71 games the previous season for the Brandon Wheat Kings in the Western Hockey League. The quiet 20-year-old meshed well with the remaining Broad Street Bullies—Clarke, Bill Barber, Reggie Leach, Rick MacLeish, Bob Kelly, Jimmy Watson and Moose Dupont.

"I think I looked at it as I was going to help any team I could get to," Propp said. "Going later in that first round helped me to be with a more competitive team. I was just happy to contribute, but I knew I would really be able to help them out."

The rookie impressed early in training camp and earned a prime opening-night assignment.

"My first linemates were Bobby Clarke and Reggie Leach," Propp said, still amazed that's how his career started. "They helped me to adjust pretty quickly."

The season opened with a tribute to Bernie Parent, who had been forced into retirement during the previous season due to a serious eye injury.

Parent's No. 1 was raised to the rafters, never again to be worn. In a sense of irony, teammates presented their teammate with a hunting rifle.

The Flyers won opening night as Paul Holmgren, Propp and Al Hill scored in a 1:41 span in the second period, and the Flyers cruised to a 5–2 victory against the New York Islanders.

Two nights later, though, the team was thoroughly outclassed in a 9–2 loss to the Atlanta Flames.

Quinn was confused as to how his team could beat the high-flying Islanders one night, then get embarrassed in Atlanta the next. But he would have time to get over the loss, because it would be a while before he had to worry about another one.

Al Morganti was in Atlanta for that defeat. It was the young reporter's first season on the Flyers beat for the *Philadelphia Inquirer*. At the time, the press was viewed as seeing the team through rose-colored—or orange—glasses. When Morganti was given his new assignment, he was told to be extra critical.

"I was brought in to be a little rough on them," he said. "They said, 'Al, we need a little more critical coverage.' But I got to cover one loss, then it's like, how am I going to criticize this?"

"This" started with a home game against the Toronto Maple Leafs on October 14, 1979. Holmgren, Leach, and Propp scored 5:29 apart in the first period. After the Leafs pulled within one on goals by Lanny McDonald late in the first and Darryl Sittler 33 seconds into the second, Kelly scored an insurance goal with 3:16 left in regulation, making McDonald's penalty-shot goal with 10 seconds left irrelevant.

Next, Leach scored twice as the Flyers beat visiting Atlanta 6–2. Two nights later, the Flyers made their last visit to Detroit's Olympia Stadium a victorious one, as Holmgren, Propp and Leach all scored twice as the Flyers took home a 7–3 win.

A STREAK OF TRAGEDY

When people think of Flyers streaks, they think of the 1979–80 team.

That team, though, doesn't own the longest win streak in club history. While their 35–game unbeaten run remains the North American professional sports standard, the most consecutive wins they ran off was nine.

Rather, it was the tragedy-laced 1985–86 team that set the club mark with a 13-game win streak, from October 19 to November 17, 1985.

The numbers the Flyers put up during their 13-game win streak were nothing short of amazing. They scored at least five goals 12 times, and Tim Kerr had 16 goals in the 13 games.

Above all else, though, they pushed the streak three games higher while being little more than skating zombies following the death of their friend and teammate, Pelle Lindbergh.

The next night, the Flyers jumped to a 6–2 lead midway through the second period against the Montreal Canadiens before hanging on for a 6–6 tie.

Barber scored twice that night and said after the game: "We have the speed, we have the movement now. Pat's system is letting us go where we want to go. Sure, it's contributing to some mistakes, but hopefully we'll cut down on them. I have this feeling we're coming on, just like my first year here."

Their unbeaten streak at four after the tie with Montreal, the Flyers only would know victory in their next nine games. New players stepped up nightly. It was Propp and Leach scoring 12 seconds apart in the third period against the Rangers, capping a rally from a 2–0 first-period hole en route to a 5–2 victory. Propp, Dennis Ververgaert and Leach scored third-period goals to turn a 2–1 deficit against the Red Wings into a 4–2 lead, then used Leach's goal with 60 seconds left to win it 5–4.

Barber scored early in the third period to break a 3–3 tie and send the Flyers to a 5–3 defeat of Montreal as the Flyers snapped a 16-game winless streak against the Canadiens, and push their own streak to eight in a row.

Brian Propp and the Flyers separated themselves from the rest of the league in the 1979–1980 season by going on an astounding 35-game unbeaten streak.

The unbeaten streak reached 11 on November 10 when the Flyers traveled to Nassau Coliseum to play the New York Islanders. Barber scored twice, sandwiching goals by Leach and MacLeish, and Clarke added a goal late as the Flyers skated away with a 5–2 win.

It was notable that members of the old Bullies team had scored all the goals. "[The Islanders] said something in the papers last year, that we aren't the Flyers and just don't have it anymore," MacLeish told reporters with a we'll-show-you joy.

Wins against Vancouver and Edmonton pushed the unbeaten streak to 13 and the winning streak to nine in a row, five short of the NHL record, when the team arrived in St. Louis on November 17. The Blues scored twice in the first period and led 2–0 early in the third before Norm Barnes, Barber and Leach scored 7:29 apart in the third to put the Flyers ahead. But a Barnes giveaway led to a Blair Chapman game-tying goal with 2:32 left. The win streak was over, but the team won four of its next five to enter December unbeaten in 19 straight.

At this point, more people outside the locker room began to notice what was happening. Mentions of the NHL record of 28 straight without a loss, set by the 1977–78 Montreal Canadiens, began popping up in more and more newspapers.

"It was around 18 or 19 games into it [that] we started getting more and more press," Propp said. "And we were getting closer to Montreal's record. When we hit 18 or 19 games, everyone was out to beat us. But it was just fun."

Wearing a bull's-eye and getting every team's best effort just because they wanted to be the ones to say they stopped the streak didn't make things easy.

"Every night someone became a hero," Morganti said. "It was an astonishing thing. The longer it got, you got really immersed in it."

Three straight ties, capped by a two-goal second-period rally to tie the Boston Bruins, pushed the streak to 22. That game against the Bruins saw Leach score his 19th goal, and just 1:08 later Holmgren added his 10th. Two nights later the Flyers spotted the Los Angeles Kings a 3–0 first-period lead at the Spectrum, then scored the next nine in a 9–4 victory. After a tie with the Chicago Blackhawks, the Quebec Nordiques took a 3–1 lead 7:52 into the third period, but the Flyers scored the next four en route to a 6–4 victory, pushing the streak to 25.

"They can put on the tap when they want to," Quebec coach Jacques Demers told reporters.

The scoring was flowing from everywhere.

"It wasn't like it was one or two guys contributing," Propp said. "It was all four lines contributing when it counted."

Twenty-five games into the streak (now the second-longest in NHL history), Leach had 24 goals despite missing two games. MacLeish, demoted to a fourth-line role, still had 17 goals, while Barber had 15 and Propp 13. Ken Linseman had 32 points, Clarke had 27 assists and Holmgren had 21 points.

"Somebody stepped up every night," Propp said. "That's why we had such a good team. We had four solid lines, and everybody knew their role. It was a total team effort."

MacLeish had the game-winner in a 3–2 defeat of Buffalo on December 15, and the next night, at Madison Square Garden against the Rangers, goalie Phil Myre stopped 34 shots, including a late glove save on New York's Ron Greschner, to preserve a 1–1 tie and push the Flyers within one game of the Canadiens' record.

With a spot in the history book at hand, Quinn told reporters: "We've been saying it's not affecting us, but you know that's a crock. This is a once-in-a-lifetime opportunity. You might play 100 years and never get another chance at something like this."

They almost missed their shot at history, which came December 20, 1979, against the Pittsburgh Penguins. The Flyers played like a team trying not to lose, but they were on their way to doing just that, trailing 1–0 entering the final five minutes of the game, with 17,077 fans at the Spectrum yearning to witness history.

With 4:39 left, the Penguins' Bob Stewart was sent off for hooking Hill. On the ensuing power play, Behn Wilson slipped behind Pittsburgh's Gregg Sheppard in front of the Penguins goal and knocked Ververgaert's pass through the crease into the goal with just 4:08 left.

The game ended tied, and balloons fell from the ceiling along with coupons that read "You Were There."

The team arrived at Boston Garden on December 22 with a chance to break the record against their old nemesis.

Boston legends Phil Esposito and Bobby Orr were gone, but the Bruins remained a tough, talented team. They were led by rookie defenseman Ray Bourque and featured aging but still-talented Jean Ratelle, as well as tough guys Terry O'Reilly and Stan Jonathan.

It was that toughness that Quinn hoped would enliven his team.

Five minutes into the first period, Clarke lifted Al Secord's stick deep in the Bruins' end and took the puck away. Taking two strides into the right faceoff circle, his wrist shot went between Kelly's legs and into the Bruins net for a 1–0 lead.

An extra roughing penalty on the Bruins' John Wensink after a fight with Holmgren put the Flyers on the power play, and a slashing penalty assessed to Bobby Lalonde a little over a minute later gave them a five-on-three advantage. It took the Flyers just 12 seconds to take advantage as Barber's slap shot from the point went through traffic and past Gilles Gilbert to make it 2–0.

In the first minute of the second period, Jimmy Watson started a rush out of the Flyers' end, and as he crossed the Boston blue line he dropped a pass for Linseman. Linseman made a nifty move to pull the puck out of the reach of Mike Milbury, cut to the outside, and when Gilbert failed to come out to cut down the angle, Linseman wristed a shot inside the far post to make it 3–0.

The Bruins got on the board when Tom Songin banked a shot off Bob Dailey's skate at 3:03, and 67 seconds later Milbury's point shot bounced off Myre's stick and into the net.

After the ensuing faceoff, the Bruins' Dwight Foster intercepted Linseman's pass to Mel Bridgman, but his hurried clearing attempt was stolen back by Mike Busniuk. Busniuk slid the puck to Watson at the left point, and the defenseman rifled a low shot past a surprised Gilbert at 4:40 of the second to restore the two-goal lead.

Busniuk made another nice play midway through the third period when he knocked down Brad McCrimmon's pass behind the Bruins' net and Kelly scored to make it 5–2. The win not only earned the Flyers a spot in the record book, but a standing ovation from the Boston Garden crowd.

"There's a tremendous feeling of relief," Clarke told reporters that night. "Nobody can say we came in the back door. We set the record against one of the top teams and we did it in their building."

The record was broken exactly 70 days after their last loss. Remarked Linseman, "I've almost forgotten what it feels like to lose."

The Flyers returned to Philadelphia the next night to start a home-and-home set with the Hartford Whalers. The Spectrum crowd rewarded the Flyers with a thunderous ovation.

"The fans were always tremendous," Propp said. "They knew what was going on. And the support was awesome."

Propp rewarded them by scoring the first two goals of the game in a 4–2 victory. The Whalers played better three nights later at their temporary home in Springfield, Massachusetts.

Propp scored twice, and Mel Bridgman's goal early in the third gave the Flyers a 4–2 lead, but Mark Howe, set up by his father, Gordie, pulled the Whalers within a goal, and then Brian Hill scored to tie it. The Flyers held on over the last 13 minutes to preserve the 4–4 tie as the streak reached 31.

Wilson, Leach and Kelly scored third-period goals as the Flyers held off the Winnipeg Jets 5–3 on December 28, and after an overnight flight from Winnipeg to Denver, they jumped to a 3–0 lead against the Colorado Rockies on goals by Propp, MacLeish and Dailey, but had to hold on late for a 3–2 victory.

After a six-day break, the Flyers opened 1980 by storming to a 5–0 lead against the Rangers at Madison Square Garden en route to a 5–3 victory January 4 that pushed the streak to 34. It also broke the North American all-sports record of 33 straight games without a loss set by the Los Angeles Lakers.

Joked Rangers defenseman Carol Vadnais: "We play them again the last day of the season. We'll break their streak then."

January 6, 1980, saw the streak carry the Flyers into Buffalo for a game against the second-place Sabres. Hill scored to put the Flyers up 1–0 midway through the first, but they trailed 2–1 after Danny Gare's goal 5:44 into the second. Ververgaert scored with 3:14 left in the second to tie the game, and Barber and MacLeish added goals in the third as the Flyers shuffled off with a 4–2 win and more stunned amazement in both locker rooms.

"You look at the travel, the schedule, the balance of the league, and it's impossible," Sabres coach Scotty Bowman said. "But it's not impossible. They've done it."

The streak was at 35 when the Flyers arrived in Minnesota on January 7, 1980. The hockey hotbed had 15,962 screaming fans, as well as 20 skaters, dying to end the streak.

"We were like every team waiting to play them," Craig Hartsburg, then a North Stars defenseman who later became a Flyers assistant coach, said in *Full Spectrum*. "We hoped they would keep winning so we could be the ones to end the streak."

It looked like that opportunity would fall to someone else as Barber scored 3:49 into the game, but Minnesota came back to take a 3–1 lead after one period.

Holmgren, a St. Paul native, scored midway through the second period, but the goal was wiped out as the Flyers were whistled for having too many men on the ice. Just 63 seconds later, Hartsburg's power-play goal made it 4–1, and 21 seconds after that Mike Polich scored to make it 5–1.

The North Stars added two more goals, and finally, after 35 games spanning 81 days, the streak ended in a thudding 7–1 defeat.

The final numbers on the streak are as mind-boggling now as they were then. The Flyers won 25 of the 35 games. They won six one-goal games and 11 two-goal games. They beat second-overall Buffalo three times. They rallied from a two-goal deficit eight times and a three-goal hole once; they came from behind in the third period to prolong the streak on six occasions.

"It was a magical ride," Quinn recalled in *Full Spectrum*. "With that team, with that defense, there was no reason to think we could even put a 10-game streak together."

The 1979–80 Flyers are remembered almost as much for what it did—the 35–game unbeaten streak—as for what it didn't—win the Stanley Cup.

"We knew they either would be the streak team or the Cup winner," Morganti said. "It became their whole headline. It's their whole identity—it's the streak team."

Propp, though, disagrees.

"That's going to be looked at as one of the longest streaks in sports history," he said. "We still made it to the [Stanley Cup] Final that year, and unfortunately lost in Game 6. We could have won it all that year. But it didn't take away at all from what we did during the season. I think if you ask most of the players, it's an accomplishment that will be there for years and years, and everyone on our team has to be very proud of it."

MR. PLUS, MARK HOWE

In their 45 years the Flyers have had a number of really good defensemen pull on the sweater, from original Flyer Joe Watson straight through to the classy, consistent Eric Desjardins and Kimmo Timonen.

None, though, were better than Mark Howe.

The son of hockey legend Gordie Howe, Mark Howe is viewed by many as the greatest defenseman never to win the Norris Trophy. But on August 20, 1982, when the Flyers traded for him, he was the greatest member of the Hartford Whalers' doghouse.

Howe's problems dated to December 27, 1980. In a game against the Islanders, he fell into the goalpost and one of the metal spikes used at the time to anchor the post to the ice pierced his buttocks.

Howe was taken to the hospital, where he said doctors told him, "an inch one way, and [the metal] could have gone into my spinal cord; an inch the other way, it would have pierced my sphincter muscle and I would have been walking around with a colostomy bag."

He lost nearly three and a half pints of blood, developed an infection which necessitated a second surgery to drain an abscess that had formed at the injury site, and his weight plummeted from 192 pounds to 176.

Howe should have sat out the rest of the season, but rushed back after 17 games despite feeling less than 100 percent. Promised he would be worked back into the lineup slowly, he wound up playing 26 minutes a night. He was in the top 10 in league scoring when he got hurt, so his final numbers for the 1980–81 season (19 goals, 65 points, plus-10 rating in 63 games) don't show just how much he struggled when he returned.

"Things were different then," Howe said. "You didn't have the same workout facilities they do now. That made a difference."

The next season Howe's numbers plummeted—eight goals and 53 points in 76 games—as did his desire to stay in Hartford.

He said a trade was something both parties needed.

"They were a little disgruntled with me and I was getting a little disgruntled with them," he said. "The people that were running the team then, they were unhappy with me, they thought I was underachieving, not playing well, and I was not playing well."

Howe had a no-trade clause in his contract, but told GM Larry Pleau he would waive it to go to one of four teams—the Boston

Though others are worthy of consideration, Mark Howe is the greatest defenseman in Flyers history.

A BEAST GONE TOO SOON

Brad McCrimmon partnered with Mark Howe to form the best defensive pair in Flyers history. From 1985–87, the duo was a combined plus-373 and helped the Flyers reach the Stanley Cup Final in 1985 and 1987.

Their partnership ended in 1987 when McCrimmon was traded to Calgary. He played until 1997 and then got into coaching. In May 2011, he was hired as coach of KHL team Lokomotiv Yaroslavl, and was killed along with the rest of the team in a plane crash in September of that year.

An outpouring of support flowed in from around the NHL, with a number of former teammates remarking how vital McCrimmon's presence was to their own performance.

"Brad was one of my three closest friends," Howe told NHL.com. "A man of his word. Best partner I ever had on the ice, but a better friend, husband and father off the ice. A sad day for the hockey world."

Bruins, New York Rangers, New York Islanders, or Philadelphia Flyers. Philadelphia, though, was his first choice.

The reason? Simple. "They won," he said.

"I had always played on winning teams, championship teams, my whole life," he said. "Hartford went a couple years, they didn't make the playoffs. I'm not a guy who so much loves to win as I hate to lose. And to me, they [Hartford] weren't making strides to get better at that time."

The Flyers were, and they sent forwards Ken Linseman and Greg Adams, plus two draft picks, to Hartford for Howe.

"I was something they didn't have," Howe said. "They had a big, strong, tough defense, but they didn't have a guy with a lot of mobility. I think they were looking for a guy to play the point on the power play. I'm in the business now of scouting, and you look for certain players for certain roles and I think I was a guy—I was young, I was 28 at the time—I could fill a role they needed at the time."

Howe immediately made the Flyers a better team and raised the caliber of play of any defense partner to career-best levels.

His first partner was Glen Cochrane, an heir to the tough-guy mantle previously held by Dave Schultz and Paul Holmgren. Cochrane had rung up 200-plus penalty minutes in his first two Flyers seasons.

"Before the [1982–83] season, Bob [McCammon, coach] calls [Cochrane] and me into his office," Howe recalled in a story on the Flyers' website. "He says, 'Mark, your job is to move the puck and run the power play. Cocher, make sure no one touches him.' When we left, Glen put this big arm around me and said, 'Don't worry. No one's gonna lay a hand on you.' That was music to my ears. In Hartford I used to get run 20 to 25 times a game. In Philly, I could just do my thing."

With the extra room, Howe had 20 goals, 67 points and a plus-47 rating. He won the first of his four Barry Ashbee trophies as the team's top defenseman, earned a spot as an NHL First-Team All-Star and helped Cochrane to 24 points and a plus-42 rating.

In 1984–85 Howe skated with Brad McCrimmon, and it wasn't long before the pair was ranked the best defense pairing in

MORE THAN HALL-WORTHY

It took 13 years, but Mark Howe finally found his place in the Hockey Hall of Fame when he was enshrined in 2011.

He had 742 points in 929 NHL games, but when you add in his numbers from the World Hockey Association, he had 1,246 points in 1,455 games.

He had the bulk of his NHL points with the Flyers, as his 480 points is the highest total of any Flyers blueliner ever. He also leads all Flyers defensemen in goals (138), assists (342), plus/minus (plus-349), power-play goals (39) and shorthanded goals (24), all accomplished in 590 games.

Howe's big moment also led to the retirement of his No. 2 sweater, which occurred March 6, 2012.

He made sure to thank the fans during his special moment.

"Over the course of 10 years I wore my No. 2 jersey in front of a sold-out Spectrum crowd," he said that night. "Sometimes I succeeded, sometimes I failed. But you always stood by my side. For that I thank you."

the NHL. Howe had 18 goals, 57 points and a plus-51 rating, while McCrimmon added 43 points and was a plus-52 as the Flyers reached the Stanley Cup Final.

The next season the duo was even better—Howe finished a league-best plus-85, while McCrimmon was a plus-83. Even more amazing was that besides Howe and McCrimmon, the Flyers did not have another defenseman who played more than seven games finish as a plus player. Howe also had his best offensive season, totaling 24 goals and 82 points. He was a finalist for the Hart and Norris trophies, but won neither (Wayne Gretzky took the Hart, Paul Coffey the Norris). He did, though, earn his first Bobby Clarke Trophy as team MVP, as well as another Barry Ashbee Trophy.

The 1986–87 season marked the final stretch of a three-season arc for the Howe-McCrimmon pairing. Playing through a bad back, Howe finished with just 15 goals and 58 points, but had a plus-57 rating, while McCrimmon was a plus-45.

Howe again won the Barry Ashbee Trophy and again was a finalist for the Norris, this time finishing second to Boston's Ray Bourque.

After the season McCrimmon was traded to Calgary; in three seasons together, the Howe-McCrimmon pairing helped the Flyers reach two Stanley Cup Finals and made life easier for goaltenders Pelle Lindbergh, who won the Vezina Trophy in 1985, and Ron Hextall, who won the Vezina and Conn Smythe Trophy as playoff MVP in 1987.

In their three seasons together, Howe was a plus-193, while McCrimmon was a plus-180.

"We were plus-200 in three years [actually, plus-373]," Howe said of his time with McCrimmon. "I don't think Brad ever got the credit he deserved. Brad was a very quality hockey player, but just because players are great players doesn't mean they play well together. We had a great chemistry, we roomed together, we basically did everything together. It was great. You never had to think of the game; everything was instinct. We knew where each other was going to be. And even though we'd both screw up, have bad nights, nobody ever pointed the finger at each other. We'd always take the blame even if maybe the other guy deserved it. We were true teammates in every sense of the word. And we had the abilities to go along with it, and we had the team to go along with it.

"It's not to say the other guys were bad, and the stats sometimes work in your favor, but it's hard to deny the fact that when over three years you're [plus-373]. They can take away 10 percent, but they can't take away them all."

HEXTALL SHOOTS ... HE SCORES!

Most goalies use their sticks to deflect shots on net, or to make short outlet passes.

Ron Hextall, though, changed all that. The grandson of Hall of Fame forward Bryan Hextall and the son of former Rangers forward Bryan Hextall Jr., Ron inherited his family's skating and stickhandling ability, but not their position. Instead, he redefined how a goaltender plays the game.

Hextall had size (6'3", 192 pounds) and athleticism previously unseen at his position. He also had intensity to spare, and certain peculiarities, like slamming his stick off the goalposts like a Keith Moon on ice.

"Sitting in between periods, he was so intense, he would sit and rock the whole intermission," Kjell Samuelsson said. "Then he would put his gear on and go out. It's like every period he walked into a fight. That was his thing. Every time he stepped on the ice, he was full out."

Added Dave Poulin: "He played to the edge of what he had to get out of him what he had. When he was at his best, he could play at that edge without going over."

Toeing that edge on the slippery ice wasn't always possible, as Hextall often would slide from the sublime to the violently ridiculous. Ask Kent Nilsson what happened to those who strayed too close to the Flyers' goal.

"He was extremely intense, a lot more than most people," Dave Brown said. "He's an easygoing guy away from the ice, but that's how he played. To me, it's all the emotion of the game, and sometimes things like that happen. I don't think it's such a bad thing, in my opinion. Everyone goes off once in a while."

He nearly went off in his first NHL game. The 22-year-old rookie was handed the starting job to open the 1986–87 season, and his first game came against the Edmonton Oilers.

When Wayne Gretzky came in on a breakaway, Hextall dragged a pad to stone the Great One. Gretzky said to Hextall, "Who the hell are you?"

Hextall shouted right back, "Who the hell are *you?*"

Hextall backstopped a 2–1 win that night, and cruised to a 37–21–6 record in 66 games, with a 3.00 goals-against average and a .902 save percentage. He won the Vezina Trophy and finished second (to the Los Angeles Kings' Luc Robitaille) for the Calder Trophy as league rookie of the year.

He was even better in the playoffs, starting all 26 games and going 15–11 with a 2.77 GAA and .908 save percentage. For nearly singlehandedly carrying the Flyers to Game 7 of the Stanley Cup Final, he was awarded the Conn Smythe Trophy as playoff MVP. He was the first losing netminder, and the second rookie goalie, ever to win the award.

"For a full 80-game schedule, that was the best goaltending I've ever seen," Mark Howe said. "He was incredible his first year. For the most part, especially in the [Stanley Cup] Final, as good as we played and as close as we came, we wouldn't have been that close without Ron Hextall, there's no doubt about it."

"There was a kid in Edmonton who was a stick boy," Hextall recalled. "He said, 'I love the way you play, but you'll only be able to keep it up for five years.' I said I wanted to play for 20 years or 30 years if I could, and I'd still want to be the best."

He certainly didn't play his best in the 1987–88 season. He rejoined the team after his eight-game suspension for slashing Nilsson across the legs during the Cup Final, but the Flyers didn't play like a team expected to battle for a Stanley Cup.

When the Boston Bruins arrived at the Spectrum on December 8, 1987, the Flyers were limping along at 9–13–4, and they were wracked by a growing hatred for coach Mike Keenan.

Hextall, who had just signed a new eight-year contract, was an abysmal 5–8–3.

"We're a disgrace to the uniform," he told reporters after a game in November. "And I'm a lot of what's going wrong right now."

Things started going right that December night against the Bruins.

With the Flyers leading 4–2 with 1:43 left, Boston pulled goalie Reggie Lemelin for an extra attacker.

"The media kept asking me, 'Are you going to score?' and I said, 'Yeah, I'll score at some point,'" Hextall recalled. "It wasn't something I thought about. I felt like I was going to, [but] it's not like it was high on my priority list. It wasn't like it was something I was going out to do."

Only once had an NHL netminder been credited with a goal— the Islanders' Billy Smith in 1979, because he was the last Islander to touch a puck a Colorado Rockies player shot into his own net.

In 1971 Michel Plasse of the Kansas City Blues of the Central Hockey League became the first goalie ever to shoot and score a goal, and Darcy Wakaluk of the Rochester Americans of the American Hockey League had shot and scored just three days before the Flyers and Bruins took to the ice.

When the Bruins' Gord Kluzak dumped the puck into the Flyers' end, Hextall saw an opportunity. He played the puck off the backboards just to the left of the cage, and with the closest Bruin more than 15 feet away, he wristed the puck down the ice, 20 feet in the air. It dropped a foot from the Bruins' blue line and skidded into history just inside the right post.

As Derrick Smith dug out the puck, teammates jumped off the bench to mob Hextall.

"I remember when I scored the whole team came off the bench. It was like we were kids in a candy store," Hextall said. "The fact the whole team was excited was a thrill to me."

Another thrill would come a season later. The Flyers faced the Washington Capitals in the Patrick Division Semifinals and were looking for revenge for Washington knocking them out of the playoffs the previous season.

The series was tied 2–2 when the teams met at the Cap Center in Landover, Maryland, on April 11, 1989. The Flyers scored three times in the third period to turn a 5–4 deficit into a 7–5 lead with 4:28 left to play.

When Jeff Chychrun was whistled for cross-checking Dino Ciccarelli, the Caps went on a power play with 2:33 remaining. Caps goalie Pete Peeters was pulled to make it a six-on-four advantage.

When Scott Stevens dumped the puck into the Flyers' end, Hextall saw another shot at history. He moved behind his goal to play the puck, took a step toward the goal line, and from next to the left post, let fly. The puck landed on the Washington side of the red line and slid inside the right post.

With 1:02 left to play, Hextall became the first goalie to shoot and score a goal in a Stanley Cup Playoff game.

"Somebody told me the other day that it had been over 100 games since I had scored," Hextall joked after the game. "I guess it was time."

The Flyers rode the momentum of Hextall's historic goal to a series-clinching win two days later at the Spectrum, and advanced to the Wales Conference Finals.

That was the last hurrah for Hextall as a Flyer. Injuries limited him to just eight games the following season, and he was traded to the Quebec Nordiques in the blockbuster Eric Lindros deal in June 1992.

He came back to the Flyers in 1994, but the temper and talent both had diminished. He backstopped the Flyers to the 1995 Eastern Conference Finals, and split time with Garth Snow as the Flyers went to the Stanley Cup Final in 1997.

When he retired after the 1998–99 season, Hextall left as the Flyers' all-time leader in games played by a goalie (489) and wins (240), and his 18 shutouts are more than only Bernie Parent's 50 (Roman Cechmanek has since passed Hextall with 20). He's also the team's all-time leader in playoff games (84) and playoff wins (45). Besides the numbers, Hextall embodied all that Philadelphia hockey stood for.

"He was not a lunatic," Brown said. "He was extremely competitive. He was extremely serious about winning games. He was the kind of guy you wanted on your side, because no matter what you think of him, he competed every night and he was there for you and he gave you everything he had every night."

TIM KERR, SULTAN OF THE SLOT

Prior to 1979, the age for eligibility for the NHL draft was 20. It was changed in 1979 to allow 19-year-olds to be selected, and while the pool of players was increased, the selection process remained at six rounds, meaning a number of good players went unpicked.

One of them was Tim Kerr, who was playing for the Kingston Canadians of the Ontario Hockey Association. Top scout Jerry Melnyk hadn't been impressed by the 6'3", 230-pounder, but eastern scout Eric Coville convinced Melnyk to allow him to offer Kerr a contract.

"There were three teams that we were negotiating with," Kerr said. "When I was at my training camp in Kingston for my last year of junior, Eric Coville came to the practice one day and we went out to lunch and dinner and he kind of swayed me to choose Philadelphia."

Kerr made Coville look smart by scoring 40 goals in 63 games in his final junior season, and he added six points in a seven-game stint with the Maine Mariners, the Flyers' American Hockey League club.

Kerr made the Flyers out of training camp the next season and scored 22 goals, but injuries limited him to just 68 games.

Aches and pains became the early story of Kerr's career. In his first three NHL seasons, he had a total of 54 goals while playing just 153 of 240 games.

"My first two years I had good years, scoring over 20 goals," Kerr said. "The third year is when I had a knee injury. I rehabbed it and missed six weeks. Then my first game back it went out on me and I had to have surgery on it. I worked with [trainer] Pat Croce all year long and really built up my leg strength, which had never been done before. I think that propelled me to the next year and the next level."

The next year and next level were ones of historic proportions. In 1983–84, Kerr showed just what he was capable of when healthy, scoring a career-high 54 goals while playing 79 games. He spent the 1984–85 season proving his previous season was no fluke.

"It's an easy game to be a 20-goal scorer," Kerr said. "You have to score just once every four games. When you're counted on to score, there's extra pressure."

No one anchored themselves in front of the opposing team's goalie better than the burly but soft-handed Tim Kerr during his days with the Flyers.

If he felt pressure he certainly didn't show it, as he again scored 54 goals. He had five hat tricks and three times scored four in a game.

His biggest frustration from the previous season was the 1984 playoffs, when he was held without a point in a three-game loss to the Washington Capitals in the Patrick Division Semifinals.

He let all those frustrations out in the 1985 postseason.

The Flyers entered Game 3 of the best-of-five Patrick Division Semifinals on April 13, 1985 with a 2–0 series lead on the New York Rangers, but they trailed 3–2 after Kerr's tripping penalty led to a Willie Huber goal at 9:18 of the second period.

The deficit wouldn't last long, as Kerr more than atoned for his penalty. At 9:41 of the period, Mike Rogers was sent off for tripping Peter Zezel. With the Flyers on the man-advantage, Mark Howe rimmed a puck behind the Rangers goal to Ilkka Sinisalo along the right wall. He pushed the puck to Zezel, who set up below the goal line to the left of the Rangers goal and threw a pass in front, where Kerr reached out and swept the puck past goalie Glen Hanlon to tie the game at 3–3 at 10:06.

Less than five minutes later, Murray Craven forced Hanlon to blindly throw the puck into the corner to his left. Kerr was there and fired a shot that went off Hanlon and the side of the net and bounced back into the slot. Rogers got a piece of it, but it pinballed to Kerr in the right circle, and he rocketed a wrister past Hanlon to give the Flyers their first lead, at 14:58 of the period.

When Bob Brooke was penalized for dragging down Rick Tocchet, the Flyers again capitalized. On the ensuing offensive-zone faceoff, Kerr beat Larry Patey, winning the puck back to Howe at the left point. Hanlon stopped Howe's drive, but the rebound went to Zezel in the corner. He threw the puck into the slot, where Kerr shrugged off Barry Beck and backhanded the puck in for the natural hat trick.

Another penalty by Brooke, who was called for roughing when he punched Craven, gave the Flyers another power play. Zezel carried the puck across the attacking blue line, and as the Rangers closed on him, he dropped a pass to Kerr in the high slot.

His one-timer found daylight under Hanlon's glove at 18:22 of the period, giving the Flyers a 6–3 lead.

The Rangers got two goals early in the third, but Pelle Lindbergh kept it a one-goal game the rest of the way and the Flyers closed the series with a 6–5 victory.

Kerr's stunning performance set or tied four NHL records. He still owns the mark for fastest four goals in a playoff game, at 8 minutes, 16 seconds, and his three power-play goals in one period remains the NHL standard. His four goals in one period and four points in one period tied NHL marks.

"It was one of those games where the puck was finding me," he said in a drastic understatement. "When you're in the heat of the game you don't really follow up on what's going on. It was pretty quick how it happened. Certainly it was great for the team. We were able to get through the first round that night. It was kind of magical what happened there."

He turned in another star performance a week later, assisting on the Flyers' three first-period goals in a 5–2 win against the Islanders in Game 2 of the Patrick Division Finals. But that would be Kerr's last shining playoff moment, as sprained knee ligaments suffered in Game 1 of the Wales Conference Finals against the Quebec Nordiques knocked him out for the remainder of the series. He returned against Edmonton in the Stanley Cup Final and scored twice in the first three games, but knee pain sidelined him for the final two games.

An infection he picked up during the preseason settled in the lining of his brain and kept him in the hospital and off the ice until the day before the start of the 1985–86 season. Once the season started, though, nothing could slow him as he scored a personal-best 58 goals, including a single-season NHL-record 34 on the power play. The glory was overshadowed, though, by Lindbergh's death.

The following season Kerr again was outstanding. Highlighted by the fifth four-goal game of his career—coincidentally, on the night of his bachelor party—he again finished with 58 goals. In NHL history, Kerr is one of just 10 players to score 50 in four or more consecutive seasons, joining a list that includes Mike Bossy (nine straight), Wayne Gretzky (eight), Guy Lafleur (six), Phil Esposito (five), Brett Hull (five), Marcel Dionne (five), Michel Goulet (four), Jari Kurri (four) and Steve Yzerman (four).

Kerr kept scoring when the 1987 playoffs started. He had three goals in the Flyers' first-round win against the Rangers, and in the Patrick Division Finals against the Islanders he had a hat trick in a Game 1 win and two power-play goals and an assist in a Game 4 victory.

Those two goals, though, would be his last. Persistent shoulder problems meant that for a second straight time, Kerr had to watch the Flyers in the Stanley Cup Final. "It wasn't a pain thing, it was just the ligaments were stretched," he said. "It got to a point in that Islanders series, my arm sitting by my side, [the shoulder] would separate. I couldn't even hold a stick."

Over the summer Dr. John Gregg operated on the back of Kerr's shoulder to tighten the ligaments, and two weeks later performed the same procedure on the front of his shoulder. During the second operation, Gregg inserted a screw to help stabilize the joint, but during a check-up six weeks later, Gregg noticed the pin had shifted because it wasn't long enough. He removed it and inserted a longer screw.

When training camp started, Kerr felt feverish, had lost weight and still was struggling with weakness in his shoulder. "They thought I was addicted to pain killers," he said. Further examination, though, showed the screw had become infected and needed to be removed. But first the infection had to be dealt with. "I was on IV antibiotics," Kerr said. "They would change my antibiotics three times a day."

Five surgeries and months of rehab later, Kerr finally returned to the lineup in mid-March, scoring three times in eight games. He also got into six playoff games but was a shell of himself. The player nicknamed the Sultan of the Slot resembled a slot machine—a one-armed bandit.

Despite losing a season in the prime of his career, Kerr said he holds no ill-will toward Gregg.

"It was unfortunate," he said. "I don't look back. Dr. Gregg thought he put the right length screw in. Maybe I did something to pull it out. It was unfortunate. Then the infection thing, that was crazy. It was just kind of a wash-out year."

A summer of rest reinvigorated Kerr, and he scored 48 goals in 1988–89, and kept going in the postseason. He had four goals in the six-game opening-round win against Washington, and in the next round against Pittsburgh went on a scoring binge. He had a hat trick in a 4–2 win in Game 2, two assists in a 4–3 overtime loss in Game 3, a pair of power-play goals in a 4–1 win in Game 4, and two goals and two assists in a wild 10–7 loss in Game 5.

With the Flyers trailing the series 3–2, Kerr's two first-period goals—his third straight two-goal game—propelled the Flyers to a 6–2 series-tying victory, and two days later they closed out the Pens in Game 7.

But a broken thumb suffered in Game 6 left him unable to do more than grip his stick, and he was held scoreless as the Flyers lost to Montreal in the conference finals. His efforts, though, did not go unrecognized, as he was awarded the Bill Masterton Trophy for perseverance and dedication to the game.

That would be Kerr's last star moment with the Flyers. In November 1989 he had arthroscopic surgery on his shoulder to remove two bone chips, decompress a bone spur and fix a tear in his biceps tendon. He was limited to 40 games, but still totaled 24 goals and 48 points.

The shoulder, though, didn't ache as bad as his heart on the morning of October 16, 1990. Kerr was awakened in his Pittsburgh hotel room by a call from a doctor at Pennsylvania Hospital, who told Kerr his wife Kathy, 10 days after giving birth to the couple's daughter, Kimberly, had died due to a pelvic infection that had caused what the hospital called a "sudden cardiopulmonary complication."

Kerr took two weeks off, but a broken heart was complicated by a broken knee, as torn cartilage limited him to just 10 goals and 24 points in 27 games.

He was left unprotected in the 1991 expansion draft, where he was chosen by the San Jose Sharks and then immediately dealt to the New York Rangers. He played one season with the Rangers and spent a final season with the Hartford Whalers before retiring after the 1992–93 season.

Kerr ranks third on the Flyers' all-time list with 363 goals and sixth with 650 points, despite playing just 601 games in 11 seasons. He's also the club's all-time leader with 145 power-play goals and 17 hat tricks.

Most of those goals came from within inches of the net.

"There was no secret to where I was going to go," Kerr said. "For me it was a game within a game. That [front of the net] was my territory. People like Peter Zezel and Dave Poulin and Pelle Eklund, they knew where I was going to be and it was their job to get the puck to me and they did a great job. That's the only reason you're successful, because of the players around you."

"IT'S GOING TO BE AN INTERESTING SERIES"

The Flyers and Pittsburgh Penguins arrived in the NHL as part of the same 1967 expansion class. However, there really was no significant bitterness in the rivalry until 2005, thanks to the arrival of Sidney Crosby in Pittsburgh.

The seeds of enmity were planted early in the 2005–06 season, when Flyers defenseman Derian Hatcher marked Crosby's second game in Philadelphia by smacking the rookie center in the mouth with his stick, breaking two of his teeth. Crosby came back that game and scored in overtime, and Flyers-Penguins games have been appointment viewing ever since.

If Hatcher's dental work on Crosby was the first spark, things really caught fire in 2008 when the teams met in the Eastern Conference Finals, a series won in five games by the Penguins. They met a year later in the first round of the playoffs, with the Penguins again winning, this time in six games. That series saw the Pens take a 3–1 series only to see the Flyers win the fifth game and lead Game 6 3–0 at home early in the second period. In what became the key moment, the Penguins' Maxime Talbot goaded the Flyers' Daniel Carcillo into a fight, and while Talbot—memorably shushing the crowd as he skated to the penalty box—lost the battle, the Penguins found the motivation

"IT'S GOING TO BE AN INTERESTING SERIES"

Record-setting Performance

Leading the Flyers' run through the 2010 Stanley Cup Playoffs was their record-setting top line of Danny Briere, Scott Hartnell and Ville Leino.

Briere led all players with 30 points, and also set a team record for most points in one postseason. Twelve of his points came during the Stanley Cup Final, one shy of Wayne Gretzky's championship-series league record.

Leino had 21 points in the postseason, tying the NHL mark for most playoff points by a rookie.

Was it really in?

There was a delayed reaction after Patrick Kane scored the Stanley Cup-winning goal in the 2010 Final, as the Chicago forward began dancing down the ice, but everyone else was slow to react.

"I looked behind me and I could see [the puck] stuck inside the net under the pad," Michael Leighton said. "Me and Kane were the only ones to actually realize it went in."

Leighton attempted to use the moment of confusion to his advantage.

"My first thought was 'Okay, it's over, but can I get this puck out of the net without anyone knowing?' ... I went over and picked the net up real quick and the puck was there and I kicked the puck over."

His ruse didn't work, as replays clearly showed the puck zipping under Leighton and into the net, where it got stuck under some padding.

needed to win the war, scoring five straight goals to close the series with a 5–3 victory.

The 2011–12 season saw the nastiness reach a boiling point, culminating in a wild game April 1, 2012 in Pittsburgh. By that point in the season the teams knew they likely were going to meet in the first round of the playoffs, so each team was looking to do what it could to gain an upper hand. In the second period Brayden Schenn cross-checked Crosby from behind, knocking him face-first to the ice, and then with 1:03 left, a full melee that saw multiple scrums and ejections broke out after Danny Briere was leveled by a Joe Vitale check at center ice. While the players scuffled, the real highlight was off the ice, as Flyers coach Peter Laviolette and Penguins assistant coach Tony Granato stood on the ledges between the benches screaming at each other.

"Guys were pretty emotional at the end of the game there," Claude Giroux said. "Obviously it's going to be an interesting series."

Giroux couldn't have been any more right.

The series started in Pittsburgh, and the Penguins gave their home fans a jolt, taking a 3–0 lead after one period. But the Flyers battled back as Briere scored in the second and again in the third, and Schenn tied the game with 7:37 left when he re-directed a Scott Hartnell shot past Pens goalie Marc-Andre Fleury.

The game went to overtime, but not for very long. Just 2:23 into extra time Fleury stopped Matt Carle's wrist shot from the left side, but the rebound went to Jakub Voracek, who crept in the backdoor to tip the puck in and give the Flyers a 1–0 series lead.

Game 2 two days later started much the same way as Game 1. Crosby scored on the game's first shift and Chris Kunitz added a goal at 9:27 to make it 2–0. Talbot, who switched sides in the rivalry in July 2011, scored shorthanded to put the Flyers on the board, but the Pens' Paul Martin answered late in the period to make it 3–1 after one.

The second period was a complete reversal as Giroux scored a power-play goal and a shorthanded goal to singlehandedly tie the game. Kunitz's power-play goal six seconds later put the Pens ahead again, but Flyers rookie center Sean Couturier knotted the game when he banged in a Braydon Coburn rebound with 2.8 seconds left.

Tyler Kennedy put the Pens ahead 1:04 into the third, but Couturier answered 17 seconds later when he intercepted a Ben Lovejoy pass deep in the Pittsburgh end and beat Fleury to make it 5–5.

Midway through the period Jaromir Jagr jumped on the rebound of a Pavel Kubina shot to score and give the Flyers their first lead of the game, and then Couturier tapped in a Giroux feed with 1:49 left to complete the hat trick, making him the youngest player since Ted Kennedy in 1945 to have a hat trick in a playoff game. Not to be out-done, Giroux closed the game with an empty-net goal for a hat trick of his own (he also had three assists), as the Flyers won 8–5 and took a 2–0 series lead.

Couturier set up Giroux's empty-net goal, but his night wasn't just all offense. The 18-year-old went 12-for-19 on faceoffs, was a plus-4 with three hits and threw a blanket over the league's leading scorer, Evgeni Malkin, limiting him to two power-plays assists and just two shots on goal.

"I don't know if I know any words to describe his game today," Jagr said. "Awesome—maybe something better than that. He was unbelievable."

If Game 2 was wild, Game 3 back in Philadelphia redefined the word.

"I thought the first two games in Pittsburgh were crazy, but this one was even wilder," Danny Briere said.

Once again the Flyers gave up the first goal, but their dominant special teams again came through, as Talbot scored short-handed and Briere added a power-play goal to make it 2–1. Briere scored again in the first to make it 3–1, and after James Neal and Matt Read traded goals, the Flyers led 4–2 after 20 minutes.

All the scoring, however, paled in comparison to the physicality in the game. There was a dust-up after Talbot's goal, when Pittsburgh's Matt Niskanen shoved him in the back of the head while Talbot was down after scoring, and Giroux immediately jumped Niskanen. Meanwhile, Carle squared off with the Pens' Matt Cooke while other players paired off in pushing-and-shoving matches.

All control was lost with 7:58 left in the period after Ilya Bryzgalov trapped a puck along the ice with his glove, and Crosby took two extra whacks at it. That angered a number of Flyers, which led to a pile-up of bodies behind the net. While Giroux and Crosby went nose-to-nose, Voracek and Pittsburgh's Steve Sullivan paired off but were separated before anything bad could happen.

In the melee Voracek lost one of his gloves. As Voracek bent down to retrieve it, Crosby pushed the plunger on the dynamite, childishly knocking the glove away from him. Kimmo Timonen didn't like it and slashed Crosby to let him know it. They started pushing and shoving, which drew the attention of the rest of the players on the ice. Giroux grabbed Crosby for a superstar-on-superstar fight, while Timonen and Pens defenseman Kris Letang dropped their gloves near center ice. The result was fighting majors for Giroux and Crosby, while the blueliners each received game misconducts.

The period was capped when Brayden Schenn ran over Paul Martin, and the Pens' Arron Asham responded with a cross check to the Philadelphia rookie forward's face, and then punched him in the back of head, earning himself a match penalty and later a four-game suspension.

Pittsburgh's Neal scored midway through the second to make it a one-goal game, but Read scored to steal back the momentum. Jordan Staal scored to get the Pens within 5–4, but Wayne Simmonds responded to give the Flyers back a two-goal lead.

Just 27 seconds into the third, Giroux iced the game, snapping a quick wrist shot past Pens backup goalie Brent Johnson to make it 7–4.

The final blow of the game was sent by Neal, who elbowed Couturier in the head with 5:20 remaining. No penalty was whistled on the play, but on the next shift Neal was assessed a charging penalty for a head-high run at Giroux and another free-for-all broke out between the benches when Malkin threw elbows at Talbot and Voracek as he was leaving the ice, and again all 10 skaters paired off.

Talbot scored a power-play goal with 2:46 left to make the final score 8–4.

The final tally was 12 goals, 158 total penalty minutes and suspensions to Asham; Neal, who received one game for his hit on Giroux; and Craig Adams, who was suspended for one game for an instigator penalty in the final five minutes of a game.

Crosby summed up the hard feelings on both sides when asked about the glove incident, telling reporters after the game: "I don't like any guy on their team. So [Voracek's] glove was near me, he went to pick it up and I pushed it."

When asked why, he said simply, "Because I don't like them. ... I don't like any guy on their team."

While the Flyers players didn't have many kind words for Crosby, the team's marketing department had their own answer— the giveaway orange T-shirts prior to Game 4 simply read: "Guess what? We don't like you either!"

With the chance to close the series in Game 4, the Flyers scored first when Giroux stuffed a Jagr pass into the Penguins' net just 1:16 into the game. However, that was all that went right for the Flyers. Staal's goal with 2:31 left in the first period snapped a 3–3 tie and continued a run of eight straight Pittsburgh goals as the Pens stayed alive with a 10–3 rout. It was the first time the Flyers had allowed 10 goals in a playoff game since Game 5 of the 1989 Patrick Division Finals, when they lost 10–7 to a Mario Lemieux-led Penguins team.

Game 5 back in Pittsburgh again saw the Flyers score first, on Carle's power-play goal, but again they couldn't protect the lead, as a Sullivan power-play goal tied the game. Hartnell's extra-man goal gave the Flyers a 2–1 lead after one period, but that lasted just 6:15 into the second when Staal scored. Kennedy put the Pens ahead for good with a blast from the right circle that beat Bryzgalov with 10:07 left in the second. The Flyers pressed late, at one point throwing seven shots on Fleury during a third-period power play, but the series returned to Philadelphia with the Flyers now clinging to a 3–2 lead.

The players remained a confident bunch, however, with Giroux saying the day after the game, "We know we can beat them [and] we know we can outwork them."

And it was Giroux who made sure of it.

Laviolette said Giroux came to him before the game and demanded to have his line start. Then right before the puck dropped, Giroux skated by the bench and told Briere to pay attention.

"About 10 seconds before the puck dropped," Briere said, "he came over and told me, 'Watch the first shift.'"

Giroux didn't disappoint. He won the opening draw, and when the Flyers dumped the puck into the Pittsburgh end, he leveled Crosby with a crushing check that lit up the sold-out Wells Fargo Center crowd. Then Giroux sealed his ascension to superstardom, intercepting a Sullivan pass in the Pittsburgh end and ripping a shot past Fleury, giving the Flyers a 1–0 lead just 32 seconds into the game.

A deflated Penguins team couldn't respond, and Hartnell and rookie Erik Gustafsson, playing in place of an injured Nicklas Grossmann, scored to give the Flyers a 3–0 lead 5:25 into the second.

Defensively the Flyers were bulletproof, blocking 40 shots. And anything that did get through, Bryzgalov stopped, as the goalie had his best game of the series with 30 saves on 31 shots. Only a Malkin shot midway through the second got past him, but Briere answered to make it 4–1, and Schenn added an empty-net goal for a 5–1 final score and a series-clinching win for the Flyers.

After the game, all the talk was focused on Giroux's tone-setting opening shift, topped by Laviolette pronouncing his center the game's best player.

"When the best player in the world comes up to you and says, 'I don't know who you plan on starting tonight, but I want that first shift,'" Laviolette said, "that says everything you need to know about Claude Giroux."

Giroux finished the series with six goals and eight assists in six games, with his 14 points one off the team single-series record of 15 set by Tim Kerr in the 1989 Patrick Division Finals. Giroux also was the first player since Crosby in 2010 to have 14 points in a single series.

And Giroux had two fewer points than Crosby and Malkin combined (16).

"There's no doubt he's in their class now," Briere said of Giroux, "if anyone was doubting before."

But Giroux's numbers weren't the only memorable ones from the Flyers-Penguins first-round matchup.

The Flyers outscored the Penguins 30–26, with the 56 total goals the most of any 2012 playoff series. In fact, only one other series saw both teams combine for more than the 30 goals the Flyers scored. And the eight goals the Flyers scored in Games 2 and 3 made them the first team since the 1993 Los Angeles Kings to score eight or more in consecutive playoff games.

The Flyers set a team record with 12 power-play goals in the series, and scored them on just 23 chances for a remarkable 52.2-percent success rate.

The teams also combined for 314 penalty minutes (165 for the Flyers), among them six major penalties, 11 misconducts, four game misconducts and a match penalty.

It was a series for the ages, and as much fun as it was to watch, it was just as much fun to play in.

"It was great," Hartnell said. "... They were physical, they were dirty, they were everything in a playoff game you want. We're just happy that we are moving on."

THE FAT LADY SINGS

BOBBY CLARKE WINS IT IN BOSTON

There was some irony to the fact that the Flyers had so much trouble winning at Boston Garden. It was Ed Snider seeing long lines of Bruins fans outside that building, waiting to buy tickets to a last-place team, that inspired him to start the Flyers.

Since winning there November 12, 1967, their first trip to Boston, they hadn't won at the Garden in 18 games, losing 16 of them. In the 1973–74 season, the Flyers had lost all three regular-season trips to Boston, part of the reason they finished with one fewer point than the Bruins, ceding them home-ice advantage in the 1974 Stanley Cup Final.

The Flyers' personal Boston Massacre reached 17 losses in 19 games when the Flyers dropped Game 1 of the series.

With Bill Barber off for interference, Wayne Cashman opened the scoring for the Bruins 12:05 into the game. Fifty-six seconds later, Gregg Sheppard made it 2–0.

The Flyers battled back. Orest Kindrachuk broke through when he poked in a rebound at 7:47 of the second period, and at 5:32 of the third Bobby Clarke jammed at a loose puck hard enough and long enough for it to slither under goalie Gilles Gilbert.

That seemed to swing the momentum in the Flyers' favor, and in the game's final minute Clarke led a three-on-two rush. He left a pass for Cowboy Bill Flett, who faked Gilbert out of the net but pushed his shot into the post. Orr smothered the rebound, and off

303

the ensuing faceoff, led the charge into the Flyers' end. Ken Hodge fed a pass back to Orr at the point, and his shot went through traffic and between Bernie Parent's pads with just 22 seconds left on the clock.

Despite the final-minute loss, the Flyers were upbeat. "We'd outplayed them, and they knew it," Clarke said in *Full Spectrum*. "We were in better shape than the Bruins."

Parent was even more positive. "We were still living in the New York series in the first period," he told reporters, referring to the Flyers' win against the Rangers in the semifinals. "But when we went back to our system in the second period, you saw what happened. We'll beat those SOBs the next game."

It looked like empty confidence when Game 2 started. Cashman opened the scoring at 14:24 of the first period, and Phil Esposito made it 2–0 just 3:18 later.

But just like Game 1, the Flyers again took the play to the Bruins in the second period. Clarke brought them within a goal at 1:08 of the second when he tipped a Flett shot past Gilbert, but that would be as close they would get until the game's final moments.

As time was running out, coach Fred Shero pulled Parent for an extra attacker. Ross Lonsberry dumped the puck into the Boston end and then rushed to harass Orr in the corner. Orr pushed the puck along the wall to Hodge, but Clarke jammed him up, and the puck slid down to Rick MacLeish in the corner.

As MacLeish and Orr fought for the puck, the Flyers' forward heard an unlikely voice screaming for it: Moose Dupont. Without looking, MacLeish threw a perfect pass onto the Moose's stick as he reached the hash marks. A stunned Gilbert didn't have time to square himself, and Dupont was into his Moose Shuffle as the red light came on.

There was just 52 seconds left on the clock.

Both goalies reverted to their impregnable selves in the extra session. Gilbert made in-close saves on MacLeish, Simon Nolet and Terry Crisp. John Bucyk, sent in alone by a Sheppard pass that bounced off referee Art Skov, went to his backhand, but Parent made a pad save.

As overtime reached its midpoint, Dave Schultz jumped over the boards for a shift with Flett and Clarke, his first ice time of overtime.

Schultz raced after an Ed Van Impe dump-in and forced Carol Vadnais into a bad clearing attempt. Terry O'Reilly had the puck, but Clarke sealed him against the boards and forced him to push it back into the Bruins' end. Schultz pulled the puck off the wall and sent a pass into the high slot for Flett. The Cowboy tried getting off a backhander, but instead passed between the skates of Bruins defenseman Dallas Smith to a cutting Clarke, who had beaten Andre Savard off the half-boards. A belly-flopping Gilbert stopped Clarke's backhander, but the Flyers' captain wouldn't be denied on the rebound. With an empty net, Clarke casually flipped a forehand shot into the top of the net at 12:01 of overtime.

As Clarke leaped into the air to celebrate the goal, the hopes of his team and the burgeoning Flyers Nation of fans rose with him.

"I don't see how anybody could have doubts about us now," Clarke told reporters after the game. "We know we can beat them."

And that's just what they did 10 days later.

The Flyers swept a pair of games at the Spectrum to take a 3–1 series lead back to Boston for an elimination Game 5. The Flyers' Garden win streak was ended at one, though, as the home team took a 5–1 decision.

In Game 6 at the Spectrum on May 19, with Parent playing the game of his life and MacLeish's incredible hand-eye coordination providing the game's only goal, the Flyers won their first Stanley Cup.

DAVE POULIN

Dave Poulin wasn't good enough for Canadian junior hockey. He wasn't good enough to be recruited by a major NCAA Division I hockey program. He wasn't even good enough to play for a top-level team in Europe.

But Dave Poulin was good enough to play for the Flyers. He certainly was good enough to captain a pair of teams to the Stanley Cup Final. And he was good enough to become one of the toughest, proudest, most dignified people to pull on a Flyers sweater.

Poulin's first introduction to the ice was as a figure skater. But when his family moved from Timmins, Ontario, to Mississauga, a suburb of Toronto, Poulin ditched his figure skates for hockey footwear.

At 165 pounds, he was considered too small for major junior hockey. Through a friend, he earned a hockey scholarship to Notre Dame, where he spent four years playing well on the ice and excelling in the classroom. He was so good, he earned a spot in the prestigious Proctor & Gamble management training program.

Before moving into the business world, he got married and spent a six-month hockey honeymoon playing for Rogle, a second-division team in Sweden.

Once the European season ended, Poulin was ready to put away his stick for good. But Ted Sator, his coach in Sweden, recommended him to Flyers coach/GM Bob McCammon, who was looking for late-season help for the Maine farm club.

It didn't take long for the Flyers to see they had stumbled across a gold mine.

Poulin had 16 points in 16 AHL games and was called up to the Flyers for the last two games of the 1982–83 season. In his first game, in front of his hometown fans at Maple Leaf Gardens, Poulin scored on his first two shots.

His success continued with four points in the club's three-game playoff loss to the Rangers.

Days later Poulin received a letter from his boss-to-be at Proctor & Gamble. The letter included a newspaper clipping from Poulin's performance in Toronto and a note: "Obviously our paths are going different ways. I'm happy for you. Best of luck."

The next season Poulin centered a line with Brian Propp and Tim Kerr and finished with 31 goals and 76 points in 73 games.

Despite his breakout season, Poulin received little recognition outside the Delaware Valley.

"When I got my first hockey card," he said, "I had a great rookie year, scored a bunch of points. On the back it said, 'Works

Dave Poulin's pre-NHL background helped him become an excellent all-around player and prepared him to be captain for the Flyers.

hard.' I wanted it to say I scored 30 goals, played on a good line. It just said, 'Works hard.'"

Those two words, though, defined Poulin's career. "It's a skill that translates to whatever you're doing," he said. "Fast skater or hard shot doesn't always translate to other things, but working hard translates."

And while the hockey (or hockey-card making) world might not have noticed, others did. Poulin's road roommate was Bobby Clarke, and the pair quickly grew close. Poulin and his wife, Kim, were on vacation with Clarke and his wife, Sandy, when Clarke was named GM of the Flyers. And it was Clarke who convinced Mike Keenan to name Poulin was team captain in 1984, just before the start of his second full NHL season.

"There were a lot of moving parts in that," Poulin said. "Darryl Sittler was on the team, but after the luncheon to kick off the year he was traded. Billy Barber was there but he was hurt and it was unclear where his career was with his knee injury." There were other veterans, like Mark Howe and Brad McCrimmon, who had served as alternate captains with other teams, but it didn't take long for players to discover that Poulin was a perfect leader, equal parts tough, smart and skilled. Little short of an armed militia could slow him down, and his willingness to play through pain became legendary.

"I think that's sort of the only reason that I could be in the league," he said. "I had to push myself to do that. That's the way I functioned."

In the 1985 playoffs Poulin suffered a slightly torn ligament in his left knee in the opening series against the Rangers. He sat out the final game of that series and the entire next round, returning for the conference finals against the Quebec Nordiques. He scored a goal in Game 2, but suffered cracked ribs when he was sticked in the chest by Mario Marois. Poulin sat out Games 3 and 4, but returned wearing a flak jacket in Game 5, which the Flyers won to bring themselves home to the Spectrum one game from the Cup Final.

Despite the win, Poulin wasn't happy with his teammates' effort, and let them know it at a meeting before practice the next day.

"In order to win we knew we needed everybody going, and that wasn't happening," he told reporters. "We're a confident, secure group of people, so we could talk over our problems honestly and openly."

The ultimate leader, Poulin turned up his own play in Game 6.

The Flyers took a 1–0 lead on Rick Tocchet's goal late in the first period, but the Flyers got into trouble at the start of the second. Joe Patterson was sent off for a penalty in the first minute of the period, and Brian Propp followed Patterson to the box 37 seconds later, leaving the Flyers two men down against the high-powered Nordiques.

Poulin, the Flyers' best defensive forward, lost a faceoff in his own end. The puck went back to Marois, who was working the point with Peter Stastny.

"We talked about how they kept collapsing into the box," Poulin recalled. "Those guys had gone across the top so well, Marois and Peter Stastny. Your natural thought is to compress into a triangle and get deeper and deeper. I just stepped out."

With his simple move, he was able to get a stick on a Marois pass at the top of the circle. He jumped on the loose puck with nothing but open ice ahead of him.

"I had such a long way to go on the breakaway," Poulin said. "From the top of the circle, it was such a race."

"It was just a reaction," he said to reporters after the game. "You rely on your reflexes out there. It hit my stick at a perfect angle and I got the breakaway, although somebody was coming fast. I could hear the chop-chop of a skate. It was near the end of a shift, and I haven't played much in the last five weeks so I wasn't sure I'd get there first."

He drew extra energy from a roaring Spectrum crowd.

"It shook," he recalled of the building that night. "You wonder sometimes at the peak of sound how can it get louder, and it gets louder."

Poulin said he didn't decide where he was going to shoot the puck until he got about five feet in front of goalie Mario Gosselin.

"I decided to put it upstairs because our scouting reports said you have to go upstairs, top of the building, to beat him," Poulin said.

He didn't just beat Gosselin with the goal. The series was over the minute the red light went on.

"It was a killer for them. It demoralized them and gave us a lift," he said that night. "I think because of the potential it had for them—they were looking at scoring one, maybe two goals and going ahead ... it had to be demoralizing."

Poulin believes that despite the long run-up from one end of the ice to the other, Gosselin wasn't ready for him.

"He was probably thinking he had two minutes off at that point," Poulin said. "You're up on a five-on-three in a very intense series. ... I'm sure human nature says there's a sigh of relief there."

Despite the joy from winning the series, it wasn't enough to cure Poulin's ailing knee or aching ribs, and the Flyers fell in five hard games to the Edmonton Oilers in the Cup Final.

The next season put Poulin's leadership abilities to the test when it fell to him to inform teammates of Pelle Lindbergh's car accident and then help guide his teammates through the aftermath of his death. "Clarke called me into the office and said I had to do the eulogy [at the funeral]," Poulin said. "He didn't ask, he said I had to. I said okay. At that point you didn't start thinking about it. I didn't start thinking about it until the night before. I remember sitting at the table with my wife and we were just staring at the paper. She went up to bed, and at 3 in the morning, it all came to me." Poulin said he still has that eulogy.

There was more pain on the ice in the 1987 Stanley Cup Final when Poulin again suffered broken ribs. However, he refused to miss any time.

"I watched him every night," Mark Howe recalled. "He'd be in the locker room a half an hour before everyone else, and they'd spend a half an hour freezing, doing a complete [nerve] block, on his rib cage just so he can play games. The needles were so long I thought they were going to come out the other side. That's the dedication."

To Poulin, though, it was just the nature of the game.

"You're in the locker room and you've grown with these guys," he said. "You were going to play if you could. As soon as you got medical clearance that you were going to be fine, you played."

By the 1989–90 season, with Paul Holmgren as coach and the Flyers close to missing the playoffs, Poulin lost first his captaincy, then his spot with the Flyers. He was traded to the Boston Bruins in a deal Clarke ranks among the worst and most painful of his career.

"Crushing," is how Poulin recalled feeling on that March day in 1990 when he was moved out of Philadelphia. "But it was the best thing that happened. You needed a change at that time, even though you didn't know it. Afterward, you learn that's the harsh reality of the business. I had a lot going on in my life. It was a whole lot of things. I came very close to retiring at that time. I had a business going on. I had worked in the offseason and had a good business situation I was in—stock brokerage."

Instead, Poulin stayed in the game, helping the Bruins, along with the expatriated Brian Propp, to the 1991 Cup Final, where they lost to Mario Lemieux and the Pittsburgh Penguins. He also played for the Washington Capitals before retiring in 1995.

THE GAME THAT WOULD NEVER END

Game 4 of the 2000 Eastern Conference Semifinals wasn't a must-win for the Flyers, but it was pretty close.

After losing the first two games of the series in Philadelphia, the Flyers needed overtime in Pittsburgh to win Game 3 on Andy Delmore's goal 11 minutes into the extra session.

With just one day to recover, the Flyers hit the ice in Pittsburgh for Game 4 on May 4, 2000.

Alexei Kovalev gave the Penguins a 1–0 lead with a wicked low slap shot just 2:22 into the game, and Pens goalie Ron Tugnutt nearly made that lead stand up. Finally, though, the Flyers answered 4:47 into the third period. Four seconds into a Flyers power play, Daymond Langkow beat Jan Hrdina on an offensive-zone faceoff, pushing the puck back to Eric Desjardins. Desjardins' slap shot through traffic went off John LeClair's stick and into the back of the net, and after a replay review to make sure it wasn't knocked in by a high stick, the goal counted. The game was tied and headed for overtime.

LeClair then nearly helped win it on the first shift of the extra session, stealing the puck from Tugnutt behind the Pens' goal, wheeling in front and sending a pass into the slot to Langkow, but he rang a one-timer off the crossbar 31 seconds into overtime.

There would be other scoring opportunities, but Tugnutt and the Flyers' Brian Boucher stood tall, and the game wore on and on.

Three overtimes. Four overtimes. Five overtimes.

The contest became less of a game and more of a war of attrition. Players sounded more like Civil War soldiers from a Ken Burns documentary, writing home about dwindling supplies as food and beverage stocks disappeared.

"After the second overtime, third overtime period, we're out of power gels, power bars, Gatorade," Keith Primeau recalled. "We were looking for food. We were literally looking for food to come into the locker room because you needed to get something into your system."

"Guys were coming in and saying, 'Somebody just end it, please,'" Boucher recalled. "Guys went through the pizza we ordered for after the game."

Were it not for that team's closeness, the night would have been even harder.

"We had a special bond," Primeau said. "We weren't the most talented group. Our lineup included Craig Berube and Keith Jones and Rick Tocchet and Chris Therien. We had a really loose group of guys."

With concessions stands closed in Mellon Arena, Tocchet tried having pizza delivered to the building, but no pizzeria would believe a professional athlete was calling.

"Ran out of everything," LeClair said. "Food was a big issue for some guys. There were some guys who were really struggling with it."

Some, like Jones, were struggling more than others.

"Between the second and third [overtimes]," Primeau said, "Jonesy wasn't playing very much at all, but you thought he was about to die of starvation."

JOHN LECLAIR SCORES SIX-HOLE

John LeClair scored a lot of goals for the Flyers, but only one led to a change in the NHL rulebook.

On April 14, 2000, at 4:53 of the second period, LeClair one-timed a Dan McGillis shot on Buffalo goalie Dominik Hasek. The red light went on, and the Flyers went on to win the game 2–1.

One problem: LeClair didn't score. The puck went into the net through a hole in the netting outside the right post—call it the six-hole—but was ruled a goal because the league didn't have access to the ESPN camera angle that clearly showed the puck not passing between the posts. After that, referees were instructed to check the netting on the goals before each game.

"I got in a groove where I was changing for him for a while," LeClair said of Jones. "He'd go about 10 feet and come back to the bench and say, 'That's all I've got.' He was cutting it short. It was funny."

Jones didn't dispute that comment on the Flyers' 40th anniversary DVD, when he said, "I can remember going on for a shift, standing at center ice right in front of our bench, looking one way, looking the other way, and saying, 'Change.'"

The players skated so hard for so long, they passed the point of exhaustion and entered the realm of the bizarre.

"I remember it being comical at times," LeClair said. "I went to the bench at times, and you get past the point of being tired. It almost got to the point, halfway through [each overtime] period, 'Let's just get through this and get back to the locker room.' I was taking IVs to keep from cramping. Jonesy was hysterical. I'm laughing at him, and he's cracking jokes. He complained about everything."

After the game, *Courier Post* reporter Chuck Gormley said, "I remember Keith Jones saying, 'I'm like a bear, I'm living off my fat.'"

It wasn't just the players getting desperate, either. Food was scarce for everyone.

"They ran out of any food in the press box," Gormley said. "I think there were PR guys from the Pens running downstairs and getting water bottles for us. It was comical."

"After a while," Gary Dornhoefer, who was working the telecast for Comcast SportsNet, said. "You don't even know what time it is, you don't know how many periods you played."

His play-by-play partner, Jim Jackson, recalled one of the funnier moments of the night was watching Dornhoefer munch on a slice of pizza when the announce crew was told they were going back live on the air sooner than expected. As Jackson was speaking, he noticed pizza sauce dripping out of the corner of Dornhoefer's mouth.

Steve Levy, doing the TV broadcast for ESPN, read a pre-written promo early in the fourth overtime, touting the next show

Keith Primeau recalls teammates scrounging for something to eat between periods during the incredible five-overtime win against the Penguins in Game 4 of the 2000 Eastern Conference semifinals.

after the game. He then laughingly said, "Yeah, sure, SportsCenter is next. Whenever next is."

Next didn't come for another period and a half.

It wasn't until Primeau jumped on the ice midway through the fifth overtime that the game came to a merciful conclusion.

Said Primeau on the Flyers' 40th anniversary DVD: "Two other times earlier in the game I had gone wide on [Penguins defenseman] Darius Kasparaitis only to get cut off at the net. So I faked like I was going to go outside on him again, and once he crossed his feet over, I was able to pull the puck back on my forehand and get a shot off."

"I think Preems tried that same move maybe four or five times that night, and each time the puck rolled off his stick," Boucher said. "He was able to pull it off, and it ended up being a great shot and a great goal."

The puck rocketed over Tugnutt's glove and into the middle of the net, ending the game at 2:35 a.m., after 92 minutes, 1 second of overtime. At a total time of 152:01, it was the longest game in the NHL's modern era (only a pair of six-overtime games in the 1930s went longer).

Boucher didn't need to see the winning goal; he heard it clearly from 200 feet away.

"There's a different sound when it hits the front bar [crossbar] and the back bar," he said. "The front bar, it's more like a ping, and the back bar is more like a clunk, and you can hear it go clunk, and you could hear it clear as day."

"I think it was a combination of [relief and joy]," Primeau said of his historic goal. "At the time I just looked at it as we had given ourselves an opportunity to get back in the series. I told people that until I retire … I don't think I'll understand the magnitude of the game until my playing career is over, and I'll look back at it as a memorable moment in my career.

"It's was one of those nights you remember vividly. I remember [Langkow] hitting the post on the first shift of the first overtime. He scores there, none of this happens. Then it goes five [overtime] periods. It's amazing, especially against a team as skilled as that team. For Brian to hold them from scoring for five periods was really a feat in itself."

Boucher said it was a good thing Primeau scored when he did. He finished with 57 saves on 58 shots, but when the fifth over-time began, the rookie netminder said he had no idea how much he had left in him.

"I know, for me, that eighth period was enough. I can remember scraping my crease at the start of the period and my hips cramping up," he said.

The win made for a fun trip back across Pennsylvania. There wasn't much celebrating, though, as Primeau remembers. "The flight home," he said, "all I can remember is hearing Eric Desjardins dry-heaving in the bathroom."

Boucher said the most celebrating he did was on his way down the ice to join his teammates: "I remember skating down, and I tapped [referee] Rob Shick on the head, like I was celebrating with him. It was an awesome feeling."

Of the unique evening, Gormley said: "It was comical but intense. It wasn't like watching the Devils. It wasn't like nobody had any chances. There were end-to-end rushes, there were incredible saves, missed nets. And it was great. It was great action. That game was incredible."

NEVER A DOUBT

Before the 2009–10 season started, numerous hockey experts had the Flyers among the favorites to be playing for the Stanley Cup.

That they got to the Final wasn't a surprise. The route they took there, however, had more twists and turns than a pretzel factory, more ups and downs than a moon bounce.

The season started with the additions of veterans Chris Pronger and Ian Laperriere and the full-time lineup installation of prom-ising youngsters James van Riemsdyk and Claude Giroux. And reclamation project Ray Emery—last seen fighting with his team's trainer during a Russian league game—was signed to play goal.

Things started well—Emery had a shutout opening night in Carolina and won his first three games.

The good times ended quickly, though. A trip to the west coast in November saw them lose three of four and started a downward spiral that nearly sabotaged their season. It didn't help that during the trip Emery was diagnosed with a torn abdominal muscle; surgery would keep him out until January.

Coach John Stevens was fired December 4, replaced by Peter Laviolette. It was seen not only as a move to right a listing ship, but a chance to shake up key members of the team—notably Mike Richards and Jeff Carter—who were perceived as being too chummy with their coach.

The coaching change didn't seem to change much, though, as the Flyers were pasted 8–2 by the Washington Capitals in Laviolette's first game, and they bottomed out December 21 as a 4–1 loss to the Florida Panthers dropped the Flyers to 14th in the Eastern Conference standings and 29th in the league.

They also lost goalie Brian Boucher to a broken hand, leaving the crease to journeyman Michael Leighton. He played for the Flyers during the disastrous 2006–07 season, but after being claimed on waivers, he lasted a month before being waived again. So there was little reason to expect Leighton to help much when he had been claimed on waivers again December 15 and thrust into the lineup.

"It was one of those things where it just wasn't working out in Carolina," Leighton said. "Eventually they put me on waivers. My agent called Homer [GM Paul Holmgren] and said with Ray Emery being hurt, he knew that there was an opening for at least a little while. My agent told him I would be willing to go there until Emery gets better and then they can send me to the minors and I'll go to the minors and willingly play there just because I needed a place to play. Homer agreed and they got me on the re-entry waivers."

The temporary job turned into a full-time role as Leighton played his way into the top job, and with him playing almost every game, the Flyers went 17–7–1 heading into the Olympic break. The good times came to a crashing halt, though, when Leighton injured his ankle March 16 in Nashville.

"A guy came over the red line and he flipped the puck in the air and it was bouncing toward me," Leighton said. "Sometimes as a goalie when you see a puck in the air you want to get to it before it bounces. ... I went out and kind of dragged my one leg behind me and went to catch it on the bounce. It hit my glove and some guy kind of got tangled up with me and I ended up falling backward on my left ankle. I felt a pop and it was a really weird feeling, it felt like blood was rushing to my leg. I got up but my leg was not feeling ... it felt like it was crooked. It felt really weird. At first I thought I broke it, then I thought that feeling would eventually go away if I skated around, so I was trying to shake it off. But it wasn't happening."

An MRI showed a high ankle sprain, with the ligament torn in three places. His regular season was over, and with Emery now out with a hip injury, Boucher was thrust back into goal. The Flyers staggered down the stretch, but entered a final-weekend home-and-home series with the New York Rangers needing just one win in the two games to bump the Rangers and clinch a playoff spot. They lost the first game 4–3 in New York on Friday, setting up a winner-take-all final-day duel in Philadelphia on Sunday.

Jody Shelley scored early for the Rangers, but Matt Carle's goal in the third period tied it. When overtime didn't decide things, the game went to a shootout.

The Flyers, however, were prepared for the occasion.

"Not too many people knew that coach Peter Laviolette made Richards, [Simon] Gagne, Claude Giroux, Carter, and myself watch video of Rangers goalie Henrik Lundqvist on breakaways, and after Saturday's practice that he made the five of us practice our shootout moves at the end of the workout " Danny Briere said.

Briere shot first and scored for the Flyers, finding room under Lundqvist's glove, and Boucher stopped Erik Christensen. In the next round Lundqvist denied Richards, but PA Parenteau beat Boucher over his extended left pad to tie it up.

Giroux was next, and he snapped a quick wrister between Lundqvist's pads to put the Flyers ahead. That left it to one final shooter and one final save to get the Flyers into the playoffs.

Rangers center Olli Jokinen skated at one end of the ice, building up speed, while Boucher waited in his net at the other end.

"I was just telling myself to be patient and that's it," Boucher said. "I didn't think about the repercussions if I didn't stop it. I knew if I stopped it, we won. I didn't think about what happens if I don't stop it."

It was a helpless feeling for the rest of the players.

"I was almost sick," Scott Hartnell said. "It was just incredible. I literally was almost sick."

"It's like we could be done right away if he scores," Gagne said. "You're just like, you can't believe it's April 11 and this might be the end of your season."

Jokinen came straight up the middle of the ice, cut to the right, and then stepped back toward to middle to try and deke Boucher's pads open, but the goalie stayed up and easily stopped a backhand attempt, igniting the crowd and sending Boucher into a fist-pumping, one-legged victory jig as teammates spilled onto the ice.

"You're taught as a hockey player not to get like that, especially the goaltender," he said. "You have to play the next night, you have the next game ahead of you. You don't celebrate the victories as much as you might think. You have to get ready for the next shot, the next game. But the enormity of the situation, I think it was called for to have that type of celebration, especially at home."

After a few days of rest, it was on to the postseason, starting with the second-seeded New Jersey Devils. All the energy built up from the last-day win was like spinach for Popeye and the Devils didn't stand a chance. Boucher, starting his first postseason series in a decade—the 2000 Eastern Conference Finals against New Jersey—allowed just eight goals in five games as the Flyers, the last team into the playoffs, was the first to advance to the second round.

Victory had its price, however, as Gagne broke his right big toe blocking a shot in Game 4, and Carter, who had missed two weeks just before the end of the regular season with a broken left foot, broke his right foot when he was hit by a Pronger shot.

Then, during the Flyers' 3–0 series-clinching win in Game 5, Laperriere was hit in the face blocking a shot for the second time that season. The latest blow hit him just above the right eye, leaving the forward's face drenched in blood.

"When I grabbed Jimmy [McCrossin, trainer], I asked him if my eye was still there," Laperriere told reporters after taking 70 stitches along his right eyebrow. "He said, 'Yeah, there was just so much blood.' I was a little bit in panic mode, I couldn't see out of my right eye. It's one thing to see, but when you don't see anything, you kind of panic. But after laying on the medical table for two minutes once I got inside, I started to see shadows and then everything came back to normal."

Besides the stitches, Laperriere suffered a non-displaced fracture of his orbital bone and a brain contusion, and it was assumed at the time his playoff run—and likely his career—were over.

"It was scary," Daniel Carcillo said of Laperriere's injury. "I've never seen someone sacrifice their body the way he does, in this league or anywhere, for that matter. It's pretty amazing. ... He's always the guy that we could look to for blocking shots and sacrificing. You want to have the courage to be able to do what he does."

The Flyers moved onward, with the Boston Bruins next in the second round. A nine-day layoff, however, left the Flyers rusty and it showed early, as they trailed 4–2 midway through the third period. They got up off the deck, however, and goals by Richards and Briere forced overtime.

In the extra session, however, Boston's Marc Savard, in his first game in nearly two months due to a concussion, beat Boucher for a 5–4 Bruins victory.

Milan Lucic scored late in Game 2 to give the Bruins a 3–2 win, and the series shifting to Philadelphia for Game 3 didn't help as the Flyers lost 4–1 to fall into a 3–0 series deficit.

In the darkest hour, however, this Flyers squad didn't panic. Even though it only had been accomplished twice previously—by the 1942 Toronto Maple Leafs and 1975 New York Islanders—the Flyers felt confident.

"I never doubted we'd come back against Boston, even being down 3–0 in the series," Briere said.

Game 4 started with a bonus, as Gagne was a surprise entry into the lineup. Then the Flyers bolted to a 3–1 lead, and after Boston tied it in the third, looked poise to hold on when Ville Leino scored with 5:40 left. Instead, Mark Recchi's sharp-angle goal with 31.5 seconds left forced overtime.

Rather than be despondent, the mood in the Flyers' locker room during the intermission surprisingly was positive.

"It's almost like we said we've got nothing to lose," Gagne said. "Nobody expected us to get back. It was positive. We had the feeling it was going to happen."

And it was Gagne who made it happen. In similar fashion to Savard in Game 1, Gagne was the Game 4 hero, returning from injury to score the winner from in close at 14:40 to give the Flyers another breath.

The elation of Game 4 didn't last long into Game 5. With a 1–0 lead halfway through the game, a pile-up in front of the Philadelphia net saw Boucher get bent over backward, with his skates caught under the weight of his body as well as two other players. The result was sprained ligaments in each knee.

Leighton, dressed for his first game since spraining his ankle in Nashville two months prior, was tossed right into the fire.

"I didn't want to put the team in a situation that if I ended up getting in I would hurt the team," Leighton said. "We had to pick a date wisely. ... It got to the point where we said all right, we think you can jump on the bench now and contribute to the team if you can play. Sure enough, second period I see Boosh go down. Right away I looked at Lavi and he looked at me and he said get out there and start stretching."

Moments after entering the game Leighton stopped Patrice Bergeron on the doorstep, and then stopped everything else en route to a 4–0 victory that got the Flyers within 3–2 in the series.

Leighton stopped 30 of 31 shots for a 2–1 win in Game 6 to the stage for a historic Game 7.

"We've fought all the way back to tie it, but we still need one more win," Richards said the day before the game. "It's a Game 7 and it's going to be tough. We have to be prepared for it."

They didn't look prepared early as Boston took a 3–0 lead just 14 minutes into the game. After the third goal, Laviolette called time out, gathered his team at the bench and delivered a Rockne-esque speech that hit just the right note with his team.

"The message was, 'Just score one goal,'" Laviolette said. "Get on the board, get in the game. That first goal, for me, was huge."

Moments later, van Riemsdyk scored his first of the playoffs. Hartnell and Briere added goals in the second to tie the game, and then Gagne scored in the third to put the Flyers ahead. From there Leighton did the rest, and improbably, the seventh-seeded Flyers advanced to the Eastern Conference Finals against the eighth-seeded Montreal Canadiens.

"There's things in your life you're always going to remember, and that's one thing that was amazing the way it happened," Leighton said. "Being down 3–0 [in the series] and being down 3–0 in Game 7, it's just almost like it was meant to be the way it happened."

In Games 1 and 2 against Montreal, Leighton did his best brick wall imitation, shutting out the Canadiens. When Mike Cammalleri scored 7:05 into Game 3, it ended Leighton's shutout streak at 172:55, dating to from late in the first period of Game 7 against the Bruins. However, that night the goals came in bunches, as the Habs put five past Leighton.

That would be their best moment in the series, as Leighton came back with a 17-save shutout in Game 4, which also featured the improbable return of Laperriere after a month-long absence.

The Canadiens took a 1–0 lead just 59 seconds into Game 5, but Richards responded with a shorthanded goal, Arron Asham scored a pretty goal early in the second, and Carter, in his second game back from his foot injury, scored twice as the Flyers cruised to a 4–2 victory and a berth in the Stanley Cup Final for the first time since 1997.

"It's been great so far," Richards said after the game. "Obviously the journey hasn't ended. Hopefully we have a little of a Cinderella story here at the end. We have to prepare for Chicago now. It feels good."

The feeling wasn't as good after Game 1 of the Cup Final. The Flyers had three one-goal leads, but the Blackhawks came out ahead in a wild 6–5 win. Game 2 turned in a 28-second span in the second period as Marian Hossa and Ben Eager scored in succession, and after the fireworks of Game 1, all the Flyers could get past Antti Niemi was Gagne's third-period power-play goal in a 2–1 loss.

That game nearly ended in a melee as Pronger scooped up the puck at the final horn for the second game in a row. When Eager yapped at him, Pronger flipped a towel a fan had thrown onto the ice at Eager, which enraged the Chicago fourth-liner.

The Flyers scored first in Game 3 as Hartnell, falling to the ice, slipped a perfect pass to Briere, who scored for a 1–0 lead. Chicago's Duncan Keith scored to tie the game early in the second, but Hartnell deflected a Pronger shot that crossed the goal line for a split second—but long enough to earn approval after video replay.

Brent Sopel scored late in the second to tie it for Chicago, and Patrick Kane's breakaway goal early in the third put the Blackhawks ahead. Just 30 seconds later, however, Leino scored to make it 3–3.

The game went to overtime, and at 5:59 the Flyers caught Chicago on a line change and Giroux cut through the crease to tip Matt Carle's shot behind Niemi.

The good times continued in Game 4 as the Flyers stormed to a 4–1 lead in the third period and held on for a 5–3 victory.

Game 5 in Chicago was a one-sided affair won 7–4 by the Blackhawks. Leighton was pulled after 20 minutes, and Pronger had the worst game of his professional life, being on the ice for six goals and in the penalty box for a seventh. However, the big defenseman answered the post-game media deluge with his usual aplomb: "I'm day-to-day with hurt feelings."

He didn't have long to recover. First, Laviolette had to decide on a goalie for Game 6 after Leighton and Boucher had allowed three goals each in Game 5.

After a day of thought he opted for Leighton, and was offended when the media dared question his decision.

"Our goaltender has the best numbers in the playoffs," Laviolette said. "I didn't think I had to announce it."

The statistics defended Laviolette's choice, as at the time Leighton had a playoff-leading 2.34 goals-against average and three shutouts, and a second-best .918 save percentage. In home playoff games, he was 6–0 with a 1.48 GAA, .949 save percentage and two shutouts.

"I'm very confident in Michael," Laviolette said. "He's played excellent in the playoffs. His home numbers are terrific. I'm very confident in Michael."

The players were confident in themselves, with a seemingly bottomless well of resolve to draw from. Being down actually got to feeling like a natural position.

"It's kind of where our season has been," Carle said the morning of Game 6. "We've been faced with some tough times. If we're going to win this series, this is how we'd do it."

They faced even more adversity when Dustin Byfuglien scored from in front with 3:11 left in the first, but moments later Hartnell banged in a puck in the crease to tie the game.

In the second Hartnell got away with a pick on Keith that allowed Leino to reach a puck floated in by Pronger and send a pass across to Briere, who scored to give the Flyers the lead. It didn't last long, though, as Patrick Sharp beat Leighton to tie the game, and then Andrew Ladd tipped a Niklas Hjalmarsson shot behind Leighton to give Chicago a 3–2 lead.

Down but not out, the Flyers got off the canvas one more time. Late in the third, Leino split a pair of Chicago players to enter the attacking zone. He cut wide down the right side around Keith and then threw the puck in front, hoping. The wild pass went off Brent Seabrook's skate, Hossa's shin pad and Hartnell's stick—nothing but net, and a tie game with 3:59 to play.

Moments later Carter had a sensational chance in the slot, but Niemi lunged forward and swatted it away with his blocker with just 1:29 remaining.

"We had the feeling we were going to win the game and go win Game 7," Gagne said. "That's the way we believed this year.

We felt it was made for us to make history. We thought it was going to happen right to the end."

The end nearly came 20 seconds into the extra session. Richards tipped a lazy Keith pass that Niemi pushed into the corner. Richards got to it first and threw it into traffic in front. The bouncing puck got to Giroux, but he couldn't get enough on the shot and Niemi was able to stop it.

"The puck bounced over two sticks and went up to me," Giroux said. "I tried to swing at it and hit a skate. What are you gonna do?"

That was their last chance, as the Blackhawks were able to land one final blow that not even this most resilient of hockey teams could get up from. Four minutes into overtime, Brian Campbell held in a Darroll Powe clearing attempt at the left point, moved toward the middle and slid the puck to Kane on the left side. Like a basketball player going one-on-one, he made a couple head fakes to attempt to rid himself of Kimmo Timonen. Timonen stayed with him, and as Kane got to the bottom of the left circle he put a shot on net along the ice. Leighton couldn't get down in time and the puck zipped under him.

"He [Kane] got to the point where he was at a bad angle and there was a guy driving the net a little bit," Leighton said. "As a goalie you have to make that save but you also have to realize there's a guy backdoor. I went down thinking that I was going to get my paddle down, or if he passed it I was going to push across and be ready for that backdoor pass. I just didn't get down fast enough. He got it under my paddle as it was going down."

The Flyers were left to watch as the Blackhawks celebrated. They had lost, but they were far from losers.

"I'm very proud," Pronger said that night of his teammates. "The way we battled to come back time and time again, there was no quit in this team, even tonight."

THE FLYERS FAMILY

BOBBY CLARKE

No story can be told about the Philadelphia Flyers without a sizable chunk being devoted to the club's all-time greatest player, Bobby Clarke.

From second-round draft pick to Hall of Fame player to championship team builder, Clarke's face is prominently carved into the Flyers' version of Mount Rushmore.

"We have been [joined at the hip]," team chairman Ed Snider said. "And I'm proud of it."

For those who don't know Clarke, he can give off an aloof, almost intimidating aura, a degree of inapproachability. He was all fire and brimstone on the ice, and almost the same as a manager.

"He's revered," Rod Brind'Amour said. "He's a god-like figure. I was always nervous around him."

"I think he speaks his mind," Keith Primeau said. "I think he does it in a style that's very small-town Canadian. What you see is what you get. If what I say offends you, it's your problem, not mine."

Rick Curran, an agent who went toe-to-toe with Clarke many times in contract negotiations, said, "I really like Clarkie. There's a person that's not always right, but you know one thing—whatever he says and does comes from his heart."

Getting to know Clarke, what you find is a grandfather who loves his family and hockey—especially Flyers hockey—in equal parts. He only listens to oldies music and programs the same radio station into all his car stereo pre-sets—when he can get the buttons to work.

"He actually returned a car because he couldn't make the buttons work," his daughter, Jody, who works at the Flyers' practice facility in Voorhees, said.

She added, "He only listens to the same three CDs over and over: Patsy Cline, Roy Orbison and his all-time favorite is Gordon Lightfoot. I have to keep the CD in my house for when my dad comes over."

Despite his outstanding numbers in junior hockey, Clarke slipped to the second round of the 1969 NHL Draft due to his diabetes. Snider pushed for his selection anyway, but it nearly blew up in his face. Snider arrived that fall at training camp, and on his first day watching Clarke, the player fainted. Clarke had overslept and skipped breakfast in his haste to get to the rink on time. It was the only time in his career he had such an occurrence.

"As long as I looked after myself, the diabetes wouldn't affect my game," Clarke said. "I was playing in Flin Flon [Manitoba], and I guarantee you the travel and the hockey life up there was a lot tougher than the hockey life in Philadelphia. And the travel was a lot easier [in the NHL] than it was in Flin Flon. So if I could play junior in Flin Flon, and if I was good enough to play in the NHL, it was a lot easier to play in the NHL than it was up there."

And he certainly was good enough for the NHL.

No player defined the Broad Street Bullies era more than Clarke. He captained the team to three straight Stanley Cup Finals and two championships. He had the finesse to score 358 goals and dish out a Flyers record 852 assists for a team-best 1,210 points.

"Bob Clarke was a great, great hockey player," Snider said. "They talk about [Wayne] Gretzky seeing the ice, Clarke was the same way. When he went into the corner with somebody, he either came out with [the puck] or nobody did. He never lost a battle in the corners."

CLARKE CONTRACT

Despite leading the Flyers in scoring in the 1969 preseason, Bobby Clarke went into the final exhibition game without a contract.

He had rejected the club's first offer, a two-way deal that would have paid him one amount if he played in the NHL and a lesser amount if he was in the minors. Clarke's objection to the deal wasn't the NHL salary; it was the minor-league end.

"I was working in the mines [at home in the summer], and I was making $10,000, and you're offering me $7,500 to play [in the minors]? That's not fair. Why should I take a pay cut?" he said.

The morning of the final game, in Hershey, Pennsylvania, GM Keith Allen made another proposal, in the parking lot outside the arena: $14,000 for the season if he was in the NHL, $10,000 if was in the minors, and a $5,000 signing bonus.

Clarke signed the deal while leaning on the trunk of Allen's car.

He also ran up 1,453 penalty minutes, fourth all-time on the franchise list, and many who watched him or played against him called him one of the dirtiest players in the game.

"If I hadn't learned to lay on a two-hander once in a while, I'd never have left Flin Flon," he once told a writer.

The people who didn't like Clarke never played with him. Those who did play with him call him an inspiration, a captain who motivated the players around him to lift their games.

"Just a tireless worker," Bob Kelly said. "In practice and in games. Played through a lot of pain, took a lot of hits."

"No one worked harder on the ice than Clarke," Gary Dornhoefer added. "He led by example, and that's what you want a captain to do. He never gave up. The fights for the puck, the aggressiveness in the corner, he did whatever he had to do to win a hockey game. His attitude and how he played rubbed off on everyone else."

Clarke understands his place among the game's greats, but it's a chore to get him to talk about himself.

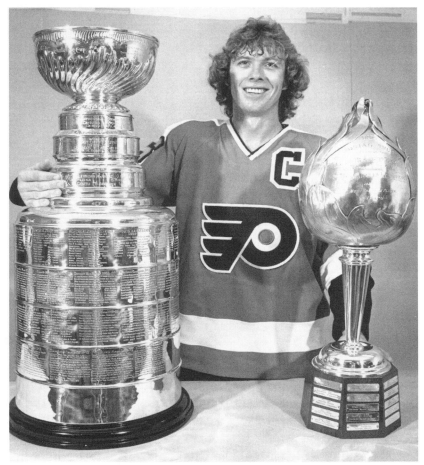

Bobby Clarke is unquestionably the Flyers all-time greatest player.

"I've tried to understand what they call leadership when it relates to me, and I really can't," Clarke told Jim Jackson in *Walking Together Forever*. "When I played, I just played."

He played to a Hall of Fame level for 15 seasons, winning a pair of Stanley Cups, three Hart Trophies as league MVP (1973, 1975, 1976), a Lester B. Pearson Award as the league's best player as voted by the players (1973), a Bill Masterton Trophy for commitment to hockey (1972), and the Frank J. Selke Trophy as the league's best defensive forward (1983).

With Clarke at the forefront, the Flyers became the most successful of the original six expansion franchises, a draw at home or on the road. You can turn on an NHL game being played anywhere in the U.S. or Canada, and there's a better-than-average chance you'll see a fan in a Flyers sweater. While some complain the Broad Street Bullies were the worst thing that ever happened to the glorious history of hockey, there's no question fans on both sides of the border loved their brawling style.

"I thought it was exciting," recalled Dave Brown, who grew up a Flyers fan in Saskatoon, Saskatchewan. "I remember where I was the first year they won the Cup. I would have been 11, 12 years old. I was at my uncle's, we were up at the lake and listening to it on the radio. I remember when they won it. We identified with them because we liked that style."

"Growing up, it was kind of neat," Tim Kerr, who grew up a Flyers fan in Windsor, Ontario, said. "You'd turn on *Hockey Night in Canada* and you'd see some fights and some aggressive play."

Another Ontario native extolled Clarke's virtues to his son, who ended up playing for Clarke's Flyers in the 1990s. The man's name was Carl Lindros.

Clarke was 34 when the 1984 playoffs ended, but the Flyers were going through a transitional phase and coach/GM Bob McCammon had been fired, leaving a hole in the team's front office. Team president Jay Snider had a list of one to fill the GM position—Clarke.

"I still intended to play," Clarke said. "I think I was I still one of the better players when Washington beat us [in the 1984 play-offs]. In those days 34, 35, was getting a lot older for a player, but defensively I was still a really capable player, capable of helping this team."

But the offer was made, and Clarke knew it wouldn't last forever.

"Had I kept playing, which I could have done, I don't know, maybe I would have stayed in hockey—scouting, coaching. I had no vision of what I was going to do. Jay Snider offered me this position, and I knew I could play for a few more years, but I knew the end was coming. If that's what the Flyers thought was right for me, then okay."

As he said the day he was introduced in his new role, "Brighter minds than mine thought I was capable of doing this, so I jumped at it."

Clarke took the job as seriously as he took his playing career. The wild, shaggy hair was tamed and trimmed to a professional length; the false front teeth that seemed to have a homing beacon on teammates' beer mugs stayed in their owner's mouth; and the hockey sweater and skates were replaced by a suit, tie and dress shoes. And Bobby was shortened to the more corporate-sounding Bob.

The love of the game and the loyalty to the organization, though, never wavered. His first stint as GM ran from 1984 to 1990. In that time, the team went to Stanley Cup Finals in 1985 and 1987, and earned five playoff appearances in six seasons.

In his first major decision, he hired Mike Keenan to coach the team. He drafted key players like Scott Mellanby, Kerry Huffman, and Dominic Roussel, and made trades for Murray Craven, Kjell Samuelsson, Chico Resch, and J.J. Daigneault.

There also were misses, including bad trades that sent away stalwarts like Lindsay Carson, Doug Crossman, Brad McCrimmon, Peter Zezel, Dave Brown, and two months apart in 1990, Dave Poulin and Brian Propp.

Clarke got little in return in those deals, and more often than not, his drafts were failures. With the final pick in the first round of the 1985 draft, Clarke took center Glen Seabrooke, who played 19 NHL games, passing on Joe Nieuwendyk and Mike Richter. In 1986 he selected Huffman with the 20th pick of the draft rather than Adam Graves, who went two picks later. He chose Darren Rumble in the first round in 1987 and made Claude Boivin the 14th overall choice in 1988. The top choices in 1989, second-round picks Greg Johnson and Patrik Juhlin, played a total of 56 games with the Flyers—all by Juhlin.

It all culminated in a 30–39–11 record in the 1989–90 season. The 71 points were the fewest for the club since the 1971–72

LICENSE PLATE

There are Flyers fans who go a little too far in their worship.

Jody Clarke, Bob's daughter, recalls working at the Jersey Shore one summer as a teenager when she met an older man who worked in the same building. When he found out who her famous father was, he made a confession.

"He told me that when they won the Stanley Cup, he stole the license plates off my mom and dad's Corvettes," she said. "I went home and said, 'Mom, do you remember anyone stealing your license plates?' She said, 'Do I remember? They didn't just steal them once, they stole them three times.' Same guy. He said I found out where you lived and I kept stealing their license plates.

"I said [to my mom], 'You gotta come meet this guy who works in the building with me, he's the one who stole your license plates.' She couldn't understand why someone would keep stealing them. They weren't vanity plates, they were normal license plates."

season, and the Flyers missed the playoffs for the first time since 1972.

"Through most of it, we were always competitive, we were always good, we were always trying to do the right things to try and win the Cup," Clarke said. "We made mistakes. I made mistakes along the way, but some of the things I did were right, too."

But with fans chanting "Bob Must Go," Jay Snider knew something had to be done.

On April 16, 1990, Jay Snider called Clarke in for a short meeting, where the club president told the face of the franchise it was time for a facelift. He asked Clarke to stay on in a yet-to-be created position, but Clarke refused and asked for the move to be announced as a firing.

When Jay Snider fired Clarke, Ed Snider was at his home in California with his new wife and daughter. Despite being 3,000 miles away from the battle lines, the owner knew there was dissension in the ranks.

"It was like having two sons that were squabbling," he said. "I tried to patch things up, and I couldn't."

When pushed, Ed backed his birth son over his adopted favorite, and just like that, the unthinkable had become reality.

Clarke said that in hindsight, getting fired wasn't as awful a thing as he thought at the time.

"Getting fired was the worst and the best," he said. "It's an awful feeling to get fired, but I was still young and I was basically just getting going in this job. In hindsight, if I was going to continue in this job, I had to go somewhere else, get with other people. I was so committed to the Philadelphia Flyers that losing a game tore me apart and I couldn't do nothing about it and I didn't know how. I didn't know how to handle the job as the GM … and all of a sudden, I couldn't do anything. You try but you don't really know.

"After I got fired and went to Minnesota, I re-grouped, re-organized in my own life. I didn't have to go to Minnesota; I could have decided I'll go somewhere else in my life. But once you make the decision that you're going to try and stay in the management end of the sport, I knew I had to change the way I lived, the way I treated it. I couldn't go on the way I was because it was killing me. I wasn't handling it the way you have to handle it if you're going to live in this world. … There was no fun from a win, but there was hell from a loss, and you have to have a way better balance. You got to learn to find a way to get some pleasure from the good, and you're responsible for the bad, but you can't let the bad eat you up or you'll never survive. I'm not the only one who found that happening to them."

Clarke built a winner in Minnesota, as the North Stars reached the Stanley Cup Final in his first season, and after a short return to Philadelphia, he spent 15 months building the expansion Florida Panthers.

He always stayed close to Ed Snider, though, and in 1994, after the Flyers missed the playoffs for a fifth straight season, the owner decided changes were needed.

"He said, "Do you want to be the manager? I'm going to take over the club,'" Clarke recalled. "'We've struggled for a while, but

FARWELL SQUEEZED OUT

Bob Clarke was viewed as the savior when he replaced Russ Farwell as GM in 1994 and promptly got the team back to the playoffs in his first season.

A lot of the chips Clarke cashed, though, were won by Farwell.

Players Clarke won with that Farwell acquired included Mark Recchi, Rod Brind'Amour, Mikael Renberg, and, of course, Eric Lindros.

"There were a lot of things building-wise that I'm not ashamed of, but we had four years out of the playoffs, and Jay's dad was most comfortable with Bob," Farwell said.

I think you and I have been able to work together in the past, and I think we can again.'"

Clarke was comfortable in South Florida, but, "This is still Mr. Snider and still home."

On June 15, 1994, Ed Snider welcomed Bob Clarke back to the Philadelphia Flyers, naming him team president and general manager; he sweetened the deal by giving Clarke a small ownership stake.

"I'm hoping he once again leads us to the Promised Land," Snider said at a press conference.

As good as he was, Clarke was no Moses and never led the Flyers to that hoped-for third Stanley Cup. But in his second, 12-year run as Flyers GM, there were a number of accomplishments and memorable moments.

He traded for John LeClair and Eric Desjardins and built a core group that got the Flyers to the 1997 Stanley Cup Final. He dealt for Keith Primeau, and watched Primeau nearly single-handedly carry the team to the 2004 Cup Final. He signed stud free agents like Joel Otto, Jeremy Roenick, Derian Hatcher and Peter Forsberg.

His drafts, criticized in his first tenure with the Flyers, became more productive as the team picked players like Brian Boucher, Dainius Zubrus, Simon Gagne, Antero Niittymaki, Justin Williams, Joni Pitkanen, Jeff Carter and Mike Richards.

There were misses, like the misguided free-agent signing of Chris Gratton in 1997, the way he badly misread the change in the game coming out of the 2004–05 lockout, and his bargain-basement shopping spree in the summer of 2006, which helped send the Flyers into the abyss in 2006–07.

There was the coaching carousel—he went through Terry Murray, Wayne Cashman, Roger Neilson, Craig Ramsay, Bill Barber and Ken Hitchcock in 12 seasons, with only Murray and Hitchcock lasting more than two full seasons—as well as the franchise-engulfing Eric Lindros soap opera.

But when his time finally ended, on October 22, 2006, the good far outweighed the bad. There were five division titles, four trips to the conference finals, and the 1997 Eastern Conference title in his second tenure.

"I don't think Bob Clarke has done a perfect job, but I don't know any general manager who has," Ed Snider said. "I'm sure Bob would like to take back some of the decisions he made. Maybe he wasn't the greatest at picking coaches. But we were always competitive. We were always in the top level of the league under his stewardship."

In 17 full seasons (not counting the 2004–05 lockout, or his aborted stint in 2006–07), his Flyers teams went to the playoffs 16 times, played for the conference title seven times, and made three Stanley Cup Finals.

But there was just one thing missing.

"I deeply regret not bringing a Stanley Cup here," Clarke said the day he retired from the GM post. "We got there a few times, but we couldn't close."

FAMILY BONDS

Traditionally, the shelf life of an NHL player is not a long one. Most players come into the league in their early twenties, and by their mid- to late thirties, it's time to start looking for another occupation. When that time comes, some organizations will thank a player for his service, wish him luck, and tell not to let the door him in the back on the way out.

And then there are the Flyers.

"I have a special affection for most players," team chairman Ed Snider said. "Hockey is a rough sport. If I have the opportunity to give back, then I will."

And Snider has spent more than 45 years giving back to his players.

"They've always said the Flyers are like family," former Flyers defenseman and coach John Stevens said. "Some places try to say that, but [with the Flyers] it truly is."

The Flyers' front-office depth-chart reads like an all-time roster—general manager Paul Holmgren; assistant GM and director of hockey operations Ron Hextall; senior vice president Bob Clarke; head of pro scouting Dave Brown; director of player personnel John Paddock; assistant coaches Kevin McCarthy and Craig Berube; player development coach Derian Hatcher; director of player development Ian Laperriere; Adirondack Phantoms coaches Terry Murray, Kjell Samuelsson and Riley Cote; scouts Dennis Patterson, Ilkka Sinisalo, Mark Greig, Neil Little, Jack McIlhargey and Simon Nolet, who was one of the original Flyers; pro scouts Al Hill and Ross Fitzpatrick; and scouting consultant Bill Barber. But former players aren't just given those traditional post-playing jobs or hired for glamorous broadcasting posts like current TV analysts Bill Clement and Keith Jones or radio analyst Chris Therien. Bob Kelly works in community relations, as do Bernie Parent, Gary Dornhoefer and Todd Fedoruk. And Joe Watson is a senior account executive, selling tickets not just for the Flyers, but for all events at the Wells Fargo Center.

"I could get my foot in the door where a lot of salesman couldn't because of who I was," Watson said in *Walking Together Forever*. "It worked out very well because people wanted to talk hockey and talk sports, and that was one thing I was always good at."

"These guys earn their living," Snider said. "They do a good job, they work hard. There's not one guy that we've given a job to that we don't feel has done the job."

"It's a loyalty," former Flyers captain Keith Primeau said. "That's why historically [the Flyers] are recognized as such a great organization. Mr. Snider doesn't have to do that. He could say you served your purpose, now go out in the real world and find something else to pay your bills. He doesn't. He recognizes and appreciates the effort these guys have put in for him in the past and is willing to say, 'Whatever the cost it is to me, it's such a menial cost for what [the players] have brought.' And that's why he's such a great man and why he's so well respected by his players."

"Organization-wise, the way the Sniders run the Flyers, it's absolutely first-class," Tim Kerr said. "The loyalty has always gone both ways. You're always treated first-class, [and] players give that back. It's got to be one of the greatest organizations in sports. They were always there for the players and their families. I don't think there's a better organization to play for than the Flyers."

Those outside the team recognize it, also.

Howard Eskin, who has covered Philadelphia sports since the 1970s, said, "[Ed] Snider is as loyal a person as you'll ever see and meet."

Agents, those trying to reach deep into Snider's pockets, also respect the man.

"The general impression of Mr. Snider is someone who has presence, someone who you can't help but respect," Rick Curran, an agent based in the Philadelphia suburb of Devon and who has represented a number of Flyers players over the years, said. "You don't always agree with him, but he always has the right intentions with his organization and fan base."

Loyalty always has been a hallmark of the Flyers organization, and the Flyers' family is a very real concept. It's not just former players working for the team; Jody Clarke, Bob's daughter, works as a receptionist at the Flyers' practice site in Voorhees. A son, Luke, works as an equipment manager, while another, Wade, is a scout; Lauren Hart, daughter of the late Gene Hart, the team's legendary broadcaster, has sung the National Anthem before every home game since 1997; Mary Ann Saleski, wife of former Flyer Don Saleski, is the senior vice president of the Comcast-Spectacor Foundation and the Flyers Wives Charities.

"I don't think I know what it's like not to feel like that," Jody Clarke said of the warm embrace of the Flyers' family. "It's all I've ever known. They've treated us like family, and in return my dad

After playing the majority of his career in Philadelphia, Bob Kelly returned there to retire and became a team ambassador in 2003.

BOB THE BUILDER

Can he build it? Yes he can.

Bob Clarke's legacy as a team-builder is borne out not just by his success with the Flyers, but by his record with other organizations.

After being fired by the Flyers in 1990, he took the GM post for the Minnesota North Stars; in his first season, the team went to the 1991 Stanley Cup Final.

In 1993 he signed on to run the expansion Florida Panthers, and though he stayed just 15 months before returning to the Flyers, the team recorded the best-ever debut season for an expansion team and played for the Stanley Cup in 1996, featuring a number of players he had acquired.

has treated other alumni like family. I guess the difference being when my dad did work for Minnesota and Florida, it wasn't true. They didn't have that atmosphere. Not for their players, not for their staff, not for their alumni."

"It's still a business," Brian Hart, Gene's son, who remains in contact with the team, said, "and in the end people are let go and guys are traded, but it just operates differently. People are connected to each other, differently than other Philadelphia teams, different than other hockey teams. People know it's a good organization to work for. You're treated well and treated with respect. They try to accommodate players as much as they can. And not just the players—everybody."

"I've always considered, and will continue to consider the Philadelphia Flyers as one of those teams you can't help but have the utmost respect for, in terms of the organization, in terms of the people, in terms of the way they handle things," Curran said. "They're not beyond making mistakes, but more often than not, it's a mistake through a genuine effort to be better as a hockey club, a genuine effort to give the people of Philadelphia a winning team."

Ed Snider is the patriarch of the Flyers' family, but few have done more to foster the organization-wide family feeling than Bob Clarke.

From the outside, Clarke may seem like an iron-fisted dictator, but players knew he cared about them as people, not as cattle easily herded in and out of uniforms.

Clarke's loyalty to his players knew few bounds. After suffering his third concussion in 20 months in October 2005, Clarke helped Keith Primeau find the best doctors during his attempted recovery, and allowed him as much time as he needed to make a decision on continuing his career. He paid for Peter Forsberg to go through more than 50 pairs of skates during the 2005–06 season in his quest to find a pair that felt comfortable on his chronically sore feet, and when that didn't work, he had the club foot the bill for extensive, risky foot surgery.

While those are examples with two very prominent players, Clarke's loyalty extended to every member of the Flyers' family.

"I'm grateful for what he did for me," Samuelsson said. The defenseman was a member of the 1986–87 team that went to the Stanley Cup Final, and had two different stints with the Flyers covering nine seasons in black and orange. "He traded for me from New York [Rangers], and that's the best thing that happened to me in my hockey career. I went to Pittsburgh for three years and he signed me again as a free agent. Then he brought me back to work in the organization as a coach."

Dave Brown spent 11 of his 14 NHL seasons in Philadelphia. Clarke hired Brown as an assistant coach in 1996, and hired him again as director of player personnel in 2006.

"I've been lucky in that the Flyers have been good to me," he said. "They do have a lot of people from the past in the organization, but I like the idea that you have some type of history with the organization. I think that's important. You have to grasp onto what was built there before you. The early days for me, when I came in, it was like I had to carry on what was there before me."

Stevens had similar feelings about the organization. As a player with the Philadelphia Phantoms in December 1998, he was hit in the right eye by a puck. Bones were crushed, his retina became detached, and his vision was permanently impaired. Just like that, his career was over, just 25 games into his 15th pro season.

"When I got hurt, it was a pretty traumatic thing," Stevens, who spent seven seasons as a player and 12 more as a coach with the organization, said. "I was dealing with a pretty serious injury that can affect you long after your playing days are over. He [Clarke] just called right away and said, 'We'd like to maintain you as an assistant coach and get you involved in that end of it and make the transition.'

"When something like that [the injury] happens, you always wonder what's next. For him to take the time to put everything at ease, to know that you can continue in a new aspect of the game and not have this big transition thing with what you're going to do, is very helpful for my wife and very exciting for me. It certainly helped me get over what I was going through."

Stevens served as an assistant coach with the Phantoms under Barber for two seasons, and became head coach in 2000 when Barber was promoted to the Flyers. Dealing with Clarke on a more direct basis, Stevens saw just how few bounds Clarke's loyalty knew.

"We've had older players in the minors that had severe injuries in the last years of their contracts and he's extended them based on character, maybe knowing they might have a tough time getting another job right away," he said. "But because their service was strong here, I think he puts a lot of onus on the character and loyalty of the players, and he rewards that.

"Guys are on the road, guys' wives are having babies. Joey Hope called me at 2:00 in the morning, his wife was having a baby. We got him on a plane the next morning, got him home so he could witness the birth of his child. I'm not sure that stuff goes on everywhere, but they certainly make it happen here. They think beyond the hockey. They treat people like people here, players like people. I think that's why they're so well-respected and that's why people love playing here."

And Stevens said his eye injury wasn't the first time Clarke and the organization helped him. A 1984 Flyers draft pick, Stevens spent six seasons with the Hartford Whalers organization, but gladly returned to Philadelphia in 1996. He wasn't back long when tragedy struck.

"My mom had a heart attack when I played for the Phantoms," he said. "They flew me and my family home at 6:00 the next morning. This was my first year back, 1996–97. They didn't even bat an eyelash."

Kelly, who was a major part of the two Cup winners, was another player who witnessed Flyers loyalty first-hand. Kelly spent 10 seasons with the club before he was traded to the Washington Capitals in August 1980. He spent of two seasons in Washington before retiring. He could have gone anywhere, lived anyplace he wanted. But there was only one kennel the Hound could call home.

"When I got traded away at the end, I never sold my home," he said. "This is my roots. I've been to all the different cities throughout North America. Everybody has a different hockey atmosphere, but here, we're so close to everything. Had we not won two Cups, maybe I'd be just another guy, but because we won the two Cups, it was 2 million people bonding here. Going home to Canada was not an option. It's awesome down here."

After ups and downs in a few different business ventures, Kelly returned to the Flyers in 2003 as a team ambassador. It's far from a ceremonial position. Kelly meets more people than a fleet of Wal-Mart greeters. He's all over the Wells Fargo Center before and during most home games, talking to fans, shaking hands, and posing for pictures. And Kelly also takes his show on the road throughout the Delaware Valley, heading the club's "Hooked on Hockey" scholastic program, leading youth hockey clinics throughout the area year-round, and he makes appearances at hospitals, golf outings and all sorts of other public events.

"Dave Coskey [former president of marketing for Comcast-Spectacor] asked me to come back and be the white World B. Free," Kelly said, equating himself to the former Philadelphia 76ers player who holds a similar position with the city's basketball team. "I'm not allergic to work."

"In my mind, I represent the Flyers and Comcast-Spectacor," Kelly said in *Walking Together Forever*. "It's certainly not a job where I shuffle papers. I am expected to be out and about. I'm getting a chance to do things with kids, go to hospitals, to do clinics, whether it be roller hockey or street hockey, or I can do meet-and-greets. I'm thankful to have a job with this organization and do my best for them."

The Flyers' family won't hesitate to wrap its arms around a person. And in return, those people have shown the same loyalty in return.

"This is a first-rate organization," Primeau, who has made Voorhees the permanent residence for him and his family, said. "It's run first-class. They treat their players as good as, or better than, any other organization—not just in professional hockey, but in professional sports."

"They [the Flyers] are very demanding," Stevens said, "but they're very fair and they treat you with great respect and they take care of you while you're here. I think that's all anybody can ask for. I think you get treated better here than anywhere else."